DECOLONISING COMMUNITY EDUCATION AND DEVELOPMENT
Understanding the Past, Learning for the Future

Marjorie Mayo

P

First published in Great Britain in 2024 by

Policy Press, an imprint of
Bristol University Press
University of Bristol
1–9 Old Park Hill
Bristol
BS2 8BB
UK
t: +44 (0)117 374 6645
e: bup-info@bristol.ac.uk

Details of international sales and distribution partners are available at policy.bristoluniversitypress.co.uk

© Bristol University Press 2024

British Library Cataloguing in Publication Data
A catalogue record for this book is available from the British Library

ISBN 978-1-4473-6756-7 hardcover
ISBN 978-1-4473-6757-4 paperback
ISBN 978-1-4473-6758-1 ePub
ISBN 978-1-4473-6759-8 ePdf

The right of Marjorie Mayo to be identified as author of this work has been asserted by her in accordance with the Copyright, Designs and Patents Act 1988.

All rights reserved: no part of this publication may be reproduced, stored in a retrieval system, or transmitted in any form or by any means, electronic, mechanical, photocopying, recording, or otherwise without the prior permission of Bristol University Press.

Every reasonable effort has been made to obtain permission to reproduce copyrighted material. If, however, anyone knows of an oversight, please contact the publisher.

The statements and opinions contained within this publication are solely those of the author and not of the University of Bristol or Bristol University Press. The University of Bristol and Bristol University Press disclaim responsibility for any injury to persons or property resulting from any material published in this publication.

Bristol University Press and Policy Press work to counter discrimination on grounds of gender, race, disability, age and sexuality.

Cover design: Clifford Hayes
Front cover image: Getty Images/Angel Pietro. The red carnation on the cover was the symbol of the movement that overthrew the Portuguese dictatorship in 1974, leading to a democratic transition in Portugal and freedom for the country's former colonies.

Readers should be aware that quoted material in Chapter 8 contains racial slurs.

Contents

Glossary		vi
Acknowledgements		viii
1	Introduction: Learning from contested histories	1
2	'Culture wars', competing ideologies and the development of critical consciousness in movements for social change	11
3	Decolonising the curriculum: knowledge and whose knowledge counts	30
4	Exploring the contested histories of adult community education and development	47
5	Learning from struggles for freedom and justice in South Africa	66
6	Co-creating knowledge and learning from labour movement histories	86
7	Communities, social movements and municipal strategies for equalities and solidarity	104
8	Learning through the arts: cultural strategies for decolonisation	123
9	Conclusions: Bringing it all together again	141
References		151
Index		163

Glossary

AAM	anti-apartheid movement
ABCA	Army Bureau for Current Affairs
ANC	African National Congress
ARV	anti-retroviral (drugs)
BAME	Black and Minority Ethnic
BCM	Black Consciousness Movement
BSA	British Sociological Association
CEO	chief executive officer
CDJ	*Community Development Journal*
CDP	Community Development Projects (British)
CLES	Centre for Local Economic Strategies
CND	Campaign for Nuclear Disarmament
colonialism	control of one country by another through direct control of the state
CPP	Convention People's Party (Gold Coast/Ghana)
cultural Marxism	Label typically applied (generally with pejorative implications) by the Far Right to academics and others concerned with the development of critical consciousness
CWED	Chicago Workshop for Economic Development
END	European Nuclear Disarmament
financialisation	increasing dominance of financial interests
GLC	Greater London Council (now reshaped as the Great London Authority)
GLEB	Greater London Enterprise Board
imperialism	control of one country by another country and/or external economic interests, economically and/or politically
ICFTU	International Confederation of Free Trade Unions
K4C	Knowledge for Change Training Consortium
LIS	London Industrial Strategy
MCF	Movement for Colonial Freedom (now Liberty)
MML	Marx Memorial Library
NCLC	National Council of Labour Colleges
neo-colonialism	effective, if indirect, economic and/or political control of one country by another and/or by corporate interests
neoliberalism	dominance of market forces with minimal provision by the state
NGO	non-governmental organisation
NRA	National Rifle Association
NVLA	National Viewers' and Listeners' Association

Glossary

PAC	Pan-African Congress
PAR	participatory action research
PRIA	Society for Participatory Research in Asia
RDA	Ruvuma Development Association (Tanzania)
SASO	South African Students Union
SPA	Social Policy Association
TAC	Treatment Action Campaign
TGWU (T&G)	Transport and General Workers Union (now part of UNITE)
TUC	Trades Union Congress
TWIN	Third World Information Network
UDF	United Democratic Front
UHP	Unite History Project
UN	United Nations
UNESCO	United Nations Educational, Scientific and Cultural Organization
USSR	Union of Soviet Socialist Republics
UWC	University of the Western Cape
WEA	Workers Educational Association
WETUC	Workers Education Trade Union Committee
WFTU	World Federation of Trade Unions
woke	alerted or 'woke' to racial and other forms of discrimination and injustice (generally used by the Far Right with pejorative implications)

Acknowledgements

My warmest appreciation to all who have contributed to this book in their different ways, responding with such generosity to my requests for information, feedback and advice. I should like to express very particular thanks to the following: Darlene Clover, Mary Davis, John Foster, Budd Hall, Christabel Gurney, Adrian Judd, Astrid von Kotze, Colin Leys, Roger Seifert, Nick Sharman, Viviene Taylor, Shirley Walters, Michael Ward and Adrian Weir. I am so grateful to you all for your contributions and for your insightful comments.

I should also like to thank students on the MAs in Applied Anthropology and Community and Youth Work, Community Development and Community Arts, Goldsmiths, University of London.

My special thanks to Ines Newman, who read and commented on draft chapters at every stage. I am enormously indebted to her for her critical insights and for her continuing encouragement.

Finally, my appreciations to Portuguese participants at the Adults' Policy Studies conference in Funchal, Madeira, 29 February to 2 March 2024. They drew my attention to the Red Carnation, symbolising the transition to democracy, accompanied by freedom for Portugal's colonies. This book's cover depicts the Red Carnation emerging from the shadows of the past.

Many thanks in addition to the team at Policy Press, and to Sophia Unger and her colleagues at Newgen Publishing. Their professionalism has been so supportive, making such a difference to the final product.

Any remaining errors are, of course, down to me.

My family has also been continually supportive, as always. This book is dedicated to them with love and appreciation.

1

Introduction: Learning from contested histories

Not everything that is faced can be changed, but nothing can be changed until it is faced.

James Baldwin, n.d.

Who controls the past controls the future: who controls the present controls the past.

George Orwell, *1984*

Reasons for writing this book

Culture warriors have been re-enforcing divisive and discriminatory attitudes and behaviours, posing disturbing threats to social solidarity. And progressive social movements have been facing mounting pushback in recent years, vilified through Far Right cultural warriors' toxic attacks on the very basis of their claims for social justice, challenges that have been effectively re-enforcing rather than confronting racism, discrimination, exploitation and oppression. These ideological battles raise many questions for community education and development, questions that are particularly acute for those committed to the pursuit of strategies for transformative social change.

Cultural warriors fundamentally question the theoretical underpinnings of transformative approaches. Their perspective on cultures, identities and the development of critical consciousness are at odds with the contributions of key thinkers such as Paulo Freire, whose writings have had so much influence on the development of debates on adult community education and community development for social transformation. It is precisely these types of approaches that are most threatened in the contemporary context.

In addition, cultural warriors' attitudes towards the colonial past pose major challenges. These need to be explored more broadly and set within the context of debates about decolonisation. The histories of slavery and colonialism have been central to the development of community education. These histories date back to the post-slavery reconstruction period in the United States through to the British government's strategies for decolonisation after the Second World War. Their impact continues to be felt today and so needs to be critically examined and re-evaluated. The Black Lives Matter (BLM) movement has been centrally important here, drawing attention to the continuing legacies of slavery and colonialism in the context of Far Right and White supremacist ideologies in the US and internationally.

There is now a greater awareness of the shameful legacies of the past, with enhanced recognition of the continuing impact of slavery and colonisation in the contemporary context. Conversely, there has also been a significant backlash involving attempts to undermine such criticisms, to trivialise them as 'woke' or to deny their significance altogether. 'All lives matter', as a slogan, effectively denies the specific experiences of people of colour, for example, despite the continuing evidence of police brutality and extrajudicial killings disproportionately impacting on people of colour, both in Britain and elsewhere. There are important implications here for community education and development, both in theory and in practice. The continuing impact of these legacies needs to be faced, confronting the past in order to develop effective strategies for change; challenging racism, discrimination and xenophobia; and promoting equalities, diversity and social solidarity for the future in their stead.

These challenges are being taken up in a variety of ways as previously accepted understandings are being increasingly questioned. There have been community mobilisations to protest about the injustices of the past and present. And curricula are being decolonised across a range of subject areas, including subject areas with direct relevance for community education and development, such as anthropology, development studies, educational studies, history, human geography and social policy. Through decolonising the curriculum, these subject areas have been developing their own challenges to previously accepted narratives and discriminatory assumptions. Decolonisation emerges as an ongoing process as a result, one of the three themes that are to be explored throughout the chapters that follow.

Relevance for community education and development

Community development has been defined as 'a practice-based profession and an academic discipline that promotes participative democracy, sustainable development, rights, economic opportunity, equality and social justice, through the education and empowerment of people within their communities, whether these be of locality, interest or identity, in urban or rural settings' (International Association for Community Development/ IACD website, https://www.iacdglobal.org/about/brief-history/) – enabling people to have a voice effectively, facilitating collective action to address their concerns and to care for the planet. Community education has been defined in comparable terms, with popular education more specifically defined as attempting, wherever possible, to forge a direct link between education and social action (Crowther et al, 2005), drawing upon Paulo Freire's approach to education for transformation (Freire, 1972, 1996).

These aims have, of course been contested and continue to be contested, both in theory and in practice. The reality has been more complex, in other words. Community education and development can be – and have been – promoted in order to contribute to the management of peoples and the containment of conflicting interests. Community-based interventions can be promoted to enable communities to cope with self-reliance, as best they can, within existing constraints rather than challenging the underlying causes of their problems. Alternatively, however, community education and development interventions can be promoted to enable communities to cope within their existing constraints while *also* contributing to the development of critical consciousness, building solidarity for alternative futures; education for social transformation, in other words (Freire, 1972, 1996). These debates run through the histories that are explored in subsequent chapters, with a particular focus on community education and development for social transformation, the perspective that is being most directly threatened in the contemporary context.

This book sets out to challenge culture warriors' divisive, racist and xenophobic narratives, exploring alternative approaches for community education and development as well as its potential to contribute to the promotion of equality, social solidarity and social and environmental justice (West, 2016). Community education and development cannot, of course, achieve these objectives on their own, but they can make a valuable contribution.

Starting with a reflection on the role of ideas in processes of social change, this book goes on to explore the development of critical consciousness. This includes questioning the nature of knowledge itself, exploring whose knowledge counts and identifying ways of enriching history by including previously marginalised voices. These theoretical discussions set the scene for reflecting on the contested histories of adult community education and development more specifically, raising questions about what can be learnt from these varying experiences and their contributions to movements for liberation, equalities and social solidarity. Most importantly, these discussions have implications for the development of policies and practices, working more inclusively within and between communities, whether these are communities of place, communities of interest or communities of identity.

Three overarching themes

1. *The role of ideas in the promotion of social change*
   How might cultural strategies contribute to the development of critical consciousness? And, in turn, how might the development

of critical consciousness contribute to the promotion of community-based strategies for freedom, equalities and social solidarity?

The contributions of cultural theorists have particular relevance here – theorists who have provided critical understandings of the role of cultures and the development of critical consciousness and processes of emancipatory social change (Williams, 1963; Thompson, 1980a; Fieldhouse, 2013). Although few, if any, of these would have described themselves as 'cultural' Marxists, as defined by cultural warriors from the Far Right, their theoretical frameworks have resonance with the writings of Gramsci on ideologies and cultures and the ways in which communities can be stimulated to challenge previously accepted norms that re-enforce oppressive, exploitative and discriminatory social relations (Gramsci, 1968; Freire, 1972, 1996). Other theoreticians who have drawn upon these frameworks include popular educationalists from a variety of contexts (Crowther et al, 2005; Hall et al, 2012; Laginder et al, 2013) and cultural and feminist educationalists (Clover and Sanford, 2013, English and Irving, 2015). Whatever their differences, they share affinities with approaches developed by Freire and others, approaches with significant relevance for community-based responses to the challenges of the contemporary culture wars.

2. *Decolonisation*

Decolonisation has been understood in varying ways, starting from the achievement of national independence with the ceremonial lowering of the colonisers' flag. But this represents no more than the beginning of the decolonisation process. At the time of writing Britain still has powers over a dozen overseas territories, including Anguilla, Bermuda, the British Virgin Islands, the Cayman Islands, Gibraltar and the Turks and Caicos Islands. These are far from anachronistic residues from a bygone age; territories such as these provide tax havens, offering opportunities for international companies to make exceptional profits. Britain has been described as the 'butler to the world', pivotal to the ways in which tycoons, tax dodgers, kleptocrats and criminals frustrate government attempts to tackle corruption and money laundering, diverting resources from public service provision towards the realisation of private super profits (Bullough, 2022). Britain is not the only former colonial power to retain influence overseas. Curaçao (a former colony of the Netherlands) has similarly been cited as a base for shell companies, providing financial obfuscation via questionable, if technically legal, practices. Decolonisation has so much further to go, it would seem, in terms of challenging the neoliberal present as well as facing up to the colonial past.

Franz Fanon's writings have particular relevance here. Aspects of his thinking have been controversial, to say the least, including his reflections on the emancipatory role of violence in struggles for colonial freedom. But his writings on decolonisation have been widely influential, especially those concerned with community education and development. In Fanon's view, the struggle for national independence from colonial rule was far from representing the end of the story. Decolonisation had to involve so much more, he argued, 'a whole social structure being changed from the bottom up' (Fanon, 2001: 27). After independence the fight would continue, he went on. This would entail the fight against poverty, illiteracy and under-development, with the rural poor as active participants in the process along with the urban poor and their allies. Fanon also emphasised the importance of political education, challenging colonial attitudes and values and building political and social consciousness in order to enable people to engage in the development process as active citizens from the bottom up. We will return to Fanon in the next chapter.

The process of decolonisation relates back to the first theme. Whose knowledge counts in these battles of ideas? How to challenge the Western biases and the omissions that have been the subject of so much criticism in the context of debates about decolonisation (Olusoga, 2017; Day et al, 2022)? And how to promote knowledge democracy (Fals-Borda and Rahman, 1991; Tandon, 2005), respecting different forms of knowledge, while maintaining processes of critical engagement and mutually respectful dialogue?

Decolonisation needs to be understood within an international context too. Former colonial powers have continued to exert influence and extract benefits from their former colonies indirectly beyond the attainment of formal independence. Such interventions have been identified in the downfall of Kwame Nkrumah, for example, the prime minister of Ghana, the first country in Sub-Saharan Africa to achieve independence from British colonial rule, in 1957 (Williams, 2021). Nkrumah himself was well aware of the challenges of neo-colonialism. He explained that this was the way in which the economic systems and policies of formerly dependent states could be directed from outside, whether by the former colonial powers or by consortiums of foreign financial interests. 'For those who practice [neo-colonialism] it means power without responsibility' he wrote, while 'for those who suffer from it, it means exploitation without redress' (Nkrumah, 1965: xi; Williams, 2021). We will encounter more on Nkrumah in Chapter 4.

Meanwhile, as Paulo Freire was also pointing out in similar vein to Fanon a decade after the latter's death in 1961, liberation needed to include the development of critical consciousness. The

> authentic solution of the oppressor/oppressed contradiction does not lie in a mere reversal of position, in moving from one pole to the other. Nor does it lie in the replacement of the former oppressor with new ones who continue to subjugate the oppressed – all in the name of their liberation. (Freire, 1972: 33)

He argued that true liberation must start in the consciousness of the oppressed and the oppressor and must involve engaging in processes of critical reflection and dialogue. Rather than offering a one-off definition of decolonisation at this point, the subsequent chapters aim to explore the different ways in which past assumptions can be contested and previous experiences can be re-appraised. And this entails unpacking the interconnections between slavery and the development of capitalism, colonialism, imperialism and racism (Williams, 2022), along with the ways in which racism intersects with other forms of exploitation, discrimination and oppression – by class, gender, sexuality, caste, religion and age.

3. *The importance of contested histories, the legacies of the past and the decolonisation of community education and development*

The history of community education and development is intertwined with the history of strategies to address the effects of slavery and colonialism, not that slavery has been eliminated. Almost 50 million people are currently trapped in modern slavery worldwide according to Anti-Slavery International, which campaigns against abuses such as human trafficking and forced labour. The main focus of the chapters that follow is the legacy of slavery and colonialism, however, including public attitudes to the past and their implications for current community education and development policies and practices. Old attitudes are slow to change, despite contemporary challenges. A relatively recent survey conducted in the UK (Smith, 2020) found that nearly a third of those polled (32 per cent) believed that the British Empire was something to be viewed with pride, with just under a fifth (19 per cent) believing that the British Empire was something to be viewed with shame. A third of those polled considered that the colonised were better off for having been colonised. And just over a quarter (27 per cent) would have liked Britain to have continued to have imperial status. Nor was Britain unique in these residual attachments to the achievements of empire. Half of those polled in the Netherlands viewed their imperial past with similar pride.

The extent to which opinions have been shifting remains to be questioned, of course. Earlier polls had revealed even higher levels of support for the imperial past in Britain. And more recent polls have revealed some evidence of further shifts in public opinion. In 2022, a YouGov poll found that four in five people in the UK believed it to be important to be 'woke' in the sense of being alive to issues of race and social justice. And 67 per cent believed that Britain had done damage in the world in the past, although 77 per cent still believed that Britain had been a force for good overall (Savage, 2022: 9).

These histories of slavery and colonialism and their legacies have continuing relevance for community education and development, whose programmes have been promoted to respond to such legacies in a variety of ways and with varying effects depending, at least in part, upon the perspectives of those involved. To what extent are programmes geared towards enabling communities to cope with resilience? How much further do they go, in addition, to facilitate the development of critical consciousness as the basis for developing more structural approaches to the promotion of agendas for liberation, equality and social solidarity? Debates about community education and development's overall aims run through these histories, illustrating their implications for public policy and community practice.

The book's structure

Chapters 2, 3 and 4, focus on each of the book's three themes in turn.

Chapter 2 focuses on the first overarching theme, starting from the development of 'culture wars' as they have been emerging in the US and elsewhere in recent decades. These debates have central relevance in relation to the theoretical underpinnings of community education and development.

Chapter 3 focuses on the second theme of decolonisation – more specifically the decolonisation of knowledge – exploring different approaches internationally. These include the specific contributions of community education and development, including the development of participatory action research (Fals-Borda and Rahman, 1991; Tandon, 2005).

Chapter 4 moves on to focus on the third theme, the histories of community education and development, their interconnections with the histories of slavery and colonialism and their subsequent legacies. This chapter sets the scene for the case studies that follow, in Chapters 5, 6 and 7.

The case study chapters explore the three themes as they cut across the histories of community education and development in specific contexts. Between them they provide illustrations of the varying ways in which the three themes can be traced through community education and development initiatives across different sectors. These chapters include case studies based in social movements and community-based settings as well as those from partnerships with universities and with local and regional authorities. And they include examples of community education and development initiatives from different geographical areas as these have developed over time.

Each chapter is based upon written sources, together with the findings from interviews and from experiences of participative action research. These include findings from the author's own research viewed through a decolonising lens.

Chapter 5 focuses on the role of ideas and critical consciousness in struggles for decolonisation, along with the contributions of community education and development in support of the anti-apartheid movement, both within South Africa and beyond. In the final years of apartheid, South Africa had vibrant adult and community education programmes aiming to take the decolonisation processes further. These programmes were committed to building a democratic rainbow nation, drawing upon Freirean approaches specifically developed for the Southern Africa context (Hope and Timmel, 2001).

The chapter includes reflections from those engaged with these and more recent programmes, particularly programmes focusing on women's concerns, along with programmes focusing on environmental sustainability in the very different circumstances of post-apartheid South Africa, characterised by the shrinkage of spaces for transformative approaches to community education and development (Baatjes and Mathe, 2004; Grayson, 2010). There are questions about decolonisation and recolonisation that need to be explored further here, along with their implications for gender equality and future sustainability in the context of contemporary policies and practices.

Chapter 6 looks at experiences of trade union education and participatory action research. The three cross-cutting themes run through this chapter in parallel, with a particular focus on questioning whose knowledge counts and the implications for the promotion of knowledge democracy, re-examining the past as the basis for developing more inclusive approaches and solidarity for the future. The labour and trade union movement has been strongly criticised for past failures to challenge racism and gender inequalities within workplaces and communities in Britain and elsewhere, and for instances of support for imperial agendas in the past. But this is far from representing the entire story. Participatory research and trade union education materials have been produced to learn from these contested histories, including learning from examples of international solidarity with movements for colonial freedom, as well as learning from challenges to the legacies of race and gender inequalities from the past.

The chapter draws on the Unite History Project, which has co-produced materials on the union's own history, including materials produced through oral history interviews conducted by trade union educators and activists themselves (Davis and Foster, 2021). These histories have provided illustrations of participatory action research in practice, exploring the union's past and evaluating previous successes, as well as reflecting on the limitations of previous achievements. The chapter includes findings from more recent interviews with trade unionists, reflecting on the ways in which such materials can be used to promote critical understandings as part of wider agendas for the promotion of social solidarity, equalities and social justice despite increasing constraints on such learning in the current context.

Chapter 7 explores the ways in which the three cross-cutting themes weave through comparative experiences of municipal strategies in Britain and US, working with communities and social movements to tackle the legacies of slavery and colonisation, promoting decolonisation in order to advance equalities and social solidarity agendas for the future (Blunkett and Jackson, 1987; Mackintosh and Wainwright, 1987; Jackson, 2021). Examples of such strategies have included community education and training initiatives to enable women and Black and ethnic minority communities to access employment and training opportunities. In parallel, they have included strategies and planning processes to improve the quality of jobs and services for communities.

There have been innovative approaches to challenging structural inequalities on an international scale through the promotion of fair trade, as well as initiatives to promote international solidarity more locally, welcoming refugees and asylum seekers. Here too there are illustrations from cities in the US as well as from cities and regions in Britain. The chapter includes contributions from those with direct experiences of such strategies, whether as policy makers or as activists, reflecting on past achievements as well as recognising their inherent limitations in contemporary contexts.

There are positive lessons to be drawn from these three sets of experiences, facilitating the development of critical consciousness *as well as* enabling communities to cope with their immediate challenges with resilience, engaging in processes of decolonisation as part of long-term strategies for social change. But the spaces for transformative approaches have been shrinking in the context of continuing marketisation and austerity, both in Britain and elsewhere. These challenges emerge from each of these case studies, pointing to the limitations of their approaches in the contemporary context.

The penultimate Chapter 8 then returns to the first theme – cultures, culture wars and whose knowledge counts. Here the focus is on cultural strategies for engaging with experiential forms of knowledge, engaging with people's emotions and building empathetic understandings through the arts. Museums and galleries can offer unique insights, for example, reaching the parts that other forms of knowledge fail to reach. Novels and films offer similar possibilities for promoting more holistic ways of knowing and feeling within communities, providing tools for use as part of a decolonising community education and development curriculum.

Films can stimulate critical discussion, for example, offering opportunities for learning about the past, whether the works in question were produced as documentaries at the time or more recently produced as feature films. Satyajit Ray's films have been used very successfully with international development students, for example, exploring the colonial past and its legacies and raising troubling questions about the roots of contemporary communal conflicts. And Steve McQueen's *Small Axe* films provide more recent examples of racism and resistance in Britain, raising significant questions for community education and community development in their turn.

There are similar opportunities for learning through the discussion of novels, from a range of African American writings about slavery and post-slavery experiences in the Deep South (Hurston, 1987). There is also much to learn from writings about more recent African American lives in the urban north. And there are numerous examples from African and African Caribbean writers reflecting on experiences of colonialism and its divisive legacies in Britain as well as its divisive legacies in the former colonies themselves.

The final chapter (Chapter 9) reflects on the potential implications for shared learning and participatory action research, bringing the three themes and their different strands together to develop more holistic understandings of decolonisation in the current context. How might such reflections contribute to contemporary cultural debates more generally while recognising that the spaces for alternative approaches have been shrinking, both in Britain and beyond? How might they contribute to the development of more inclusive community education and development policies and practices more specifically, facilitated by a decolonising curriculum? And how, despite their inherent limitations, might they contribute to wider strategies for social and environmental justice, racial equality and social solidarity for the future?

2

'Culture wars', competing ideologies and the development of critical consciousness in movements for social change

Concerns with the divisive impacts of 'culture wars' provide the starting point for thinking about the decolonisation of community education and development. Where have these 'culture wars' come from, and how do they relate to long-standing debates about the role of ideas in processes of social change? The development of critical consciousness has been centrally significant here, with particular relevance for community education and development. How to unpack these debates about cultures, the role of ideas and critical consciousness in movements for social justice and equality?

While these debates are centrally important in theoretical terms, there are also major implications for community education and development practice. Attitudes towards slavery and colonialism in the past can so readily blend into attitudes towards racism now, along with attitudes towards the desirability or otherwise of living in a multicultural society. Racism and xenophobia represent some of the most challenging issues for professionals and community activists alike in the context of increasing social polarisation fanned by politicians from the Far Right.

Cultural warriors have also been engaging with religious fundamentalist debates, whether to celebrate their traditional values or to deplore their apparent decline due to increased secularism or supposed threats to Christianity from Islam. There are potential implications here for those concerned with human rights issues such as women's sexual health and LGBTQ rights, divisive enough already in so many contexts. The toxicity of cultural warriors' interventions on such topics is not to be underestimated, with significant consequences for those concerned with building support for more socially just alternatives.

This is why this chapter sets out to explore the notion of culture itself and the role of ideas, critical consciousness and human agency, along with the idea of 'cultural Marxism' and the ways in which this term has been applied as a term of abuse by the Far Right (Finlayson et al, 2022). The chapter sets the framework for the discussion of cultural racism and the legacies of the past, focusing on the need to address these challenges via the decolonisation of adult community education and development curricula for the future.

Cultures, 'culture wars' and racisms, past and present

Cultures have long been the subject of contestation and challenge. 'Culture' is in fact 'one of the two or three most complicated words in the English language', according to Raymond Williams (Williams, 1988: 87), taking account of 'the specific and variable cultures of different nations and periods, but also the specific and variable cultures of social and economic groups within a nation' (Williams, 1988: 89). Cultures represent whole ways of life, in other words. No wonder that there have been differing understandings and competing perspectives over time. But why, in recent decades, have such debates been perceived as constituting culture wars?

The 1990s seem to have been marked by significant changes. The end of the Cold War has been described as marking a new phase in world politics. 'It is my hypothesis', Samuel Huntington has argued, that 'the fundamental source of conflict in this new world will not be primarily ideological or primarily economic. The great divisions among mankind and the dominating source of conflict will be cultural' (Huntington, 1996: 1). 'The clash of civilisations will dominate global politics' (Huntington, 1996: 1) both locally and between states.

Now that capitalism had finally triumphed over socialism, class politics was being superseded by identity politics, as traditional ethnic and religious identities came to the fore. Or so Huntington supposed. He gave particular emphasis to the significance of conflicts between Christians and Muslims, which risked becoming more virulent in his view, reflecting that although there had been some fighting between Christians and Muslims in the former USSR, for example, there had been virtually no violence between ethnic Russians and ethnic Ukrainians (or so it must have seemed to him at the time).

There have, of course, been alternative explanations for this increasing focus on cultural explanations and concerns. There was evidence that increasing Islamophobia was being associated with popular feelings of resentment and fear in the face of increasing economic, social and political polarisation (Mayo, 2020). These resentments and fears were being fanned by politicians of the Right, misleading the public (Dorling, 2018) and attempting to justify increasing insecurities by shifting blame onto 'the others', including immigrants, refugees and Muslims. Bhattacharyya and colleagues write of name calling, racist street violence and zealous anti-immigrant politics in just such a context of a security-oriented state seeking legitimacy in times of unbearable economic uncertainty (Bhattacharyya et al, 2021) and seeking political acceptance through 'othering' the outsider (Bhattacharyya, 2015).

In addition to blaming the victims, populist politicians have been focusing attention on the so-called liberal elite, the educated establishment, the politically correct 'bleeding heart' 'woke' multiculturalists, accused of supporting the rights of immigrants and refugees while despising the White working class. These types of arguments were associated with Trump's election campaigns in the US in 2016, for example, appealing to those who felt despised for being racist, sexist and homophobic. In her study of poor White people in the southern states of the US, Hochschild found that these were people who felt left behind, 'strangers in their own land, afraid, resentful, displaced and dismissed by the very people who were, they felt cutting the line' – in other words, cheating their way ahead of them (Hochschild, 2016: 218).

'The great replacement conspiracy' feeds on such fears, as perpetrators of White supremacist violence have argued in order to justify their attacks (such as the racist murder of ten people in Buffalo, New York in 2022, for example). In their view, privileged elites are conspiring to change the demographics of America, replacing White people with very different populations: people of colour and immigrants from very different cultures and religions, especially Muslims. There has been plenty of scope for playing on such fears, exacerbated by politicians from the Right, including Republican candidates when facing mid-term elections in the US, for example (Smith, 2022). The extent to which such fears impact upon the 2024 presidential election campaigns remains to be seen at the time of writing.

Inequalities have continued to grow, meanwhile, both in Britain and internationally. The situation has been exacerbated by the impact of the COVID-19 pandemic, along with further threats to living standards because of rising energy prices. The growth of precarious employment has been adding to widespread feelings of anxiety about the future. And the wars in Ukraine and Gaza have been compounding divisions on an international scale. This then has been the context for the growth of Far Right populism and White supremacist movements in many different contexts.

Whatever the underlying causes, there have been powerful processes of 'othering' at work. Whether these processes can be considered as culture wars is more contested. Extreme positions have certainly been taken on cultural issues, but whether people's views are polarised into warring factions remains questionable. However, this is in no way to underestimate the damage that can still be caused by politicians playing on popular fears, exacerbating racism, sexism, xenophobia and Islamophobia in the process.

First, though, to explore the positions in question in more detail. Melvin Tinker's *That Hideous Strength* sets out the case for the dangers of cultural wars from his particular end of the spectrum on the religious Right (Tinker, 2020). The cultural warriors driving so much political correctness in the contemporary US represented a diabolical threat to Christian values, in his view, raising the spectre of a new dark age. Those social liberals who were championing the oppressed were promoting a self-centred view of human beings rather than a Christ-centred view. Individual rights and identities were being given precedence, including the right to challenge Christian views on marriage and the family. Homosexuality was being presented as being acceptable, for example, along with same-sex marriage, as part of the all-pervading political correctness of the age. And the Church of England was being too accommodating in response, effectively colluding with these forms of secular liberalism, threatening our whole way of life with potentially disastrous social and political consequences.

There would seem to be echoes of earlier mobilisations here, reminiscent of Mary Whitehouse's National Viewers' and Listeners' Association (NVLA) campaigns against the permissive society in the 1960s and 1970s. As an evangelical Christian who had already been influenced by the Right-wing organisation for 'Moral Re-armament' in the 1930s, Mary Whitehouse became a very effective mobiliser of those who felt alienated and neglected by liberal elites in rapidly changing times. She focused her ire on social liberals who supported the legalisation of homosexuality and abortion, along with greater freedoms from cultural censorship, and waged war on the BBC, which she accused of broadcasting programmes which promoted the sexual revolution (Whitehouse, 1993). Social liberals, in her view, were trying to subvert the family and Christianity, degrading British culture, corrupting public morals with their tolerance for pornography and thus opening the way for communism.

These supposed connections between communism and the counterculture emerge as threads running through such debates from that period into more recent times, as will be suggested in more detail subsequently. These threads have continued to run despite the demise of the former USSR. Meanwhile, a number of ironies were to emerge, including the fact that in 1977 Jimmy Savile, a popular media figure at the time, had been feted with an award from the National Viewer's and Listeners' Association for wholesome family entertainment. Savile was subsequently identified as a compulsive paedophile.

James Davis Hunter's writings on culture wars also recognised their historical antecedents in religious terms (Hunter, 1991). There had been conflicts in US over cultural and religious differences in the past (between Protestants and Catholics and between Christians and Jews, for example). Since the Second World War, there had been some evidence of increasing tolerance, in his view. But cultural conflicts had not been disappearing. On the contrary, in fact, although they were occurring along new lines in the US at the end of the 20th century.

Hunter traced these lines back in terms of different and opposing bases of moral authority, between orthodoxy versus progressivism or God/the church versus the spirit of rationality and subjectivism. Although he recognised that many, if not most, Americans located themselves somewhere in the middle ground between these polarities, there was still, he argued 'a fairly comprehensive and momentous struggle to define the meaning of America' (Hunter, 1991: 51). This was a struggle between opposing views about what constituted the good society, the struggle between cultural conservatives versus cultural progressivists, traditional morality versus individual choice. He went on to suggest that these differences were replacing class politics (around economic issues) with the politics of cultures and identities in the post-Cold War context – a debatable view, to say the least, as will be suggested in more detail later in the book.

Major corporations, meanwhile, have been embracing cultural politics in specific instances with the advent of what has been described as 'woke capitalism' (Rhodes, 2022). But not to the detriment of their bottom lines – far from it, in fact. Building upon traditions of corporate social responsibility, entrepreneurs such as Amazon's George Bezos have been embracing popular causes. Rather than becoming liberal 'bleeding hearts', however, as their critics from the Far Right have suggested, 'woke' capitalists have been only too aware of the financial benefits of their actions. Supporting fashionable causes makes perfect sense as marketing tools for targeting specific demographics, as the CEOs of Quantas and Gillette discovered for themselves, supporting same-sex marriage and less toxic forms of masculinity, respectively (Rhodes, 2022). Far from challenging the status quo, Rhodes has gone on to argue, 'woke' capitalists have actually been strengthening it, undermining democracy by bypassing political structures, reducing the scope for challenging the underlying causes of inequalities and racial discrimination.

But this was absolutely not how Hunter and others had been understanding the emergence of cultural politics in the US and elsewhere in the last decades of the 20th century. From the 1980s onwards, Hunter had become concerned with the collapse of traditional Left and Right divisions with the demise of state socialism. Cultural battles were about realignment, he argued, refocusing on cultural rather than economic concerns (Hunter and Wolfe, 2006) – challenging the 'it's the economy stupid' view that Bill Clinton later expressed to summarise his own position on voters' political priorities in the US. Social class was no longer key since the demise of the USSR, Hunter maintained (Hunter, 1991). Voters were concerned with issues of culture and identity, issues that cut across traditional divisions between Left and Right.

Contestations over the right to own guns provide further examples of such conflicts, it has been argued, seen by supporters of the US National Rifle Association (NRA) as essential for individual freedoms and traditional understandings of masculinity, underpinning conservative politics on gender as well as race, the protagonists being predominantly White and mostly male (Melzer, 2009). NRA activists saw themselves as cultural warriors, according to this study, at war with evil as personified by 'Left girly men' and 'freedom-hating communists', part of the liberal media elite (Melzer, 2009). Guns were being perceived as symbols of opposition in their cultural wars against the social liberals who were challenging White men's privileges, social liberals who were favouring women, Black people and immigrants, turning White men into victims in their own country. As Hunter summarised these cultural wars more generally, the US was undergoing processes of reconfiguration, with debates increasingly focusing on issues such as abortion, gay rights and the family, along with attitudes towards race and gender equality, funding for the arts, the educational curriculum and attitudes towards the past.

Meanwhile, Hunter's critics remained unconvinced about the existence of culture wars in the first place. Culture wars existed only in the minds of journalists and political activists, not in the minds of the majority of Americans, according to Wolfe, for example (Wolfe, 2006). By implication, polarised attitudes towards race and racial equality did not occupy their minds either. In the 2004 elections, Wolfe argued, cultural issues were not key to the campaign, and nor were issues relating to race and race equality. The US wasn't much concerned with religious issues, such as the headscarf, although Wolfe did accept that attitudes could change, especially after the terrorist attack on the Twin Towers in New York on '9/11'. The notion of culture wars may have been exaggerated in his view then. But cultural issues were not likely to disappear while politicians could see the benefits of mobilising around them. And the Republican Right was being more effective than the Democratic Party here, using cultural issues for their own ends (in order to gain legitimacy for their own self-interest, in his view) (Wolfe, 2006).

Wolfe's suggestion that cultural wars may be on the decline seems somewhat more questionable in the light of more recent events. Donald Trump has been described as having pioneered a whole new politics of perpetual cultural war. Cultural issues were milked for their potentially popular appeal during the 2016 election campaign. And once elected, Trump continued to wage war on 'woke' agendas – being 'woke' in this context meaning being alert to injustice and social discrimination, especially racial discrimination. Nor did cultural wars end with the election of Trump's successor, Joe Biden, as the following reprisal story so aptly demonstrates.

A relatively recent article in *The Guardian* seemed to illustrate this point precisely. Entitled 'They're after Mickey Mouse: Biden decries Republicans' Disney reprisal', the article reported the US president's apparent disbelief that the Governor of Florida's cultural wars had reached the gates of the magic kingdom of Walt Disney World (Luscombe, 2022: 38). The governor, Ron DeSantis, was calling for the end of a tax deal which had been benefitting the Walt Disney World Resort – as revenge on the company which he was branding 'woke' for opposing his 'don't say gay' law. At that time a potential candidate for the Republican presidential nominations in 2024,

DeSantis was described as having 'pushed his legislature on several right-wing laws recently', including a ban on abortion after 15 weeks, impacting on black voters' representation in Congress and preventing the discussion of sexual orientation and gender identity in schools (Luscombe, 2022: 38) – homophobia, transphobia, misogyny and racism all mobilised in support of Far Right political ambitions for the future.

Race and racism have been central to the politics of wars on woke, in fact. The Unite the Right rally in Charlotteville, Virginia in 2017 was a case in point. At this event White supremacists gathered to build a united movement, chanting racist and antisemitic slogans, protesting against the removal of monuments to the slavery-supporting Confederate past. Unsurprisingly, violence ensued. These were very live issues, as the Black Lives Matter movement has so clearly demonstrated, both in US and elsewhere. Other issues have also been framed within these culture wars debates, including climate change and the wearing of masks during the COVID-19 pandemic. But race and racism have continued to be centrally important along with misogyny, homophobia, xenophobia and resentments against 'the other' more generally.

These have been the challenges that Far Right populism has been posing for those concerned with community education and development. How to support communities and social movements in developing their own understandings of their situations, working together to address the structural causes of inequality, discrimination and oppression? Whether these challenges are best described as culture wars remains contentious. They do involve battles over competing ideas, though, and the role of human consciousness in strategies for social change, ideological struggles that have been identified with so-called 'cultural Marxism'.

'Cultural Marxism' and the continuing importance of developing critical consciousness

These struggles between ideologies take the discussion back to the demise of the USSR and the debates that followed. Capitalism had won the Cold War, Hunter and others argued, and the class struggle had been superseded. But subversive ideas lived on in the ideology called cultural Marxism, focusing specifically on Gramsci, the Italian Marxist whose writings about the battle of ideas have resonated with those of Paulo Freire and other key influences on community education and development (de Figueiredo-Cowen and Gastaldo, 1995; Freire, 1996). 'Cultural Marxists' were to blame for what Tinker considered to be the all-pervading political correctness of the age (Tinker, 2020).

These ideas were being associated with critical theory and the Frankfurt School, along with critical race theory (more on which subsequently).

'Cultural Marxists' such as Marcuse were to be particularly vilified for their attacks on traditional values and sexual constraints. Marcuse was described as one of too many so-called 'cultural Marxists' who had achieved dominant positions in higher education and the media (Tinker, 2020), Between them these 'cultural Marxists' were questioning the very basis of previously accepted norms, the everyday common sense of the status quo that Gramsci and others had indeed set out to challenge – but in very different ways and for very different aims (Gramsci, 1968).

Gramsci was certainly concerned with the battle of ideas, questioning the norms and values associated with the status quo. Paulo Freire's writings on adult education and the development of critical consciousness have direct parallels, as he himself recognised, reflecting on his debts to Gramsci (de Figueiredo-Cowen and Gastaldo, 1995). Nor was Gramsci the first to pose such challenges to generally accepted ways of thinking. Thomas Paine's *Common Sense* (first published in 1776), set out to do precisely this. The 'long habit of not thinking a thing wrong, gives it a superficial appearance of being right', he pointed out, illustrating the continuing weight of previously accepted norms and values (Paine, 2004: 3) before going on to question the violent abuses of power that characterised Britain during the reign of George III. Paine's writings have provided inspirations to those struggling for freedom and equality since that time, from the patriots fighting against British colonial rule in the American War of Independence to the supporters of the French Revolution and onwards. Paine was an early advocate of the abolition of slavery and the promotion of human rights whose writings have had continuing relevance for those concerned with community education and development.

While they have historical antecedents – as in the writings of Thomas Paine, for example – Marxists have indeed had particular relevance for community education and development in more recent times. Although not all of these theorists would have defined themselves in these terms. Far from it, in fact. The term 'cultural Marxism' has been particularly contested given its usage by the Far Right, caricaturing the term in order to vilify progressives and continuing the Cold War by other means.

The Frankfurt School of theorists have not all been considered Marxists, let alone cultural Marxists (Bottomore, 1984). They did consider themselves as critical theorists, though, concerned with the development of emancipatory approaches. The group originated as a number of intellectuals coming together around a shared concern to develop a form of Western Marxism which would be relevant for advanced capitalist countries. They were particularly concerned to bring back considerations of human agency and the role of consciousness and ideas, including the contributions of psychoanalysis, in place of the economic determinism that they had associated with Marxism in the USSR in the interwar period. Having fled

Nazi Germany in the 1930s (many of them were Jewish refugees), they found sanctuary in the US. Some of them returned to Germany at the end of the Second World War, while others stayed in the US, going on to develop their ideas in different directions that were more or less recognisably Marxist.

As Bottomore's study of the Frankfurt School explains, a number of its adherents, including Adorno and Horkheimer, became increasingly pessimistic in the post-war period, going on to dissociate themselves from the radical student movements of the 1960s, becoming ivory tower pessimistic intellectuals, according to their critics (Bottomore, 1984). Others such as Marcuse, however, did become significant – if controversial – influences on radical student movements and movements for racial justice, challenging the all-pervasive 'system', as the status quo was being described in general (and in relation to the economy more specifically) at that time.

Marcuse's book *Eros and Civilization* (Marcuse, 1966) was particularly influential, challenging previously accepted norms on sexuality and sexual freedom. Once material scarcity had been addressed, in Marcuse's view, the focus could shift to the pleasure principle and sexual liberation, ideas associated with the counterculture of the times. There are clearly echoes here of the challenges that continued to concern the cultural warriors of subsequent decades, from Mary Whitehouse and the NVLA onwards.

Marcuse himself came to more pessimistic conclusions subsequently, however. In the preface to the 1966 edition of *Eros and Civilization*, he reflected that he had been too optimistic about the prospects for the end of scarcity. And he had underestimated the extent to which the affluent society in countries such as the US could develop more sophisticated forms of social control. 'The people efficiently manipulated and organized are free; ignorance and impotence, introjected, heteronomy is the price of their freedom' (Marcuse, 1966: xiii) – the 'democratic introjection of the masters into their subjects' (Marcuse, 1966: xv) – the oppressors inside the heads of the oppressed, as Freire and others would subsequently explain.

Conflicts were mostly taking place elsewhere, meanwhile – in Vietnam, the Congo and South Africa and 'in the ghettos of the "affluent society": in Mississippi and Alabama, in Harlem', in Marcuse's view (Marcuse, 1966: xiii). He referred to the revolts against 'the intolerable heritage of colonialism and its prolongation by neo-colonialism' with youth in revolt in the US in solidarity with the 'wretched of the earth' (the title of Fanon's classic text, Fanon, 2001).

Marcuse's own conclusions from these reflections were far from traditionally Marxist. To him, it was the outcasts and outsiders, rather than the working class, who represented the standard bearers of revolutionary change: 'the exploited and persecuted of other races and colours, the unemployed and the unemployable' (Marcuse, 1966: 199–200). 'Their opposition is revolutionary even if their consciousness is not' (Marcuse, 1966: 200), he concluded.

This was Marxism without the proletariat, in Bottomore's philosophical meditations on the defeats of the working class in the 20th century, although Bottomore did appreciate the theoretical contributions of later associates of the Frankfurt tradition, such as Habermas, for example (more of whom in Chapter 3).

The contributions of Raymond Williams and E.P. Thompson and their continuing relevance

The Frankfurt School's concerns with human agency and critical consciousness were central to the New Left more generally, though, including the writings of Raymond Williams and E.P. Thompson, where we can find many questions of relevance for debates on the decolonisation of adult community education and development and the emergence of critical consciousness. Williams and Thompson were similarly concerned with cultural issues and critical consciousness from an emancipatory perspective. Each had their differences with the other. But each made outstanding contributions to the development of ideas about history and culture, representing continuing influences on adult education, community education and community development, both in theory and in practice.

Dworkin's study of cultural Marxism (Dworkin, 1997) includes both writers within its remit, along with a number of others, including Paul Gilroy (more of whom later too) and Stuart Hall, whose contributions to cultural studies seem to have owed more to the influence of Gramsci than Marx himself (McLennan, 2021). Hall's analysis of the ways in which race and racism were being mobilised to provide the arena in which complex fears, tensions and anxieties could be projected drew upon Gramscian approaches with particular contemporary resonance (Hall et al, 2013). Hall's subsequent writings have been seen as moving further away from a socialist approach, however, let alone a Marxist approach (Turner, 2022).

Neither Williams nor Thompson would have necessarily self-defined as cultural Marxists, as it has already been suggested, although both engaged with Marxism, acknowledging its influence on their thinking about culture, society and social change. Both explored the roles of ideas and human consciousness. And both rejected mechanistic forms of Marxism, criticising crudely determinist explanations and arguing for more nuanced understandings of the interrelationships between base and superstructure and between people's material circumstances and their consciousness – or lack of consciousness – about their situations and the possibilities for social change.

Raymond Williams has already been quoted for his approach to the definition of culture as a way of life. So, cultures were linked to societies' productive bases, but not in crudely deterministic ways (Williams, 1963). Popular cultures were features of capitalist societies, but that did not mean that they were to be looked down upon by the proponents of so-called high (elitist) forms of culture. Nor were working-class people necessarily taking on middle-class attitudes and values by dint of becoming less impoverished and acquiring consumer goods after the Second World War, as Marcuse, among others, had come to conclude (Marcuse, 1966). On the contrary, in fact, majority and minority cultures overlapped and developed over time. As a working-class scholarship boy himself, Raymond Williams had respect for working-class cultural traditions as he described these in relation to 'structures of feeling' rooted in the values of mutual aid and co-operation.

These values underpinned his approach to adult education more specifically, values that he developed as a tutor in Extra-Mural Studies at the University of Oxford and subsequently as a Workers Educational Association (WEA) tutor. He was very critical of top-down approaches rooted in elitist distrust of the majority. Learners did not need to be patronised in these ways. '[T]he process of learning depends so much on the conscious need to learn, and such a need is not easily imposed on anyone', he pointed out (Williams, 1963: 318). His emphasis on respect for learners chimed with his views on the concept of community, in terms of the working-class ethics of mutual responsibility and solidarity. Learning needed to be about collective, not just individual, betterment. And cultures needed to be open to diversity, neither striving to preserve old forms nor 'as socialists trying to prescribe the new man'.

Williams has been subjected to a number of criticisms, including criticisms from E.P. Thompson, who argued that Williams under-emphasised considerations of power and class conflict in history. Ironically, perhaps, this was similar to one of the criticisms that was subsequently levelled against E.P. Thompson himself: for being too focused on human agency and consciousness and insufficiently rigorous in his analysis of underlying structures. In their essay introducing E.P. Thompson, Fieldhouse, Koditschek and Taylor described agency as his defining term, exemplifying 'his historical method but also his political and peace movement activities, and indeed his life as a whole' (Fieldhouse et al, 2013: 3). He has been described as a polymath for the breadth of his contributions, spanning history, literature, fiction and poetry, biography, socialist and libertarian politics and – most importantly for the concerns of this particular chapter – the practice of adult education.

Like Raymond Williams, E.P. Thompson was also a key figure in New Left debates in the second half of the 20th century, influenced by Marxism but concerned to develop more nuanced understandings of the interrelationships between base and superstructure, material considerations and the world of ideas, developing critical consciousness as the basis for progressive social change. He had been a member of the Communist Party but left in 1956 along with a number of other Left intellectuals, including Left historians who were disillusioned by the Soviet Union's invasion of Hungary. But he remained a Marxist (or 'a Marxist fragment', as he once described himself), reflecting that 'none would repudiate the powerful formative influence of Marx' (Thompson, 1980: 183), although Marxism was in the process of splitting into several traditions and fragments, in his view. He was particularly critical of what he considered to be the rigid, overly deterministic forms of Marxism that were being developed by Althusser and others, elitist theories that were divorced from practice or progressive movements in his view (Thompson, 1978).

E.P. Thompson's approach to the understanding of consciousness and human agency was summarised in the preface to the 1980 edition of his study of *The Making of the English Working Class* (Thompson, 1980a). Class involved class consciousness, he argued. Classes were not static entities; classes were made by human agency. 'The class experience is largely determined by the productive relations into which men are born – or enter involuntarily', he agreed. But 'class-consciousness is the way in which these experiences are handled in cultural terms: embodied in traditions, value-systems, ideas, and institutional forms. If the experience appears as determined, class consciousness does not' (Thompson, 1980a: 9). And class consciousness developed in different times and places, as his study of the making of the English working class demonstrated, tracing this back to even before the Industrial Revolution.

This was history from below, as Thompson explained. He was 'seeking to rescue the poor stockinger, the Luddite cropper, the "obsolete" hand-loom weaver, the "utopian" artisan and even the deluded follower of Joanna Southcott [a self-defined religious prophetess in the late 18th/early 19th century], from the enormous condescension of posterity' (Thompson, 1980a: 12) recognising that their aspirations were valid in terms of their own experiences. These were aspirations, ideas and values that were to be taken seriously in their own right. They formed part of what he described as 'this process of self-discovery and of self-definition' (Thompson, 1980a: 939) – the basis of his approach to the study of class consciousness, human agency and social change.

E.P. Thompson's writings on adult education provide illustrations of these ideas in practice. He referred to the deep social dialectic at the heart of the tutorial class movement, as developed within the WEA and the University Extension tradition. This was about 'the testing of academic scholarship by the action and experience of a social class too long neglected: the interplay and conflict of abstract, passive, contemplative experience and concrete, active, productive experience'. Tutors needed to engage with learners' own experiences and learning needs in processes of dialogue rather than welcoming them into our classes 'only on our own terms' (Fieldhouse, 2013: 33). Adult education should be committed to serious study, he emphasised, but this should be social purpose education based on adult education values and objectives – particularly relevant for community-based approaches to learning.

While he was keen to encourage student participation, E.P. Thompson was also realistic about the challenges involved (challenges that may also be only too familiar to contemporary practitioners). There was widespread reluctance to undertake the required reading and written work, he found, and too many students listened over-respectively and passively. These were problems that he worked on, seeking ways of engaging students by drawing on their own experiences. It was tutors' responsibility to take such contributions seriously and learn from them, in his view, acknowledging his debts to his own students, in the preface to *The Making of the English Working Class*. Universities should engage in adult education 'not only to teach but also to learn' (quoted in Fieldhouse, 2013: 41). But this was becoming increasingly problematic, as he also recognised, reflecting on the destructive impacts of increasingly market-oriented pressures on higher education in prescient ways (Thompson, 1980a).

E.P. Thompson was also an active supporter of the Peace Movement, from his early engagement via the Communist Party through to his engagement in the Campaign for Nuclear Disarmament (CND) and the European Nuclear Disarmament (END) movement. Taylor has described him as a 'social-movement' man, a perspective that was 'in harmony with the eloquent "human agency" argument which permeates his historical as well as his political writing' (Taylor, 2013: 181). He came to the feminist movement rather later in life, although he did come to recognise its importance – stimulated by the influence of his wife, Dorothy Thompson, it has been suggested, but also through the couple's friendship with the socialist historian Sheila Rowbottom. In the most recent volume of her autobiography (Rowbottom, 2022), Rowbottom writes of this long-standing friendship, describing Thompson's growing interest in feminism and the potential for bringing feminism together with other sections of the Left at that time, as she and others had been arguing in *Beyond the Fragments* (Rowbottom et al, 2013).

In summary, then, E.P. Thompson was a polymath, making significant contributions across a range of intellectual fields. His contributions to debates on culture, critical consciousness and human agency have continuing importance in particular, along with his emphasis on the roles of class and class conflict in historical processes. And he was committed to social purpose learning, starting from learners' own interests and experiences, further emphasising his specific relevance for adult and community education and development. Most importantly for the concerns of this book, he was also a supporter of movements for colonial freedom, although he was certainly not a romantic about post-colonial governments, as he demonstrated with his criticisms of Mrs Gandhi's State of Emergency, for example. He saw this as an attack on civil liberties, although there were some on the Left of the political spectrum who were nevertheless prepared to justify this at that time (Thompson, 1980b). Decolonisation was about much more than formal independence, in his view. There is not the space here to explore his multifaceted contributions further, though, let alone do them justice. Readers are encouraged to engage with his writings for themselves.

While Williams and Thompson shared some intellectual concerns, they had their differences, including differences over the significance of class conflict in processes of social change, as has already been suggested. But their differences didn't prevent them appreciating each other's contributions. Nor did such differences prevent them from collaborating with each other and with others to produce the *May Day Manifesto*, which developed a shared position statement for the Left in 1967 (Williams, 2018). This set the situation in Britain within a world perspective, taking account of the importance of decolonisation and the complexity of the ex-colonial world, recognising the ways in which colonial powers had been making concessions as part of Cold War agendas to keep their former colonies safe from communism.

Both Williams and Thompson were committed to the furtherance of social justice agendas. And both recognised the central importance of cultural factors and the development of critical consciousness. People needed to make sense of their situations in order to change them. Both were also committed to adult education, more specifically. But adult education had not been seen as uncontentious either. On the contrary, in fact, the fields of adult community education were being conceptualised in different and competing ways, as the *May Day Manifesto* recognised, taking account of the context of Cold War battles for the hearts and minds of those previously colonised. These differences of aims and approach have run through debates in the past and on to more recent times, in fact – education for active democratic participation or education to 'neuter and de-radicalize working-class students' (West, 2016: 94) – just as these debates run through the chapters that follow regarding learning for liberation or learning for pacification and social control, whether in colonial or post-colonial contexts.

Culture wars and racism: legacies of the colonial past

Culture wars have been waged with particular virulence when it comes to questions of race and racism. The very concept of racism has been repackaged in cultural forms, with cultural racism replacing long-since discredited, if still extant, pseudo-scientific versions (such as those understood and practiced in Nazi Germany). Cultural racism – or 'civilisationism' – has come to seem more respectable than raw 'natural' race hierarchies, Paul Gilroy has argued (Gilroy, 2004). His study *After Empire* quotes Hunter on the clash of civilisations, viewing multiculturalism as threatening the uniqueness of Western culture. This represented a very static view of cultures as impermeable and unchanging, in his view, rather than seeing cultures as dynamically hybrid. Gilroy's went on to demonstrate that racism continued to obsess post-colonial, post-slavery cultures, however defined.

As Gilroy explained, 'the imperial and colonial past continues to shape political life in the overdeveloped-but-no-longer-imperial countries' (Gilroy, 2004: 2). He identified patterns of denial about racist brutalities in the past, such as the brutalities that followed the Indian uprising of 1857, for instance, along with Britain's particular failures to come to terms with the loss of empire and imperial prestige. This he described as 'post imperial melancholia', a neurotic obsession with the days when Britain ruled the waves, basking in fantasies of omnipotence, images of the Second World War still circulating and still defining Britain's 'finest hour' – plucky little Britain standing up to the might of the Nazis. Far from evaporating over time, Gilroy has pointed out, this kind of nationalism has actually gained new momentum in the context of the War on Terror, marked by flag-waving expressions of patriotism from both sides of the political divide.

Nor was this only a British phenomenon. The enduring effects of European colonialism were deeply and disastrously inscribed in its neo-colonial present, characterised by ultra-nationalism and xenophobic racism in the context of the waning of the West, Gilroy argued (Gilroy, 2016). There were, of course, variations across Europe, but there were also common themes across national borders – populist politicians' weaponisation of popular fears about immigration in general and Islamic immigration more specifically.

Looking back to the time when I first read Gilroy's book, I recall feeling less than totally convinced. The generation of students that I was encountering seemed barely aware that Britain had ever had an empire in the first place. And this was the case even among young people with a colonial heritage themselves, as Sanghera has pointed out, for example, having grown up in a South Asian heritage community in Wolverhampton but with very little understanding about the colonial past (Sanghera, 2021). How, then, might this translate into post-colonial melancholia? With the benefit of hindsight, I can see how very wrong I was. The evidence of continuing denial about past wrongs is all around us still, with politicians of both major parties routinely draping themselves in the Union Jack.

But the colonial past is also being sharply contested in the contemporary context. Critics had suggested that British atrocities in Kenya described in Caroline Elkins' account (Elkins, 2005) had been an isolated and atypical case. But this was far from being the reality, as she demonstrated in her subsequent study, presenting evidence from many different contexts to support her arguments about the violence inherent in Britain's colonial past (Elkins, 2022). Meanwhile, the opinion polls that were quoted in the previous chapter clearly testify to the continuing strength of the belief that the British empire has been a force for good rather than the reverse, mirroring the views identified by opinion polls in other post-imperial countries, especially the Netherlands, even if the strength of such views may perhaps seem to be somewhat on the wane.

The effects of such beliefs can be traced through racist immigration policies and the hostile climate towards newcomers, especially, although not of course only, those who came to Britain from the former colonies, those who were here because we were there. The hostility to these unwanted settlers could be linked to the ways in which they acted as reminders of the imperial and colonial past. Government proposals to send 'illegal' asylum seekers to Rwanda provide chilling evidence of the continuation of more contemporary forms of colonialism – colonialism in reverse – forcibly sending the victims of violence and oppression off to Africa on a one-way ticket.

In contrast, Gilroy has argued for a fundamentally different approach to difference and diversity. Rather than hostilities based on racial hierarchies, he has argued in defence of conviviality, tolerance, peace and mutual regard, the right to be human and so to be treated with respect. He has been deeply critical of the ways in which cultures and identities have been presented in divisive ways, referring to Du Bois' views on the values of humanism and brotherhood, in contrast, taking account of the local and the global, cosmopolitanism from below (more of Du Bois in Chapter 4).

Among other influences, Gilroy has also acknowledged the contributions of Fanon, who was similarly concerned to move beyond previous histories of oppression and violence, recognising the ways in which the colonised could internalise their oppressors' mindset. In his preface to a relatively recent edition of Fanon's *Black Skin White Masks*, Gilroy pays tribute to Fanon's insights in these respects (Fanon, 2020), including the insights that he had gained from his psychiatric training, understanding the existential and psychosexual dimensions of racial subordination.

White people were psychically wounded by colonialism as well, a theme that Fanon went on to develop, with examples, in *The Wretched of the Earth* (Fanon, 2001). Fanon appreciated that the torturer can be dehumanised too, describing his experiences of treating just such a patient in Algeria. Decolonisation challenges all of us, in other words. This was a conclusion that Paulo Freire developed subsequently in the context of his writings on education and social change, arguing that 'the great humanistic and historical task of the oppressed' was 'to liberate themselves and the oppressors as well' (Freire, 1972: 21).

Fanon's writings have so much of relevance in relation to the importance of the development of critical consciousness – challenging the colonisers' presentations of colonialism as coming to lighten the natives' darkness, getting the oppressor out of the heads of the oppressed as well as the oppressors.

Fanon referred to the 'whitewashing' of Algerians who had the opportunity to study in France. Putting such a native bourgeoisie in charge of a newly independent state would leave it in the hands of the imperialists, in his view. Political education was crucial, he argued, if decolonisation was to lead to alternative outcomes, with new concepts and a 'new man'. In the end, he argued, everything depended on the education of the masses, but not via long political harangues delivered from time to time by leaders speaking in 'pompous tones' (Fanon, 2021: 159). On the contrary, he emphasised, political education involved opening people's minds, awakening them, developing critical consciousness through a process of dialogue, as Freire has so cogently argued in parallel.

Fanon has been described as a humanist in his early writings, although he was also influenced by both psychoanalysis and Marxism. But this was an unorthodox approach to Marxism, as he himself described his position. In the colonies, being White was associated with being rich, which was why Marxist analysis should be lightly stretched in his view (Fanon, 2021). In the colonies, he went on to argue, the proletariat had much to lose. National liberation movements needed to take account of the rural poor and displaced youth who had so much less to lose, the unemployed who had gone to urban areas to find work, only to be so sadly disappointed.

This emphasis on the role of the peasantry has a long history. The Indian Marxist Prabhat Patnaik has argued that the conception of a worker–peasant alliance dates right back to the formulations of the Bolsheviks under Lenin's leadership, representing a new theoretical departure within Marxism by recognising the revolutionary potential of the peasantry – if not specifically focusing on the potential of the unemployed in Lenin's case, perhaps. This type of approach opened the way forward for transitions towards socialism, even within societies where the development of capitalism had remained restricted (Patnaik, 2017). Fanon's scepticism about the role of the proletariat has been more controversial, based perhaps on his own (mis)understanding of the specifics of the Algerian situation (Caute, 1970).

His views about the role of violence in struggles for colonial liberation have been similarly contested, however understandable, given his experiences of the colonisers' violence in Algeria, violence that had been exacerbated by French settlers' determination to preserve their interests. Violence was certainly a feature of freedom struggles in countries with settler populations, such as Kenya. But then again, there was also plenty of violence in colonies without significant settler populations. Such controversies are beyond the scope of this chapter, however. The point to emphasise here is simply that there have been, and continue to be, many different strands of interpretation, including different strands within Fanon's thinking, just as there have been different strands within Marxist approaches more generally, in varying contexts.

These approaches have included 'Black Marxism', as Cedric Robinson's publications have also demonstrated (Robinson, 2021). Challenging what he considered to be Marx and Lenin's lack of sufficient attention to the world outside Europe, Robinson's writings on Black Radical traditions have provided inspiration to the Black Lives Matter movement. He has explored the contributions of a number of Black thinkers, including Du Bois, C.L.R. James and Richard Wright, along with activists such as Booker T. Washington (more of whom in Chapter 4).

Like Fanon and others before him, Robinson has also emphasised the importance of political education and mass consciousness, including consciousness through culture. And most importantly, he has emphasised the importance of intersectionality and transnationalism with a particular focus on the contributions of Black women in the US and elsewhere (Robinson, 2021). More of these too in Chapter 4.

Beyond culture wars? Popular education for liberation and social justice

The notions of culture wars and wokeism have been promoted from the Right of the political spectrum along with related notions of cultural Marxism. These are held to blame for the death of Western civilisation as we know it, harbingers of a new dark age. Culture wars have been described (even by a former Conservative government minister) as 'more than just an ugly political phenomenon' (Abdul, 2022: 11), linked as they have been with White supremacist views and 'great replacement' conspiracy theories. There are elements of the absurd about some of these attacks. The case of Mickey Mouse springs to mind, for example. But this is in no way to minimise the potential damage that such notions can cause, especially when used to provoke – and so undermine – the proponents of progressive agendas for racial justice and social solidarity, core to the values of community education and development.

If not culture wars, then, how about the battle of ideas? Or better still, how about leaving these military analogies aside to focus on contesting ideas through processes of deliberation and dialogue? Community education and development have been and continue to be influenced by a range of different ideas, debates *within* Marxism and debates *with* Marxism, along with debates within humanism and Christian Socialism, to name the most frequently cited influences on thinkers such as Paulo Freire, for example. Most importantly too, community education and development continue to be influenced by debates about the role of histories, cultures and critical human consciousness in movements for social change – and by debates about how these relate to the influences and impacts of material factors, the base in relation to the superstructure, to use more traditional terms.

These differences emerge within contemporary debates across a range of academic disciplines, as well as within adult education and community development. And they continue to be pivotal when it comes to popular political education – more specifically, popular education that is 'rooted in the real interests and struggles of ordinary people, overtly political and critical of the status quo [and] committed to progressive social change', as Crowther and others have defined this (Crowther et al, 2005: 2). This definition raises further questions in its turn, though, including questions about whose knowledge counts when it comes to developing strategies for social transformation. These are the issues to be explored in more detail in the following chapter.

3

Decolonising the curriculum: knowledge and whose knowledge counts

The decolonisation of learning raises significant questions in its turn, as the previous chapter has already suggested. Whose culture is defined as being more significant than others? Whose knowledge actually counts? And whose knowledge is being correspondingly devalued as a result?

This chapter moves on to focus on decolonisation and racial inequalities more specifically. Whose knowledges have been predominant and whose knowledges have been devalued as a result of slavery and colonialism in the past, along with the impacts of neo-colonialism and imperialism in more recent times? What can be learnt from strategies to decolonise the curricula in other disciplines? What might be the pedagogical implications, the ways in which a decolonised curriculum is offered to learners (Morreira et al, 2021)? And what might be the lessons to be applied to decolonising the curricula in community education and development studies in contemporary contexts? These questions will be explored more fully in subsequent chapters. While there is much to learn from the experiences of other disciplines, pioneering work of potential wider relevance has already been undertaken in adult community education and development too. This has been especially significant in relation to the development of participatory action research (PAR).

Having summarised the contributions of PAR, the chapter will conclude by revisiting the starting point: whose knowledge counts? How might different forms of knowledge – including Indigenous forms of knowledge and experiential knowledge – be valued? And how might they be critically evaluated and most appropriately employed through processes of reflexive dialogue?

Decolonising curricula and pedagogy

Decolonisation has been envisaged in a variety of ways, as previous chapters have already outlined, from decolonisation as formal independence from colonial rule through to calls for more fundamental challenges to the legacies of slavery and colonialism, and continuing structural inequalities internationally, starting from the bottom up. Morreira et al refer back to the contributions of Du Bois, Nkrumah, Nyerere, Ngugi and Fanon in this regard, emphasising the importance of calling into question both the systems of power and the systems of knowledge that have served to perpetuate oppression (Morreira et al, 2021). According to Ngugi wa Thiong'o', in fact, imperialism's biggest weapon has been the cultural bomb, which served to 'annihilate a people's belief in their names, in their languages, in their environment, in their heritage of struggle, in their unity, in their capacities and ultimately in themselves' (Ngugi wa Thiong'o, 2005: 3). He himself came to the view that he would write in his own language, Gikuyu, rather than writing in English, the language that had been imposed as part of these processes of control (more of Ngugi wa Thiong'o in Chapter 8).

Education has been and still remains centrally important here – education for domestication and/or education for social transformation, as Paulo Freire's much-quoted writings have summarised the alternatives (Freire, 1972: 21). There are significant implications here for decolonising curricula and pedagogies in the Global North as well as in the Global South.

Challenges to oppressive systems of power and knowledge have their own histories, then. Calls for decolonising curricula have been building on these heritages, whether more or less consciously, gaining new impetus in recent years. The Black Lives Matter movement has already been identified as a significant driver of change in this respect. But there have been other crucially important influences too. In South Africa similar pressures were exerted by the 'Rhodes must fall' movement which started at the University of Cape Town in 2015 with a campaign to remove the statue of Cecil Rhodes, an arch-imperialist and White supremacist who considered that to be born English was to have won first prize in the lottery of life. University staff were involved in this campaign as well as students.

There had been increasing recognition of the problems within South African universities even before this, along with widespread frustrations at the lack of progress towards equalities since the formal end of the apartheid regime in 1994. White supremacy had supposedly ended as a result of this transfer of state power. Yet inequalities remained persistent, along with their ideological and cultural underpinnings, rooted in assumptions about the superiority of Western knowledge systems. So, the campaign to remove Cecil Rhodes' statue led to wider demands for the decolonisation of the curriculum as well as demands for fees to fall. These demands then spread to universities elsewhere in South Africa and beyond, including Oriel College, Oxford, which had its own statue of Cecil Rhodes to challenge, along with its own arguments for decolonising the curriculum.

There have, of course, been very different views as to the futures of such controversial statues, whether to preserve them or whether to remove them (immersing Edward Colston's statue in a nearby dock, for example). Others have argued for displaying such artefacts in very different ways, questioning the racist, White supremacist values that these statues had been erected to represent in the first place. This was the solution that was eventually reached when Edward Colston's statue was subsequently retrieved from Bristol Dock, to be displayed in a local museum alongside placards from the protests.

There are parallels here with some of the debates that have been surrounding decolonisation initiatives more generally, themes that run through some of the discussions that follow. There have been debates about what needs to be rejected altogether, along with what needs to be re-evaluated in order to challenge racial injustice. And there have been debates about the ways in which racism and racial injustice intersect with other forms of exploitation and oppression that also need to be addressed. As Day et al affirm, 'elitism in the university is complex and intersectional in ways that no single set of initiatives – neither those pursuing diversity, those seeking inclusion nor those wanting to decolonize – can capture alone' (Day et al, 2022: 4).

In the South African context, for example, critics have argued that the limited attempts at reform post 1994 were too focused on education for economic growth within the logic of neoliberal capitalism, addressing some aspects of racism but not tackling related forms of exploitation and oppression within the university system or indeed within wider society. Similar arguments were raised in relation to the limitations of adult basic education, seen by critics as having become increasingly instrumentalised. There was correspondingly less focus on learning for democratic participation, let alone learning to address the intricacies of exploitation, oppression, exclusion and marginalisation, working for justice, freedom, care, equality, peace, stability and development. This was despite the NGO sector's resilience, critics argued, attempting 'to protect civil society from economic and political colonisation and to continue to exert influence and pressure on political society' (Baatjes and Mathe, 2004: 412). Strategies to include the contributions of Indigenous knowledge systems were insufficient by themselves, other critics argued, if they failed to address these interrelated forms of exploitation and oppression. The curriculum needed to be critically analytical as well as inclusive, in other words, unpacking the underlying causes of inequalities within the logic of neoliberal capitalism. Chapter 5 explores some of these themes in further detail in the South African context.

Drawing on experiences from different disciplines

There are many experiences from different disciplines in response to these challenges. Decolonisation has been addressed across a range of disciplines, from anthropology, cultural studies, history, political science, sociology and social policy through to education itself, to list some of the most evident. These disciplines have varying and contested histories of their own, histories of challenging the roots of racism and White supremacy along with histories of failing to make such challenges – or worse.

Anthropology was a discipline that had been deeply implicated in Britain's colonial past, for example. The cultures of the colonised had needed to be understood, along with their languages, if the colonised were to be governed most effectively (Mayo, 1975a). This had been particularly relevant for British approaches, perhaps, given British colonial strategies for governing via indirect rule, working through traditional (or what were perceived to have been traditional) structures of governance and taking account of local cultural traditions. This was the strategy that Lord Lugard had set out to explain, on the basis of his own experiences in Nigeria, for example: the dual mandate to 'civilise' while also exploiting the colonised (Lugard, 1965).

The reality has been far more contested, however, and not only in more recent times. The Anthropological Society of London's predecessor organisation, the Ethnological Society of London, had been associated with anti-slavery campaigns in the 19th century and so had its counterparts in France and the US, for instance. Ethnology and anthropology have indeed had past associations with the proponents of White racial superiority, such as Gobineau (Gobineau, 1999). But there have been significant opponents of slavery and colonialism too with critical traditions of continuing relevance in the contemporary context. The discussion of decolonisation has needed to take account of such complexities, both past and present.

As Grant has argued, in the *Political Quarterly* issue on decolonising the curriculum, universities need to constantly think about what they teach and how they teach it (Grant, 2020). Decolonisation was most certainly not about political correctness, in his view, nor indeed was this an example of Left-wing 'wokery'. Decolonisation was not about abandoning great books either, let alone about compromising academic standards. Rather this was about considering a far wider range of sources for study. Most importantly too, this was about subjecting existing sources to rigorous criticism. Non-Western materials needed to be included in the curriculum, but traditional materials also needed to be re-examined with a decolonising lens.

The critique of Eurocentrism was not necessarily a critique of European thinkers per se (Meghji et al, 2022). Nor did the critique of Eurocentrism imply the reverse, simply embracing non-Western thinkers uncritically. Each discipline needed to address these challenges as a matter of urgency, just as they needed to reflect on the ways in which their subjects were being taught in order to stimulate critical reflexivity among their students.

The Royal History Society's report on *Race, Ethnicity and Equality in UK History* has been described as trailblazing, an example of a discipline which set about addressing precisely such challenges (Atkinson et al, 2018). The report highlighted the underrepresentation of Black, Asian and Minority Ethnic (BAME) staff in history, detailing the racisms experienced by staff as well as exploring the narrowness of the scope of the history national curriculum, which was a significant obstacle to racial and ethnic diversity within the discipline. Comparable reports have been produced within other disciplines and working groups have been established to address these challenges.

The British Sociological Association (BSA) commissioned a report on *Race and Ethnicity in British Sociology* in similar vein, exploring the positioning of race and ethnicity in sociology curricula, the racial demographics of staff and students in sociology departments, the institutional commitment to change and the experiences of BAME staff, along with the roles of the BSA and other professional bodies (Joseph-Salisbury et al, 2020). The report found that there was significant underrepresentation among Black, Pakistani and Bangladeshi British academics, while BAME students were particularly underrepresented at the most elite Russell Group of universities. Almost a quarter of the undergraduate sociology degree programmes that were sampled made no explicit reference to 'race', 'ethnicity' or 'racism'. And where these were being taught, race and ethnicity were often taught as an add-on or specialist module, with little attention to 'Whiteness as a raced category'. Many respondents felt that there was resistance at institutional levels, while staff also reported student resistance, with defensiveness and denial around issues to do with race, ethnicity and racism. Clearly, much needed to be done to address these barriers, just as much needed to be done in order to support both students and staff to engage in these processes of change.

Similar issues emerged from the Social Policy Association (SPA) report titled *The Missing Dimension: Where Is 'Race' in Social Policy Teaching and Learning?* (Craig, Cole and Ali with Qureshi, 2019) which was published following an audit that was carried out between 2018 and 2019. In summary, this report suggested that the dimension of 'race' had been largely rendered invisible over the previous ten years as a direct consequence of government policy (policies based on denials of the extent of structural racism within British society, along with policies to promote a 'hostile environment' for asylum seekers, refugees and other immigrants more generally). BAME representation was found to be severely lacking in key SPA publications and activities. And respondents referred to the 'Whiteness' of social policy as a subject. Much needed to be done here too, then, if these imbalances were to be addressed and 'race' was to be regarded as a key element of the curriculum.

These reports demonstrated welcome recognition of the problems within their subject areas. While much could be achieved within particular academic disciplines, however, much else needed to change besides, as they also recognised. Universities were under additional pressures too as the result of wider processes of marketisation (Collini, 2017), as the critics of South African universities' increasing focus on neoliberal approaches to economic growth have already been quoted as reflecting (Chisholm, 2004).

Others have also pointed to the particular pressures on young academics, too often employed on precarious contracts, feeling undervalued, overworked and generally insecure (Begum and Saini, 2019), pressurised to publish in the most prestigious journals despite the challenges of doing so for those coming from non-Western or non-elite backgrounds (Day et al, 2022). Women were especially vulnerable as they tended to be allocated time-consuming caring roles on top of their regular academic commitments, looking after students' welfare while more senior male colleagues pursued their career-enhancing research and publication trajectories (Begum and Saini, 2019). Worrying attempts to rehabilitate the history of Britain's empire have also been identified in some fields, along with attempts to whitewash the academy's role in relation to racism (Begum and Saini, 2019).

The SPA report draws similar conclusions about the significance of external influences in the context of racist social policies and the 'hostile' environment in Britain. This was not just about economic policies and marketisation processes, then, but also about politicians' resorting to culture wars in the pursuit of their own agendas and interests. Educational initiatives cannot be expected to resolve structural inequalities on their own, in other words, an argument that has been applied to schooling and structural inequalities of class and gender, of course, as well to structural inequalities of race (Reay, 2017).

In summary, then, strategies have been and continue to be developed to address the marginalisation of Black students and staff along with strategies to widen the curricula accordingly. Most importantly too, decolonisation agendas have needed to address the residues of slavery and the colonial past that continue to underpin discriminatory attitudes in society more generally. As the summary of the report on the Black curriculum points out, the current history national curriculum 'systematically omits the contribution of Black British history in favour of a dominant White, Eurocentric curriculum that fails to reflect our multi ethnic and broadly diverse society' (Arday et al, 2020: 2). 'During this particularly factious time within our societal history', the report continues, 'the need for a curriculum that redefines conceptions of "Britishness" and how this aligns to our values and identities is integral towards developing an inclusive classroom'. 'The History National Curriculum in its current guise continues to disassociate Britain from a legacy that has oppressed black people historically in favour of a more romanticized, filtered legacy that positions Britannia as all-conquering and eternally embracive of ethnic and cultural difference' (Arday et al, 2020: 2).

There are significant implications here for the development of decolonisation strategies for adult community education and development in the Global North as well as in the Global South. Whose knowledge counts when it comes to designing the curriculum? And whose knowledge and experiences have been effectively marginalised?

Participatory action research and the promotion of knowledge democracy

Adult community education and development educators have much to learn from other disciplines' approaches. But they have particular experiences of their own to share too when it comes to addressing the question of whose knowledge counts. PAR was developed in the Global South before being taken up in a variety of ways in the Global North. In practice, some of these applications of PAR have been more emancipatory than others, just as Paulo Freire's own approaches have been applied in contested ways. Yet this in no way detracts from PAR's significance as a key component of strategies to challenge predominant knowledge systems, working towards the promotion of knowledge democracy in their stead.

A number of sociologists, adult educators and development professionals have played key roles in the development of PAR, starting from the pioneering work of Orlando Fals-Borda (1925–2008). As a Colombian sociologist and activist, Fals-Borda focused on the importance of valuing what people know already, then enabling them to acquire the research skills needed in order to create new knowledge for social change. Addressing academic sociologists in 1995, four years after the groundbreaking publication of *Action and Knowledge* (Fals-Borda and Rahman, 1991), Fals-Borda put forward his case as follows:

> Do not monopolise your knowledge nor impose arrogantly your techniques, but respect and combine your skills with the knowledge of the researched or grassroot communities, taking them as full partners and co-researcher. Do not trust elite versions of history and science which respond to dominant interests but be receptive to counter-narratives and try to recapture them. Do not depend solely on your culture to interpret facts, but recover local values, traits, beliefs, and arts for action by and with research organisations. (Gott, 2008)

This approach to PAR has been a major influence on very many adult community educators, development academics and activists over the years. Budd Hall has reflected on this, starting from his own experiences of developing adult education and action research in Tanzania, inspiring his people-centred approach to knowledge creation as a critical tool for political and cultural action. In his view, Orlando Fals-Borda's vision could be considered as a movement in the field of social research parallel even to that of Paulo Freire in the field of pedagogy. These ideas were taken up and developed by Budd Hall and his colleagues in Tanzania with the support of President Julius Nyerere (president of Tanzania from 1964 to 1985), an admirer of Gandhi's non-violent approach to the struggle for colonial freedom who was keen to promote alternative education and development strategies for the future (approaches that are explored in more detail in the following chapter).

Rajesh Tandon, Budd Hall's colleague and Co-Chair of the UNESCO Chair in Community Based Research and Social Responsibility in Higher Education, has paid similar tributes to Orlando Fals-Borda's pioneering work. The two met in person at a gathering in Venezuela in 1978, he explained, sharing ideas about taking participatory research forward. This meeting with Fals-Borda and other enthusiasts was the inspiration for Tandon to go on to form the Society for Participatory Research in Asia (PRIA) to support the development of PAR in India and elsewhere in Asia. Since then, PRIA has been providing training and practising PAR, building on local knowledge about sustainable development and gender equalities. This was the beginning of Rajesh Tandon's lifelong passion for the promotion of knowledge democracy (Mayo, 2020), valuing the knowledge, experiences and skills of everyone concerned with the promotion of sustainable development and social justice regardless of class, caste, race, ethnicity, age, ability, religion, sexuality or gender.

This commitment to PAR and knowledge democracy has been shared by many leading academics, professionals and activists. PRIA has collaborated with a range of organisations and individuals across the globe, from Miles Horton, John Gaventa and Juliet Merrifield at the Highlander Research and Education Center in the US through to PRIA's international partners in the Knowledge for Change Training Consortium (K4C), which was launched in 2017 to develop cadres of mentors skilled in the co-creation of knowledge on a global scale.

This consortium is based upon a series of hubs based in a growing number of different countries – over 20 countries from Africa, the Americas, Asia and Europe at the time of writing. These include Rhodes University in South Africa, incidentally, the launch pad for decolonisation agendas as already outlined earlier in this chapter, bringing these different strands together for progressive social change. As Budd Hall is on record as saying, 'Rajesh Tandon and I are very proud of the remarkable work which is being done at Rhodes University through your community university engagement centre and the Knowledge for Change hub. The news of the passion and professionalism of your K4C Hub is circulating all around the globe!' (Hall, 2022).

Each hub contains a higher education institution working in partnership with a civil society–based organisation to provide training for mentors. Once they have completed their 21-week course, these mentors then move on to become trainers themselves. This is about cascading the knowledge and skills for knowledge democracy on an international scale.

The training itself is provided through a combination of online learning and face-to-face learning, along with fieldwork, co-producing knowledge to tackle the priorities of the different communities in question. Communities have been concerned to address problems such as poverty, exclusion, gender-based violence and climate change, priorities in line with the wider goals of sustainable development and social justice. Since K4C's launch in 2017, the project has expanded, building on its initial successes. A trade union organisation has joined, an initiative that raises several new possibilities which are the subject of more detailed discussion in Chapter 6.

Meanwhile, PAR approaches have been continuing to contribute to the social sciences in general as well as to adult community education and development more specifically. These approaches have ranged from the use of participative techniques for business development agendas through to the use of PAR in the service of more sustainable, people-centred forms of international development. There is not the space for more detailed discussion here. Any summary would need to include the range of approaches developed by Robert Chambers and others at the Institute of Development Studies, University of Sussex (Chambers, 1983; Holland and Blackburn, 1998), who pioneered methodologies and practices in development from the bottom up.

Such a summary would also need to include the development of community–university research partnerships, both in Britain and internationally (Lepore et al, 2022). In principle (although admittedly not exclusively), such partnerships should involve participatory approaches to knowledge creation, actively involving communities in the initiation, control and ownership of the research. This is about developing mutually beneficial exchanges, as communities share their understandings, assets and needs while universities bring research resources, theoretical knowledge and expertise (Lepore et al, 2022). A 2014 UNESCO survey identified the growth of such partnerships internationally, with 95 per cent of all respondents believing that the co-creation of knowledge was their primary goal – although somewhat disappointingly, these were still very much top-down initiatives, with only 15 per cent having had their origins in their communities (Lepore et al, 2022).

There have been a range of such initiatives in Britain too, some sponsored by universities, reflecting their commitment to becoming more socially relevant, as in the case of the University of Brighton's Community University Partnership Programme. Some have been in response to external pressures to demonstrate such relevance. And others have been promoted in the past via government programmes to tackle social problems, from the British government's Community Development Projects (CDP), launched in 1969, through to more recent programmes to promote active citizenship (Mayo and Annette, 2010; Mayo et al, 2013). Each of these initiatives has had its critics, however, questioning the extent to which British governments have been prepared to address the structural inequalities that were underpinning communities' problems. There are many reasons why such initiatives have been limited in the past – and why community–university research partnerships face such challenges in the contemporary context, with increasing pressures for marketisation within institutions for higher education. There is not the space to go into further detail here, although the following chapter picks up on some aspects of these arguments in further detail as part of community development's history in the UK.

The point to emphasise here is simply that whatever their inherent limitations, such public policy initiatives can open spaces for popular education and PAR. Despite its inherent limitations, for example, CDP triggered a number of critical analyses about the underlying causes of poverty and deprivation (including *The Costs of Industrial Change*, CDP, 1976), as well as facilitating research and community action from the bottom up. There have been similar lessons to be learnt from subsequent programmes, including the above-mentioned programmes to promote active citizenship and community–university partnerships (Mayo and Annette, 2010; Mayo et al, 2013). Chapter 7 includes further discussion of these types of programmes, both in Britain and the US.

Comparable conclusions have also been drawn from more a recent research initiative on 'connecting communities through research' (Banks et al, 2019). This was to be about researching *with* communities, rather than researching *about* communities, drawing upon similar approaches to PAR and community–university partnership. These have had their inherent limitations too, especially challenging given the marketisation of higher education more widely. The teams themselves were realistic about the limitations of such initiatives in communities that were suffering the effects of austerity following on from years of industrial decline. Whatever the limitations, though, participatory research partnerships could and did bring people's experiential knowledge to the surface, enabling them to create new knowledge, it was argued, with the potential to contribute to processes of positive change (Ward et al, 2019).

Participatory action research and knowledge democracy

The development of PAR has had much to offer, despite the limitations of some of PAR's applications in practice, in particular policy contexts. PAR has at least the potential to challenge traditional views about whose knowledge counts and whose knowledge is correspondingly undervalued as a result. There are significant implications here for the decolonisation of the curriculum, co-creating new approaches to knowledge: knowledge democracy for social change.

Summarising their approach to knowledge democracy more generally, Lepore and his colleagues explain that that this 'refers to an interrelationship of phenomena that intentionally link values of democracy and action to the process of producing and using knowledge' (Lepore et al, 2022: 80). 'Firstly, knowledge democracy acknowledges the importance of the existence of multiple epistemologies or ways of knowing', they continue, 'such as organic, spiritual, and land-based systems), a diversity of conceptual frameworks arising from social movements, and the knowledge of marginalised or excluded social groups'. They go on to affirm that 'knowledge is both created and represented in multiple forms (including text, image, numbers, story, music, drama, poetry, ceremony, meditation and more)' (Lepore et al, 2022: 80). This is about co-creating knowledge as a powerful tool for taking action for a fairer, healthier world, they conclude, where the benefits of knowledge are freely available to all.

Their concept of knowledge democracy has so much to offer. Yet the very inclusiveness of their approach raises further questions in its turn, as the following section sets out to explore.

Reflexive approaches to the validation of truth claims, whatever their provenance

The notion of multiple epistemologies raises further questions that have been of increasing concern in recent years. Knowledge has been and continues to be created and represented in a variety of ways. So, how might the truth claims of such different forms of knowledge be evaluated, whatever their provenance?

The reasons for concern with these questions can be traced back to the growth of populism – particularly, although not exclusively, Far Right populism – in Britain and elsewhere. Previous chapters have already outlined a number of ways in which Far Right populist politicians have been fuelling the so-called culture wars, playing on widespread feelings of alienation, anxiety and distrust in uncertain times, peddling toxic messages of racism, anti-Semitism, Islamophobia and misogyny in response. Far Right populism has been associated with emotional appeals to notions of identity, such as national, ethnic or religious identities, including White supremacist identities, typically framed in terms of 'us' in contrast with 'the other' (Mayo, 2020). Responding to such appeals with 'the facts' simply misses the point: these appeals are not based on rational arguments in the first place.

It is not just that Far Right populism plays on people's emotions, especially people's fears and resentments about others who are believed to be doing better in challenging times – although Far Right populists can and do indeed play upon precisely such emotions. The reality is more complicated, however. Contemporary populisms have roots in aspects of postmodernist thinking over recent decades.

Postmodernist critiques have fundamentally questioned previously widespread 'grand' theories about society and social change, including

Marxist analyses of the structural causes of class exploitation and oppression. They have, in fact, rejected the notion that such overarching explanations could have validity in the first place. This was about deconstructing the grand theories of the past.

Although the sociologist David Harvey has welcomed aspects of such critiques, including their emphases on the importance of understanding social divisions in terms of gender, sexuality and race as well as social class, he has also pointed to some of their inherent limitations. In his view, the deconstruction of previously recognised approaches could lead to the 'suspicion of any narrative that aspires to coherence'. Most importantly for the concerns of this chapter, such approaches potentially challenge 'all consensual standards of truth and justice, of ethics and meaning' (Harvey, 1990: 350). Postmodernist scepticism, in other words, has been seen as paving the way for more general doubts about the very possibility of objective truth.

In the context of the rise of Far Right populism, such a possibility would seem to be deeply disturbing. If there are no objective truths, then politicians can, and indeed do, say whatever they like in order to win support for their causes, whether personal and/or political. The potentially disastrous effects of such approaches were seen only too clearly when Donald Trump's supporters claimed that the election of Joe Biden as president had been fraudulent, leading to chaotic scenes when the Capitol was stormed in January 2020. There were parallels with the mobilisations that took place in Brazil following the electoral defeat of Jair Bolsonaro in 2022. These may be extreme examples. But they do point to the potential logic of postmodernist thinking. 'If anything goes, then any interpretation is as valid as any other. So, why fuss about the facts?'

Of course, the notion of multiple epistemologies is not undermined as a result of such concerns about 'the facts'. There are indeed different ways of knowing that draw on diverse conceptual frameworks. The point is absolutely not to disregard frameworks that differ from Western Enlightenment models. Rather, the point is to explore ways in which different forms of knowledge – and different types of truth claims – can be evaluated. This, then, is not about questioning the validity of different ways of knowing per se. But it does suggest that different ways of knowing can still be subjected to critical analysis.

There are significant challenges here. If people, or indeed communities, say that they feel threatened or undermined by others, for example, then that statement has to be accepted and respected as such. It is neither logical nor indeed helpful to suggest otherwise. The people or communities involved can, of course, be invited to give reasons for their feelings, though. And such an invitation might be issued in ways that open constructive dialogues about tackling the underlying causes of their anxieties in the first place. The question is not about whether but about how to respect different ways of knowing – exploring different ways of validating truth claims, whatever their provenance.

Challenging epistemological legacies from the Enlightenment

As critics have been pointing out, the predominance of Western Enlightenment ways of knowing has been posing challenges here, too often implying that these are the only viable approaches. By implication, knowledge based upon people's personal experiences would be seen as inherently inferior, along with knowledge based upon storytelling and naming one's own reality, such as one's lived experiences of racism. It was only knowledge rooted in Enlightenment values of rationalism and progress that counted, just as it was Western theorists that provided the framework for explaining the foundations of modernity, liberalism and capitalism in the world today.

These were extremely partial views, of course, as critics such as Spickard have been pointing out (Spickard, 2022), a very skewed approach based in early social scientists' erroneous assumptions about Europe as the leading edge of world history. As Giddens and others have also pointed out, the founding fathers (such as Durkheim and Weber) concentrated on matters that explained their own situation, underplaying the role of colonialism in European ascendance in the process (Giddens, 1976). This has been described as 'epistemological ethnocentrism', the belief that 'scientifically there is nothing to be learned from "them" unless it is already "ours" or comes out of "us"' (Spickard, 2022: 158, quoting Mudimbe, 1988: 15).

Critics such as Cedric Robinson have also pointed to the ways in which Western intellectual traditions have been linked to the normalisation of social and political inequalities in contemporary times. Far from prefiguring Enlightenment values of freedom and democracy, classical texts such as Plato's *Republic* have provided what Robinson has described as 'a rhetorical cornice for later disputants about democracy' (Robinson, 2019: 127). It was not just that Plato accepted the existence of slavery without question – which he did – or the myth that he referred to, reflecting on the god-given nature of social hierarchies, the ingredient of gold in the making of the Rulers, silver in the making of the Auxiliaries and iron and bronze in the farmers and other workers (Robinson, 2019: 133). It was the influence that such ideas have held over generations of Western thinkers that Robinson went on to emphasise, from Hobbes and Locke through to more recent authorities in the US. 'Plato survives', Robinson concluded, 'because if he had not existed, he would have had to be invented' (Robinson, 2019: 142). Ideas about hierarchies have persisted in varying forms, including all-too-pervasive ideas about racial inequalities, deeply embedded in US and elsewhere, including Britain. Small wonder that critics have pointed to the contradictions inherent in Western Enlightenment traditions.

Being critically aware of such contradictions doesn't need to imply rejecting Western thinkers altogether, though, as Meghji and others have been arguing (Meghji et al, 2022). On the contrary, in their view, Marx and Weber made relevant contributions, even if their analyses were partial rather than omniscient. Similar points could be made about more recent thinkers whose work has been described as resonating with Enlightenment traditions, such as Habermas, who drew upon Marxist approaches, if only to move away from these in his later writings, as the previous chapter has already outlined.

In his later writings Habermas came to focus on questions of language and communication, exploring different aspects of rationality in the process (Habermas, 1986). In summary, he distinguished between

- *strategic action*, directed towards instrumental goals such as economic development in *the systems world*;
- *communicative action*, concerned with the expressive, emotional and aesthetic aspects of *the lifeworld*. (my emphasis)

Strategic action could be implemented through the use of economic and/or political power, whereas communicative action was based upon reason and the reconciliation of differences, rooted in shared values and norms, as experienced through churches, families and neighbourhoods, for example. This was a very different approach.

Habermas considered that the lifeworld was being colonised by the systems world. However, this did not imply the rejection of science and technology per se. He recognised that instrumental action was needed for economic development. But Habermas was specifically concerned that the space for communicative action should be safeguarded rather than colonised by the logic of the systems world. He was anxious as to whether corporate capitalism was penetrating people's everyday lives through these colonisation processes, just as he was anxious as to whether participatory democracy was being replaced with representative democracy. His own preference was for more deliberative forms of decision-making based on equal rights.

Habermas' critics have challenged the bases for these categories, pointing to the ways in which these different worlds actually overlap. Nor are values in the lifeworld as simple as Habermas seems to be suggesting. For a start, lifeworld cultures can be hierarchical and oppressive. Fundamentalist religious movements are by no means emancipatory, for example (Fraser, 2002). Nancy Fraser has particularly questioned Habermas' separation of the public from the private sphere for its unequal implications for women, re-enforcing the status quo by relegating women to the supposedly cosy world of hearth and home.

The point is absolutely not to suggest that Habermas' approach to communicative action has been unproblematic. There have been challenges aplenty, although there is not the space to develop these criticisms further within this chapter. Rather, the question is whether Habermas' interest in deliberative democracy has anything to contribute in the context of debates on rationality and competing forms of knowledge in the contemporary context.

While Habermas was concerned by what he believed to be the colonisation of the lifeworld, he was not arguing for the rejection of rationality per se. On the contrary, in his view, rationality was the quality that made action defendable against criticism. Whatever the values or opinions being expressed, those holding them needed to be able to respond to their critics with reasoned arguments. In other words, it was important not to give up on the possibility of a rational understanding of the lifeworld.

Habermas' approach to deliberative democracy has also been the subject of considerable criticism. His approach was based on the notion that agreements could be reached if participants enjoyed equality in terms of their access to information and the ability to put their views across. This would seem utopian, to say the least, in view of the structural inequalities that would need to be addressed. But this doesn't necessarily imply that the notion of deliberative approaches needs to be dismissed out of hand, offering alternatives to the toxicity that has characterised so much of the discussion of differences in the context of contemporary culture wars.

Similar arguments could be applied to the use of reasoned arguments more generally too, as Habermas himself suggested. The question was not *whether* but *how* such forms of reasoning might be appropriately applied and in what contexts. How could very different ways of knowing be debated from varying perspectives while being treated with absolute respect? And how might populist critiques of Western scientific forms of knowledge be addressed in the context of emotive debates on decolonisation? The following case study from South Africa illustrates some of these challenges in practice.

Case Study: HIV/AIDS and the Treatment Action Campaign in post-apartheid South Africa

Powerful stereotypes and prejudices have been associated with HIV/AIDS, including the racist myth that this was a 'Black disease' (Robins, 2005). It was therefore quite conceivable, it has been suggested, that African nationalists such as South Africa's President Mbeki could interpret research-based AIDS statistics as 'evidence of a long colonial and apartheid legacy of scientific racism' (Robins, 2005: 114). These could be 'read through the colour-coded lens of colonial histories of discrimination and dispossession' along with the specific histories of capitalism and the contemporary interests of the pharmaceutical industry (Robins, 2005: 114) wanting to use Africans as guinea pigs for scientific experiments with their drugs. These anti-retroviral (ARV) drugs were being described as dangerously toxic, while sex with virgins, including infants, was being advocated as an alternative form of cure.

Challenging these myths was going to be problematic, to say the least. Local myths about the most appropriate forms of treatment were being combined with conspiracy theories about the interests of the pharmaceutical industry along with distrust of scientific authority more generally in the context of documents referring to 'the crimes and falsities of "scientific" Eurocentrism, its dogmas imposed upon our being as brands of a definitive, "universal" truth' (quoted in Robins, 2005: 119). Although the president came to distance himself from these views eventually, devastating damage had already been done by these 'dissident' theories in terms of their impact on public health interventions.

Meanwhile, alternative approaches were being developed by trade union and community activists from the bottom up. The Treatment Action Campaign (TAC) that was established in December 1998 played an extraordinary role in convincing people of the case for very different approaches, building a wide coalition of forces in the process, from the community level upwards. Through the active involvement of working-class communities, trade unionists and the poor, particularly poor women, TAC challenged the myths and the cultural nationalist/identity politics that had been promoted by sections of the African National Congress leadership at the time. With widespread support from health professionals, scientists, the media and ordinary South African citizens, TAC used rights-based provisions in the South African constitution to put pressure on the government and the pharmaceutical industry in order to ensure that poor people could indeed gain access to effective AIDS treatment (Robins, 2005).

TAC's story provides a powerful example of community-based education and development in action, then, although the detail is beyond the scope of this chapter. The point to emphasise here is that TAC succeeded in addressing competing knowledge claims, engaging with popular myths and disentangling different critiques of Western science within the context of wider debates on decolonisation and scientific racism in post-apartheid South Africa, building a broad coalition in support of an effective ARV treatment programme in the process.

Conclusions

There is much to be learnt from strategies for decolonisation across a range of disciplines. While there are important lessons for community education and development, they have much to contribute in their turn, including lessons from the varying histories of PAR. Together, these experiences demonstrate the importance of understanding decolonisation as a process rather than seeing this as a one-off event, diversifying curricula *and* subjecting curricula to continuing interrogation. This needs to involve questioning the basis for previously accepted forms of knowledge as well as for more mainstream forms of knowledge, taking respectful account of multiple ways of knowing while subjecting them to critical analysis, whatever their provenance.

There are significant pedagogical implications here. It is not just about what is to be taught but how this is to be learnt if decolonisation is to engage learners in ongoing processes of critical reflexivity. Critical thinking has to be central to these pedagogies, alongside critical understandings of the roots of structural inequalities. And these need to be accompanied by respectful understandings about different ways of knowing, including experiential ways of knowing about their continuing impacts in contemporary contexts.

4

Exploring the contested histories of adult community education and development

This chapter explores the contested histories of adult community education and development per se, from post-slavery experiences in the US through to post-colonial experiences in Africa and elsewhere. Rather than attempting to provide a comprehensive review, the chapter's aim is far more modest – to identify common threads that interweave with the themes of cultural wars, the development of critical consciousness and decolonisation, with a particular focus on the threads that have relevance for more recent debates about community education and development in practice.

The previous chapter challenged a number of assumptions about whose knowledge counts and whose knowledge is correspondingly devalued as a result. This chapter explores additional questions about whose interests are actually being served when people's knowledge is enhanced through community education and development projects and programmes. Is the aim to build communities' resilience to cope with the challenges that face them, promoting self-reliance and individual advancement within the confines of their contemporary situations? Or do the aims go further, to enable them to address the underlying structural causes of their problems? To what extent have community education programmes been designed to safeguard the interests of the status quo? And how far have they been designed and delivered in more challenging ways within the context of strategies for decolonisation?

These questions have already been posed in previous chapters in relation to the contributions of Paulo Freire and others in different contexts. Here, the focus is upon projects and programmes in the post-Civil War context in the US and the post-Second World War context in Britain's African colonies. The final section reflects on potential connections with more recent initiatives to address the challenges of the legacies of Black migration from the South to the cities of the North in the US and Black and Asian migrations to Britain following the Second World War.

Community education and development in the US, post-slavery: from Booker T. Washington to W.E.B. Du Bois and beyond

Slavery was formally ended in the US in 1865 with the 13th Amendment to the Constitution. But early hopes for racial justice were soon dashed. Racial segregation and structural inequalities were re-enforced in the post-Reconstruction Southern states, including re-enforcement via mob violence in the form of lynchings. This situation continued right up to the Civil Rights Movement's challenges to segregation from the mid-20th century onwards.

This history of violent oppression formed the background context, impacting on Booker T. Washington's strategies for community education and development in the latter part of the 19th century and the early years of the 20th century. His approach has been criticised by the more radical Black leader W.E.B. Du Bois and others for being too cautious and too limited in its aspirations for Black liberation (Du Bois, 2017). Yet critics have also recognised the particular risks that have faced those who challenged White supremacy in the Southern states, especially in the most dangerous years of the post-Reconstruction period.

Booker T. Washington himself was born into slavery on a plantation in Virginia in 1856. After abolition, he managed to get an education at Hampton Normal and Agricultural Institute (now Hampton University), which had been founded to nurture thrift, industry and self-reliance among the newly emancipated populations of the region, but without fundamentally disrupting the structures of racial inequality that persisted despite the formal abolition of slavery. Coming from a very poor family, the young Washington worked as a janitor at Hampton to help to pay his tuition fees. He went on to win a scholarship and then subsequently taught at Hampton, imbibing much of its ethos in the process. This was where he stayed until 1881, when the State of Alabama provided funds to set up the Tuskegee Industrial and Normal Institute (now Tuskegee University).

As the first principal of Tuskegee, Washington set out to promote 'community development, networking and fighting against the perception of Black inferiority, at a time when racism was institutional' (Bieze and Gasman, 2012: 4). Beginning with some 30 students and one teacher, Tuskegee expanded rapidly over the coming decades, with some 2,000 students by 1911, along with an extension programme that included short courses for farmers. The emphasis was upon the development of practical knowledge and know-how, with students growing their own food as well as acquiring practical skills such as carpentry and plumbing, along with 'girls' trades' such as laundering, cooking and sewing. Night schools were also organised in Southern villages, spreading this type of approach to practical education for self-reliance, encouraging communities to build their own schools as part of the process. This was about communities pulling themselves up by their own bootstraps, in other words learning for survival, despite the continuing inequalities of the post-Reconstruction South. Zora Neale Hurston's novel *Their Eyes Were Watching God* includes a description of life in the Black community of Eatonville, founded on such principles of self-reliance in the Deep South, as Chapter 8 considers in further detail (Hurston, 2007).

At first sight, Booker T. Washington's approach seems to exemplify so many problematic aspects of community education and community development more generally. Similar criticisms were being levelled at India's Community Development programmes post-independence, for example – programmes that set out to promote economic and social betterment that would keep everyone busy, body and mind (Brayne, 1945; Mayer, 1958) yet still within their 'place' without formulating explicit challenges to existing land, property and caste relationships. As a United Nations evaluation team concluded on their visit in the late 1950s, poorer peasants still lacked incentives while richer peasants and landlords continued to appropriate surpluses as well as benefitting from the resources made available via the Indian community development programmes themselves (discussed in Mayo, 1975a).

Booker T. Washington's own position was more complex than had appeared at first, however. This helps to explain why the far more radical W.E.B. Du Bois respected Washington as a distinguished Black leader despite fundamentally disagreeing with so many of his opinions and approaches. Du Bois responded to the publication of Washington's autobiography, *Up from Slavery*, in 1901 with significant but not entirely unsympathetic rebuttals. For example, his chapter 'Of Mr Booker T. Washington and others' in *The Souls of Black Folk* recognised Washington's achievements in gaining sympathy and support from Whites in the South as well as in the North: 'One hesitates, therefore, to criticise a life which, beginning with so little, has done so much' (Du Bois, 2017: 49). Critics admired Washington's sincerity of purpose, Du Bois explained, and they co-operated with him as far as they consciously could, but honest criticism was essential to the soul of democracy in Du Bois' view. He went on to highlight the ways in which Washington represented 'the old attitude of adjustment and submission' Du Bois, 2017: 54), focusing on economic improvements within the status quo rather than going on to campaign for social and political rights, including the right to the vote on the same terms as White people.

Washington himself expressed a variety of views, though, depending upon the audiences that he was addressing. Although Tuskegee obtained funding from the State of Alabama, this was never sufficient, so he needed to appeal to Northern philanthropists' self-interest for additional funds. And Tuskegee's approach to education fitted the bill precisely – developing

Black people's practical skills while encouraging the values of hard work, self-reliance and thrift. As he himself explained, he sought to re-assure White people that 'you and your families will be surrounded by the most patient, faithful, law abiding and unresentful people that the world has seen' (Washington, 2021: 192). In the speech that he made in Atlanta, Georgia in 1895, he went even further: 'The wisest among my race understand that the agitation of questions of social equality is the extremist folly and that progress in the enjoyment of all the privileges that will come to us must be the result of severe and constant struggle rather than of artificial forcing' (Washington, 2021: 193).

He could hardly have been surprised that he was criticised for being an 'Uncle Tom' as a result, a race traitor who was selling out on civil rights for meagre material gains in the here and now (Bieze and Gasman, 2012). Yet Washington did support the goals of civil rights in principle, believing that progress could be won for the longer term through Tuskegee's 'softly, softly' approach. Industrial education and economic progress could provide the route to greater equality for the future, or so he believed at first.

In later years, he became less optimistic. Yet he remained discreet, lobbying behind the scenes against racial segregation rather than taking a more public stand. He modified his views on education too as he came to recognise the importance of book-learning as well as the importance of more practical forms of vocational learning. 'Because I have spoken so strongly in favor of industrial training', he argued, 'I would not have it understood that I undervalue academic education', which he saw as necessary the development of Black professionals' (Bieze and Gasman, 2012: 131). His support for book-learning came to include learning about Black history and culture too as part of wider struggles for Black empowerment.

Washington and Du Bois did not come much closer together, though, despite such apparent shifts in Washington's thinking. On the contrary, in fact, there were instances of personal rivalry, according to Aiello's reflections on their writings (Aiello, 2016) as they competed for leadership after the death of Frederick Douglass, the previously acknowledged leader in 1895. For example, Du Bois was a prime mover in setting up the National Association for the Advancement of Coloured People in 1909. Washington had not wished to be associated with this. He was dubious about people in the North getting involved in Southern struggles more generally too, once referring to Du Bois as 'stirring up racial strife in the heart of the South' (Aiello, 2016: 413). Du Bois didn't really understand the South or, by implication, the risks for Black activists in the Southern states, he suggested, risks that have continued into more recent times, from the racist murder of 14-year-old Emmet Till in 1955, in the run-up to the Civil Rights Movement of the 1950s and 1960s, through to the more recent killings that sparked the Black Lives Matter Movement.

Aiello's reading of their writings concluded that Du Bois was actually more generous than Washington in the end, however strongly he disagreed with the latter's views. Du Bois paid tribute to Washington's sincerity of purpose, for example, emphasising that he had a perfect right to his opinions but maintaining that he was wrong about the position of Black people in the US, underestimating their sufferings. Du Bois explained this view in what has been described as a courteous letter to the peoples of Britain and Europe (Aiello, 2016: 408), written in response to Washington's more optimistic accounts. When Booker T. Washington died, in 1915, Du Bois even described him as the greatest Black leader since Frederick Douglass.

Du Bois' ability to discuss fundamental differences with his contemporaries in respectful ways seems particularly striking – and relevant – in the context of more contemporary debates and debating styles, especially the styles associated with contemporary cultural wars. Du Bois was, however, very critical of Washington's gradualist approach to racial justice via community development and self-reliance from the bottom up, just as he was very critical of Washington's limited approach to learning, emphasising the importance of vocational education and practical skills to the detriment of more theoretical forms of learning. These differences re-emerge as continuing themes in subsequent debates about adult community education and development, demonstrating the continuing relevance of Du Bois' thinking as well as the relevance of his approach to engaging with differences in mutually respectful ways within movements for social justice and democratic change.

Du Bois' contributions to struggles for civil rights in the US and internationally

Du Bois' contributions have very many resonances, over and above his duels with Booker T. Washington on the subject of community education and development in the aftermath of slavery in the US. He was a major influence on struggles for freedom from colonial rule across Africa and elsewhere, as well as a major influence on struggles for racial justice within the US itself. The colour line was, he argued, the key problem for the 20th century, just as it has continued to be subsequently. 'How does it feel to be a problem?' he went on ask his readers, born with a veil between Black and White, with two souls, two thoughts, as a Black American (Du Bois, 2017: 8–9).

Racial injustice was the central challenge that had to be faced, with demands for the right to vote, civic equality and education freely available for all, Black as well as White. Du Bois argued that these demands could not be traded for short-term economic gains as capitalism spread with its emphasis on 'material prosperity as the touchstone of life' (Du Bois, 2017: 80). Nor could economic power be sustained for the longer term without political power and civil rights in any case, in his view. On the contrary, Black Americans were demanding equality – 'political equality, industrial equality and social equality' – and would never be satisfied with anything less (Du Bois, 2017: 45).

Du Bois also argued for a wider approach to education, including higher education. Poor schooling and a narrow, vocational curriculum had been a major feature of life for Black communities following the American Civil War. What was needed, in contrast, was a balance between 'the ideal and the practical in workable equilibrium' (Du Bois, 2017: 90), blending knowledge and culture with more vocational forms of learning. Whites' fears about educating their former slaves were understandable, he recognised, but these were challenges that had to be faced. He himself was very widely read, as his own writings testify, demonstrating his knowledge of history, the classics and the arts, writings that included his reflections on the Sorrow Songs that expressed Black experiences of exile and slavery, for example (Du Bois, 2017). He was, in addition, an original social scientist, challenging negative stereotypes about Black communities through his careful collection and critical examination of the evidence demonstrating the long-term effects of slavery. Overall, he was an activist rather than an armchair academic, although he did hold a number of academic positions and very much valued these opportunities for teaching and writing. Towards the end of his life, it was to these aspects of his work that he referred when asked what he would include in his epitaph (Du Bois, 1971: 708). But it has been for his internationalism that he has been particularly appreciated in the context of debates about decolonisation.

Du Bois had been educated in the North, eventually completing his PhD at Harvard University in 1895. Before going to Harvard, he had also spent time in Berlin on a scholarship, a formative experience which had further widened his world views. This internationalism became a defining feature of Du Bois' legacy. He travelled widely in Europe, visiting the USSR and China as well as visiting several African countries.

Du Bois was clear about the nature of the inequalities that needed to be challenged at the international level, describing empire as the domination of White Europe over Black Africa and Asia 'through political power built on the economic control of labor, incomes and ideas' (Du Bois, 1975: 96). In this summary he drew upon Marxist understandings of the interconnections between slavery and the development of capitalism and imperialism, while recognising the significance of the battle of ideas, including the battle of ideas about racism that needed to be challenged within trade unions and progressive movements as well as within the wider society.

He celebrated the contributions of the Russian Revolution in 1917 while maintaining a critical stance. The USSR did not offer the only path towards socialism in his view; he was in favour of allying with social democratic welfare states as well as with communist states. And he supported the development of co-operatives, building upon Black communities' traditions of mutual support. This approach was to re-emerge with the concept of 'African Socialism', which drew on these traditions (or perceptions of how these traditions might have functioned in the past), following decolonisation.

Du Bois played a key role in movements for colonial freedom overall, drafting the letter which went to European leaders from the first Pan-African Conference in 1900 that asked them to join the struggle against racism and to grant African and West Indian colonies self-government, as well as respecting the integrity and independence of free states such as Abyssinia, Liberia and Haiti. This was about striving for the absolute equality of races as the Manifesto of the Second Pan-African Congress demanded in 1919.

While Du Bois was very supportive of movements for decolonisation, however, he expressed some reservations about what he described as sincere but potentially misplaced 'Back to Africa' initiatives to encourage Black Americans to return to contribute to African development. After 300 years in the US, he questioned whether many of these migrants would be well equipped with the necessary skills to become pioneers in Africa. The implication was that solidarity was essential, but that Africans themselves should be in the lead in their own countries.

The African countries Du Bois visited included Ghana, having known the Ghanaian leader, Kwame Nkrumah, since the Fifth Pan-African Conference in 1945. He could not attend the Ghanaian independence celebrations in 1957, however, having been unable to obtain a passport at that stage of the Cold War. He was also keen that Ghana should play a leading role in the Pan-African movement and in post-colonial development in Black Africa more widely, views that Nkrumah shared strongly. It was on another visit to Ghana in 1963 that Du Bois died.

There is not the space here to go into further detail about the achievements of W.E.B. Du Bois and his contributions to the struggle for civil rights at home in the US as well as to movements for decolonisation and development internationally. He has, in summary, been a major influence in both respects. Political leaders who were influenced by Du Bois have included Leopold Senghor of Senegal and Jomo Kenyatta of Kenya, along with anti-racist writers and activists such as C.L.R. James, George Padmore and Aime Cesaire. Pan-Africanism has taken a variety of forms in different contexts over time, but there have been common threads emphasising the importance of solidarity across national boundaries along with pride in African histories and cultures as part of movements for colonial freedom. These are also strands that re-emerge in contemporary and more recent debates about community education and development as part of the histories of decolonisation, both in Africa and elsewhere.

Community education and community development within strategies for decolonisation

This takes the discussion to the intertwined histories of community education and development and decolonisation in the post-war period. Adult education has a much longer history by far, and so, of course, does community development, from the Settlement Houses that were developed in Britain and the US to provide services in deprived communities in the 19th century onwards to more recent times (Toynbee Hall was founded in London's East End in 1884, and Hull-House in Chicago was founded in 1889, for example). These initiatives have their own contested histories, valued for providing essential services to deprived communities yet criticised for too often doing so in top-down, paternalistic and disempowering ways.

Post-war approaches to community education and development have been similarly contested. This was a particularly significant period in the context of decolonisation, with considerable interest from the recently formed United Nations Organization as well as from Britain as a major colonial power. Future strategies for decolonisation were under way, in fact, even before the end of the Second World War. In 1944, the British Colonial Office had produced a report titled *Mass Education in African Society*, followed up by *Social Development in the British Colonial Territories* in 1948. These reports were indicative of the Colonial Office's increasing concern about the prospects for Britain's colonies.

Independence was still seen as being some way off, despite the pressures from movements for colonial freedom. There was also powerful resistance to the very idea of colonial freedom in some political quarters. But these were issues that had to be faced for the future all the same – issues that became more pressing with the advent of the Cold War. Could the colonies be kept safely within the Western fold? Or might they be tempted to ally with the socialist camp under the leadership of the USSR? There were political considerations here, as well as concerns with social and economic development. The British wanted 'to encourage democracy and local initiative' and 'to establish solid foundations for the approaching self-government', David Brokensha and Peter Hodge pointed out (Brokensha and Hodge, 1969: 164). This was about keeping the former colonies safe for Western-style democracy. Mass education and community development were central to this strategy.

The United Nations Organization that had been established at the end of the Second World War became similarly concerned to promote adult community education and community development. This was then defined as a 'process designed to create conditions of economic and social progress for the whole community with its active participation' (United Nations, 1955) – a definition that raised a number of questions in its turn. These questions involved whose benefit this process was for, and with what degree of power or influence for the communities concerned, questions that have been raised in many contexts, including that of the US 'War on Poverty', more of which subsequently (Moynihan, 1969; Marris and Rein, 1972).

Reflecting on his experiences in Ghana in the post-war period, meanwhile, Peter Du Sautoy recognised that 'Whether we like it or not the original conception of community development held within it, in spite of its emphasis on self-help and giving force to local initiative, a strong element of benevolent paternalism' (Du Sautoy, 1958: 11). These were contested approaches, then, reflecting the interests of the colonisers or former colonisers yet containing possibilities for more transformative outcomes.

The Ghanaian experience provides illustrations here. Adult literacy had been the starting point for community development initiatives, including women's projects to promote health and well-being before independence in what was then the Gold Coast. The Convention People's Party (CPP), which Nkrumah led, supported plans for just such programmes for mass literacy, mass education and community development in preparation for national independence, the first independent nation in Black Africa. Nkrumah himself subsequently reflected on the continuing importance of 'intensive education of the masses and of ourselves' (that is, political leaders and activists) post-independence, including through the development of study circles among young people (Nkrumah, 1997: 3). Mass education and community development would be able to cut both ways, it seemed, with the potential to promote decolonisation and development as well as to keep the colonised firmly in their places within Western spheres of influence.

In the event, Nkrumah was subsequently ousted by a coup. He had evidently alienated public opinion across a wide political spectrum, as well as upsetting powerful forces internationally. Whatever the criticisms of his time in office (including criticisms levelled by former sympathisers such as C.L.R. James, among others) and whatever the role that Western interests may – or may not – have played in Nkrumah's downfall, Western countries seemed fine with the results (Fitch and Oppenheimer, 1966; Williams, 2021). Ghana remained firmly within the Western fold.

As Brokensha and Hodge reflected in similar vein, in relation to US strategies in this Cold War period, by far the greatest American expenditures on community development were occurring in those countries (Vietnam, Thailand, Laos) considered to be most threatened by communism (Brokensha and Hodge, 1969). Community development could be used to win hearts and minds, then, or simply to impose settlements by force. This was the case in the context of the 'community development villages' that were imposed in Malaya as part of the British counter-insurgency programme, for example – a programme that forcibly resettled half a million people as part of British military operations against communist insurgents.

Community development programmes could be – and were – promoted for the political ends of the colonisers or former colonisers alongside neo-colonial agendas for safeguarding their economic interests. This was particularly marked in the case of Britain, which had emerged from the Second World War in a seriously weakened state, weighed down with debt from war loans. Community development schemes had particular advantages here as a strategy for increasing exports and promoting increased production through the use of self-help initiatives in the colonies. Formal independence represented no more than the first step towards decolonisation, then, with community education and development as the potential harbingers of recolonisation in the longer term.

Looking back on these debates some five decades later, these concerns seem more relevant than ever given the subsequent history of neoliberal globalisation. But there were, of course, inherent contradictions too. Outstanding educators have also made extraordinary contributions in these contexts, promoting learning for freedom, justice and social transformation.

Anti-imperialist educators

Adult community education has a contested history from the 19th century onwards, as has already been suggested, with debates about 'useful', instrumental learning versus 'really useful knowledge'. The debates centred around whether education was intended to enable learners to cope within their present circumstances or to understand the underlying causes of their problems in order to develop effective strategies for social change (Johnson, 1979). Similar debates developed within and between Ruskin College, Oxford and the Workers Educational Association (WEA) from the start of the 20th century (Mayo, 2020), debates which have continued in varying forms as marketised agendas have become increasingly influential, to the detriment of spaces for popular education for social transformation (Evans et al, 2022). Chapter 6 explores these questions in relation to trade union education more specifically.

These debates ran through the history of adult education and decolonisation during and just after the Second World War. The British government promoted education programmes within the armed forces through the Army Bureau of Current Affairs (ABCA), programmes that continued after the hostilities ended and servicemen and women awaited demobilisation. This was all part of 'building up not only an intelligent and well-informed society but an electorate which will preserve and enhance the victory we have so dearly bought' (ABCA, 1945: 4–5). For whatever reason, then – to promote active citizenship, to keep the troops occupied or whatever else – these programmes were influential, credited with building support for the development of the welfare state in post-war Britain. And they included discussions about 'The Colonial Problem' (Hinden, 1945).

Guidance for running these discussions emphasised the importance of engaging the learners and encouraging active participation. Starting by exploring learners' stereotypes about the colonies, the sessions were to move on to consider British colonial policy 'to eliminate poverty while helping colonial peoples towards self-government' (Hinden, 1945: 7). This was in Britain's interest, it was explained, recognising the importance of the colonies for a variety of reasons, including the provision of raw materials and trade, as well as the importance of contributing to world stability. 'It was undoubtedly true', it was recognised, 'that a great part of the wealth of many Colonies has been exploited in the interests of traders and financiers from overseas' (Hinden, 1945: 16). No wonder that there were colonial peoples who were critical and resentful, arguing that 'We don't want your charity. We only want you to get out' (Hinden, 1945: 15). Colonial grievances had to be remedied, then, as part of these processes of decolonisation. These sessions were clearly encouraging critical discussions about the future of the colonies. Anti-imperialist educators were to take the process further, supporting the development of adult learning in the colonies themselves.

Thomas Hodgkin made outstanding contributions in these respects. After his Oxford University education, Hodgkin spent time in Palestine before the Second World War, a relatively brief experience that confirmed him in his views as an anti-imperialist, becoming active in the League Against Imperialism as well as becoming a Marxist. He developed his interest in adult education, working for a period as a tutor for the WEA before becoming the Secretary of the Oxford Delegacy for Extra-Mural Studies and a fellow of Balliol College Oxford in 1945. These experiences – of adult education and anti-imperialism – laid the groundwork for his subsequent extension work in West Africa and elsewhere.

After the Second World War, Hodgkin went on to lobby for the development of experimental extension courses in West Africa, working with newly elected Labour MPs, including George Wigg (who had been a WEA tutor as well as having served in the ABCA). Arthur Creech Jones, who became Secretary of State for the Colonies, was also convinced of the case for expanding adult education in West Africa. As a result of these representations, two experienced tutors were sent to the Gold Coast and Nigeria. The aim was to run study groups in different centres as pilots for more extensive programmes.

Thomas Hodgkin himself left for West Africa in 1947. From his perspective, the aim of mass education was to develop critical understanding, building support for decolonisation in the process. Although he apparently met with some scepticism initially, he encountered enthusiasm overall as he engaged with educationalists and activists across the Gold Coast and Nigeria. His contacts included trade union activists as well as nationalist leaders, such as Azikwe in Nigeria and Nkrumah in the Gold Coast.

As the Cold War developed, however, there was increasing concern back home in Britain in the Colonial Office. Having supported the Oxford Delegacy's work in West Africa, Creech Jones became anxious about the influence of communists, deciding that other universities should become involved, as well as Oxford's Delegacy, in a bid to ensure that no more communists would be sent to West Africa. Thomas Hodgkin resigned his membership of the Communist Party to clear the way for his work in West Africa. But this was not enough to enable him to expand the work into East and Central Africa. In 1952 he resigned from his post at the Delegacy, becoming what his biographer, Michael Wolfers, has described as a wandering scholar – part scholar and author (publishing a major study of Nationalism in Colonial Africa in 1956), part journalist and part adult educationalist (Wolfers, 2007). He continued to be actively involved in anti-colonial, anti-imperialist struggles, including supporting activists in their struggles against apartheid in South Africa.

It was not only men who were involved in adult education for decolonisation, of course. Lalage Bown was another outstanding adult educationist, whose first university teaching post was also in the Gold Coast in 1949. Although only 22, as her obituary pointed out:

> she immediately questioned the department's British literature-oriented curriculum believing that poems such as Wordsworth's Daffodils (I wandered lonely as a cloud) had little meaning for African students, and that it was important for them to encounter writings by and about African people. Challenged by the department's senior members, who doubted such texts existed, she bet them a bottle of beer that she could produce numerous passages written in English by African writers over the previous 200 years. (Innes, 2022: 9)

She won her bet, subsequently editing an anthology containing two centuries of writings by Africans, including works by politicians such as Jomo Kenyatta and Julius Nyerere and writers such as Chinua Achebe (more of Chinua Achebe in Chapter 8).

Lalage Bown was a leading figure in the promotion of adult education in a number of African countries, including in universities in Nigeria and in Zambia, where she established a national programme with courses for trade unionists as well as for politicians. In addition, she was involved in the development of the first systematic training for adult educators in Africa. And she served as founding secretary of the African Adult Education Association. She was also passionately committed to women's education, a commitment that ran throughout her work across different African countries.

When she returned to Britain to take up an appointment at Glasgow University in 1981, Lalage Bown continued to promote adult community education with an emphasis on the decolonisation of the curriculum, bringing her learning from her African experiences back home to the colonial heartlands. This was a very innovative approach at the time, given that the importance of decolonising the curriculum in the Global North, as well as in the Global South, has only become widely recognised more recently (Day et al, 2022).

In summary, Lalage Bown promoted adult education for decolonisation, from the Global South to the Global North. Like Thomas Hodgkin, whom she described as her mentor, she worked in solidarity with adult educators, committed to developing more transformative approaches, facilitating these processes of learning rather than in any way substituting for the contributions of those actively struggling for decolonisation themselves in Africa and elsewhere.

Education for decolonisation: an African approach

Among the African independence leaders that had been in contact with Thomas Hodgkin, Julius Nyerere of Tanganyika (subsequently Tanzania when joined with Zanzibar) was perhaps the most directly concerned to promote education for decolonisation. He combined a strong commitment to internationalism, heartened by Ghana's independence in 1957, with a strong commitment to nationally relevant approaches to freedom and development. This was to be based upon African traditions of co-operation and self-reliance, the notion of Ujamaa – although Nyerere himself was also clear that pre-colonial Africa had not been an ideal place in which the 'noble savage' of Rousseau 'lived his idyllic existence' (Nyerere, 1969: 14). His approach was to be more realistic about the past, although he did believe that there were important traditional elements upon which alternative approaches to development could be built.

Nyerere was born in 1922, the son of a chief, and studied in Uganda before going on to Edinburgh University in Scotland. He became a teacher, which was how he liked to be described (as 'Mwalimu' in Swahili), indicative of his recognition of the importance of education as part of the struggle for a decolonised future. After independence in 1961, Nyerere went on to develop his own approach to African Socialism, the approach that was set out in the Arusha Declaration in 1967. Rather than relying on foreign aid (which could result in the growth of a parasitical elite, as Fanon and others had already warned), this was to be an approach to development based on mutual self-help and self-reliance, along with the development of co-operatives and a fairer distribution of wealth backed by some forms of nationalisation. Scattered rural settlements were to be brought together in co-operative Ujamaa villages to enable support services to be provided more effectively. And education was central to the whole project, as Nyerere explained, in an interview with Tariq Ali in 1986 (Nyerere, 1986). In Tanzania, he reflected, it was particularly important to prioritise what he described as 'the outstanding tasks of Socialist adult education, and of strengthening the people's self-confidence and pride' (Nyerere, 1969: 58). Paulo Freire was among those invited to Tanzania to share ideas about how to develop such approaches in practice.

The establishment of Kivukoni College (now Mwalimu Nyerere Memorial Academy) in 1961 epitomised Nyerere's own thinking, drawing upon the model of Ruskin College, Oxford (although the Ruskin model had actually been contested from the start, as Chapter 6 explains in further detail). Kivukoni College was absolutely not originally intended as a form of higher education that would produce a Western educated elite. On the contrary, Nyerere had envisaged this as a way of promoting a very different approach to development, from the bottom up. Rather than facilitating Western capitalist forms of development, in his view, this was about building the leadership for the development of a self-reliant country in which there would be 'no exploitation of one man by another', as Nyerere himself expressed his aims (Nyerere, 1969: 32). Summarising this approach, Lalage Bown had quoted Nyerere's view of the purpose of education as 'the liberation of Man from the restraints and limits of ignorance and dependency', 'to increase men's physical and mental Freedom' (Bown and Tomori, 1979: 17). This was about education for social transformation.

Although he was critical of market-driven approaches, Nyerere was also convinced that his country needed to find its own way forward towards a socialist future. There was no single path. If Karl Marx had lived in Africa, 'he would have written a different book than *Das Kapital*, but he could have been just as scientific and just as socialist' in his view (Nyerere, 1969: 42). Although he himself was very critical of doctrinaire approaches to Marxism, he was on record as commenting that 'you would be amazed if you knew how much of Marx I do accept' (Yahya et al, 2020: 274).

In the event, this all turned out to be more problematic in practice. Much was achieved in terms of promoting the development of Ujamaa villages. The original model drew from the experiences of the co-operative villages that came together through the Ruvuma Development Association (RDA), an association which had grown from the bottom up. This development has been described, by one of those who had been actively involved, as 'the continuation in Tanzania of the great movement for colonial liberation and the hope and energy it generated' (Ibbott, 2014: 13). The RDA operated on the basis of collective decision-making with the active involvement of the villagers themselves. Nyerere himself referred to the RDA as the exemplar for Ujamaa villages based on co-operation and self-reliance.

The RDA had its critics, however, including influential critics in government. In 1969 they succeeded in getting the RDA closed down and its assets taken over. Villagisation policies were to be led by professional managers in future, with backing from the World Bank. Coercion replaced co-operation as the basis for the resettlement schemes that followed, it has been argued (Ibbott, 2014), with very different outcomes as a result. Critics also pointed out that some of the subsequent population moves were achieved in great haste and too often forcibly (Ibbott, 2014).

Very few of the Ujamaa villages that survived were actually operating as self-reliant co-operatives, it was argued, even if some still had co-operative shops and buses (Komba, 1995). Meanwhile, Kivukoni College was subject to its own processes of change. Having started with the aim of training leaders who would be committed to the development of co-operation and self-reliance from the bottom up, the college became a party training college, eventually becoming re-organised in 1992 when Tanzania ceased to be a one-party state. As part of the expansion of higher education, Kivukoni College was renamed as the Mwalimu Nyerere Memorial Academy in 2005.

There is not the space to explore the history of Nyerere's attempts to build African Socialism further. Tanzania faced many obstacles that are beyond the scope of this chapter, obstacles that increased as the international economic climate worsened from the 1970s onwards, along with the pressures from neoliberal approaches to development. Rather, the point to emphasise is simply this: adult community education and development were central to Nyerere's strategic attempts to move on from the colonial past as he aimed to build a more co-operative, self-reliant and more equitable future. Whatever the criticisms of his approaches at the time, his contributions to education for transformation have been increasingly recognised subsequently.

There are continuing threads here in the history of adult community education and development, as Du Bois has already been quoted as pointing out. Self-reliance has had its place, but economic development could not be ensured without the achievement of civic, social and political rights. Conversely, political independence represented no more than the first step towards decolonisation, given the structural causes of inequalities that have needed and still need to be addressed on an international scale. There are implications with continuing relevance here for adult and community education and development in the Global North as well as the Global South.

The boomerang effect: from the colonies to the imperial heartland

Writing about Britain and the aftermath of empire, Kojo Koram has drawn upon Aime Cesaire's idea of history as a boomerang, with experiments carried out in the peripheries of the empire eventually coming flying back to its very heartland (Koram, 2022). The boomerang metaphor has wide connotations, including extremely negative ones, as Koram has gone on to suggest, bringing counter-insurgency strategies that had been developed in Kenya and Malaya back home to UK to contain the civil rights movement in Northern Ireland, for example. Brigadier (subsequently General Sir) Frank Kitson's book on combatting subversion, insurgency and peacekeeping drew upon his own experiences in dealing with the Mau Mau/Land and Freedom Army in Kenya, the insurgents in Malaya and civil rights activists in Northern Ireland (Kitson, 2010). But this was not the only example of the boomerang effect.

The context in post-war Britain was problematic, to say the least, as the country struggled to maintain its position as an imperial power in the face of strengthened movements for colonial freedom. In addition, there were economic as well as political challenges to be faced, as has already been explained, including labour shortages in key areas of the economy. So, the British Nationality Act 1948 set out to encourage immigration from the Commonwealth. But there was implicit, if not actually explicit, racism underpinning this approach. It had, apparently, been assumed that the Act would encourage skilled workers from predominantly White Commonwealth countries such as Australia and Canada to apply (the assumption being that only White people would have the relevant skills). When it emerged that Black people were also arriving, there were subsequent discussions within Churchill's Conservative government about how to draft legislation that would limit non-White immigration without appearing to be overtly racist (Olusoga, 2017)! These intertwined themes of immigration, calls for immigration controls and racism have continued to run through the histories of subsequent decades.

Black people had been living and working in Britain for centuries, as David Olusoga and others have so amply demonstrated (Fryer, 1984; Olusoga, 2017). In the aftermath of the Second World War, their numbers – and visibility – increased significantly, however. Black servicemen and women had spent time in Britain during the war, some of them returning subsequently as part of wider movements from the colonies, as in the case of the Windrush generation who arrived from the Caribbean on the *Empire Windrush* in 1948. The numbers rose over the following years, from between one and two thousand a year between 1948 to 1952 to some 42,000 in 1957 (as US immigration restrictions reduced the opportunities for moving there instead).

This was the context in which politicians from both main parties have been described as setting out 'to delineate and define the problems caused to the country by the presence of black migrants and demonstrate the negative effects the host population might face if black people continued to arrive in significant numbers' (Olusoga, 2017: 499). Their labour was in demand, and yet their presence was being seen as problematic. British employers were actively recruiting workers from the Caribbean to work in transport, hospitality and the National Health Service, among other areas. And these recruiters included Enoch Powell, who was involved in the recruitment of West Indian women to train and work as nurses, the very same Enoch Powell who delivered the infamously racist 'rivers of blood' speech in 1968.

When they arrived in Britain, then, Black workers faced racism and discrimination in the workplace and within communities. No wonder that so many memoirs of West Indian and African migrants who came to Britain in the post-war decades contained expressions of disappointment. 'They were disappointed that the nation they had been told was their "mother country" treat them so badly, disappointed that skills and talents which the nation had found useful during the war years were disregarded in peacetime and they were ushered into low status or menial jobs' (Olusoga, 2017: 503). They were also deeply disappointed at how difficult it was to find somewhere to live. The result was that they tended to find themselves living in the poorest parts of Britain's cities, too often at the mercy of predatory private landlords, such as the notorious Rachman, in areas that were being defined as problem areas. This was the context for the emergence of violence, such as in the Notting Hill riots in 1958.

There is not the space here to explore these experiences in further detail (although Chapter 8 includes some illustrations, as set out in novels and films set in this period). The point to emphasise is their significance in relation to the development of community education and development in Britain. By the mid- to late 1960s, there was increasing concern about the persistence of poverty and deprivation in Britain, despite the very real achievements of the welfare state in the immediate post-war period (Abel-Smith and Townsend, 1965). There were concentrations of social problems in some areas, particularly inner-city areas, it was argued, with too many people falling through the safety net of the welfare state. And these were the areas where so many immigrants lived, disproportionately disadvantaged by poverty and racism.

Although the underlying causes were deeply rooted, the problems of deprived areas became redefined, reduced to manageable proportions in terms of public policy interventions. This was about tackling pockets of poverty, it was suggested, rather than seeing these inner-city areas as symptomatic of more deep-seated inequalities. The inner-city areas policies that were developed from 1968 with the Urban Programme and the launch of the government's Community Development Project (CDP) in 1969 illustrated precisely this type of thinking. The challenge was how to contain socio-economic problems within manageable proportions and enlist communities' potential for self-help without explicitly addressing the underlying structural causes of inequalities and racial injustice (Loney, 1983). There were inherent contradictions here, as subsequent CDP reports so clearly demonstrated (CDP, 1976, 1977) – tensions that were inherent within the histories of adult community education and development more generally. There were also specific parallels with the War on Poverty that had been launched a few years earlier, promoting community participation in strategies to tackle poverty in the US, tensions that were so clearly spelt out by Marris and Rein in their study *Dilemmas of Social Reform* (Marris and Rein, 1972) and so studiously ignored by the policy makers who were engaged in designing the CDP initiatives at that time.

In summary, then, community development programmes were being promoted by governments as a way of mitigating rather than effectively confronting the causes of deep-seated structural problems in the context of rapid social change. These included the problems that were arising from deindustrialisation, as well as those that were arising from racism in response to changing patterns of migration, whether this was migration from Britain's colonies and former colonies or internal migration from the US Deep South to the cities of the North. These initiatives sparked off their own internal tensions and challenges, however, raising questions that have continued to feature in debates within and about community education and development and action research. CDP's critical analysis was taken forward by others and further developed in areas where the focus had been somewhat limited, including the development of an intersectional analysis of racial and gender-based inequalities alongside the inequalities arising from social class. Chapter 7 explores these themes further on both sides of the Atlantic.

Reflecting on the impact of the boomerang effect overall, Gary Craig and colleagues started from an analysis of the legacy of adult community education and development programmes in Britain's colonies as 'a means of controlling local populations', quoting Nkrumah's summary of social projects as 'a means to one end: the perpetuation of foreign rule' (Craig et al, 2011: 3). It was precisely this type of approach that Craig and his colleagues went on to critique in the context of struggles on the editorial board of the *Community Development Journal* (*CDJ*). The *CDJ*, which had emerged in 1965 – from a newsletter that had circulated largely among those returning from the colonies – was described as having been 'dominated by their perspectives and experience'. This was precisely the perspective that was to be challenged by Craig and others (including myself) joining the editorial board in the early 1970s. Although the new board members came with experience in urban settings in the Global North, several did also come with experiences from the Global South, and so were, perhaps, correspondingly aware of the limitations as well as the possibilities of community education and development in those settings.

The aim was to ensure that the *CDJ* would operate as a truly international journal, reflecting on critical perspectives and experiences from the Global North as well as from the Global South, providing 'a voice for the poor and dispossessed against ruling elites' across these international divides (Craig et al, 2011: 5–6). Community development had always had an ambiguous nature, Craig and colleagues went on to argue (Craig et al, 2011: 7). This could be empowering for communities, just as it could be 'colonised by those working with different values and objectives' (Craig et al, 2011: 7). It could promote self-help and voluntary action in response to inadequate public service provision, for example, rather than campaigning against public expenditure cuts in the first place. But these didn't have to be 'either/or' mutually exclusive choices. Neighbourhood community work could achieve immediate improvements in people's lives *and* these achievements could lead on to the development of wider understandings and challenges, building broad alliances for social justice across racial divides.

Just as community education and development have their own inherent tensions and ambiguities, so does the boomerang effect more specifically. As a result, two-way processes of learning that can become empowering rather than disempowering can be promoted across these international divides. The previous chapter's discussion of learning from experiences of participatory action research in the Global South provides an illustration of just such processes in action, along with previous chapters' discussions of the learning from experiences of popular education in the Global South.

5

Learning from struggles for freedom and justice in South Africa

The previous chapter concluded with reflections on the scope for two-way processes of learning and solidarity across international divides. This chapter moves on to explore these processes further in the context of struggles for freedom and justice in South Africa in the late 20th century and beyond, illustrating the ways in which the book's key themes run through these experiences. The role of ideas and critical consciousness emerge as centrally important in these challenges to what has been described as 'the shameful legacy of Britain's colonial past' (Scottish Education and Action for Development, 1990: 3). And so do the contributions of community education and development, including the contributions of community arts, which were significant in South African struggles for decolonisation. In the final years of apartheid, South Africa had vibrant adult and community education and development programmes that creatively engaged with community and social movement activists, focusing upon learning for decolonisation for the future. These programmes were committed to building a democratic rainbow nation, drawing upon Freirean approaches as these were being developed for the Southern Africa context (Hope and Timmel, 2001).

This chapter concludes with a focus on more recent initiatives, including holistic programmes addressing environmental sustainability, gender equality and social justice in the very different circumstances of post-apartheid South Africa. Here too, decolonisation emerges as a key theme and an ongoing process in the pursuit of social transformation and solidarity, demonstrating the continuing importance of working together for a sustainable future. These final sections draw upon reflections from three South African academics, educationalists and activists who have all made outstanding contributions to learning for social transformation: Astrid von Kotze, Viviene Taylor and Shirley Walters (reflections from personal interviews with Taylor, von Kotze and Walters are included).

Learning and building solidarity for the Anti-Apartheid Movement in the Global North: decolonisation of a special type

Social movements have their own histories of providing formal and informal learning for their supporters as well as developing initiatives to engage the wider public. Civil society organisations and social movements have varied agendas, of course, by no means all progressive: there are movements that promote exclusionary agendas and discriminatory practices, for a start (Kenny et al, 2015). The focus here, in contrast, is on social movements that are concerned to promote learning for social justice, such as the popular education initiatives that have been organised by the Landless People's Movement in Brazil and by popular progressive movements elsewhere in Latin America (Kane, 2012).

People can and do learn informally from their experiences of activism within social movements (Foley, 1999), learning about the issues that are the focus of their campaigns as well as the challenges inherent in organising for social change. They learn from sharing their stories. And they learn through the arts and cultural practices, engaging people's emotions as well as sharing knowledge and skills for social change (Clover and Stalker, 2007; Clover and Sanford, 2013). The Anti-Apartheid Movement (AAM) provides examples of a range of such approaches, building support and international solidarity in the Global North.

The South African context

There is not the space to provide a detailed account of apartheid here, simply to outline some of the ways in which South Africa was providing such an extreme case of racial discrimination and oppression. Politically, economically, socially and culturally, apartheid epitomised racial injustice. Racial discrimination had been a feature of life in South Africa under Dutch and British colonial rule. From 1948, the South African National Party systematised these injustices, exacerbating them through the apartheid policy of 'separate development', a system of institutionalised inequality. This was colonialism in a continuing form, 'colonialism in one country', as the African National Congress (ANC) described it, perpetuating the divisive strategies that have been so widely associated with White minority rule.

Under the apartheid system, people were categorised as White or Black, privileging the White minority population and disadvantaging the rest, with the greatest disadvantages reserved for the majority Black population. Black people were consigned to particular areas unless they had a pass permitting them to stay and work in an urban area. The land was distributed extremely unequally; by the time that apartheid was brought to an end, White South Africans, who formed some 10 per cent of the population, owned some 90 per cent of the land (including the best land). Economic opportunities for Black people were extremely limited. Education, including university education, was segregated, and so were sports, leisure and cultural facilities. Even beaches and park benches were categorised as to whether they were for 'Whites only' or not. Racial discrimination was enshrined in every aspect of

South African life, in other words, intersecting with other forms of division within as well as between classes (Wolpe, 1985).

Within South Africa, opposition to apartheid had been organised by the ANC and other anti-apartheid organisations and movements, including the Pan-African Congress (PAC) – only to be met with determined repression from the apartheid state. The ANC and the PAC were banned in 1960, bans that continued until 1990, when the apartheid system was being brought to an end. State repression was determined and extremely brutal, as illustrated by the deaths of 69 peaceful protesters and the injuries inflicted on up to 180 others at Sharpeville in 1960. In Soweto and other centres in 1976, thousands of Black school children were killed and injured in police shootings, although the official death toll was 176. These mass murders galvanised anti-apartheid mobilisations across the globe.

Activists in South Africa, including Nelson Mandela, were imprisoned in appalling conditions for decades. Others were killed, including the Black Consciousness Movement (BCM) leader, Steve Biko, who died in police custody in 1977 (more of Steve Biko subsequently in this chapter). And numbers went into exile in Britain and elsewhere, many of them continuing to face harassment and worse – some of them, like the sociologist Ruth First, being assassinated by the South African security forces. But the struggle for justice continued despite the appalling risks that this entailed.

The Anti-Apartheid Movement

It was this background of racial injustice that sparked the mobilisation of solidarity with the development of the Boycott Movement in Britain in 1959. Initially the focus was on the call for an international boycott of South African goods, a campaign that won some cross-party support – with the notable exception of the Conservative Party. A key speaker at the launch rally was Julius Nyerere, the Tanzanian independence leader and educator featured in the preceding chapter.

The movement really took off in Britain the following year in shocked response to the Sharpeville massacre. The campaign was renamed the AAM to reflect the movement's wider purpose, going beyond the initial call for the boycott to campaign for South Africa's total isolation. This came to involve more than campaigning for economic sanctions and disinvestment, important though these measures were. South Africa was to be isolated culturally too. And there were demonstrations against sporting links, including the Springboks' rugby tour (1969–70) and the successful campaign against the cricket tour in 1970. Given the importance of sport for White South Africans, these were powerful blows. The approach was holistic, then. And it was internationalist. The AAM supported struggles in neighbouring states, especially in Southern Rhodesia (now Zimbabwe), which remained a British colony until 1980. This internationalism included support for liberation movements in the Portuguese colonies of Angola and Mozambique as well as support for struggles for freedom in South Africa itself.

At its 1961 conference the AAM expressed the following aims: 'to promote activity of all kinds to demonstrate the continuing repugnance for apartheid felt by the people of Britain' via 'meetings, rallies, poster parades, film shows, letters to MPs and the press, resolutions at meetings and conferences', according to historian and adult educationalist Roger Fieldhouse in his account of the movement (Fieldhouse, 2005). The objective was to build support, persuading governments and international agencies to isolate the South African government in their turn. The movement used a variety of educational and agitational tools, building a social movement of powerful international significance in the process. There is not the space to provide a comprehensive account of these varying approaches here. The following examples are simply summarised for illustration.

Posters, dramas and educational packages promoting learning, building solidarity

A relatively recent exhibition, titled 'The World Must Change', displayed a range of posters by David King, a creative designer whose work included a number of iconic images, illustrating their power to engage viewers' emotions as well to inform them of the facts. This exhibition included a particularly striking series of posters depicting 'Apartheid in Practice' (King, 1978). Each poster combined some text, setting out the key facts about life under apartheid, with an accompanying picture appealing to the viewer's emotions to register the full impact of the message.

There was a poster about health and housing in apartheid South Africa, for instance, with an image of grim devastation showing the effects of the forcible removal of Black Africans from their homes. The text underneath explained the shocking differences between these experiences, and the poor health outcomes that ensued, and those of the White minority population. The poster on education showed a crowded group of Black school children sitting on the ground together and trying to learn. Underneath, the text summarised government spending on Black children's education in contrast with what it invested in White children's education. The most potentially upsetting of all was the poster titled 'Law and Order in South Africa', which showed a woman holding a dead child in her arms. This graphically illustrated the South African police's policy of shooting first, regardless of whether they were shooting unarmed protesters or defenceless children.

Drama provided another creative way of engaging with supporters' emotions as well as informing them about the nature of apartheid and the importance of supporting resistance struggles. The Sharpeville massacre was dramatised, for example, to mark its tenth anniversary in 1970. A reconstruction was staged in Trafalgar Square, using professional support to relay the sound of the guns and actors portraying the police shooting into the crowd. Others lay down in response, simulating the effects of police bullets on unarmed protesters. Unsurprisingly, this event was described as having been truly chilling.

A follow-up event was staged that evening at the Lyceum Theatre. This consisted of a series of short plays put together with the support of a number of writers, including South African writers, along with a performance by South African dancers in the interval. As Ethel de Keyser, the AAM's executive secretary, explained, it was important to find ways that would enable the movement's messages to hit home. So many potential supporters struggled to even begin to imagine the horrors of apartheid.

These are just a couple of examples to illustrate the creative ways in which the AAM built support in solidarity with the struggles in South Africa and its neighbouring states. There are many more examples to explore via the AAM website at https://www.aamarchives.org. These are set out with summaries, decade by decade, from the 1960s onwards. The written archives are in the Bodleian Library, Oxford. The International Defence and Aid Fund (IDAF)'s pamphlets provide another complementary source covering all aspects of life under apartheid to keep the conscience of the world alive to the issues at stake, as the IDAF explained its mission.

Meanwhile, of course, more explicitly educational materials were also being developed. The Southern Africa Resources Project set out materials that were produced by and for teachers in Sheffield, for example. With support from the Jordanhill Project in International Understanding (based in the Jordanhill College of Education, Glasgow), these teachers produced a package that included materials on racism in contemporary Britain along with materials to support debates on the sports boycott, for example. This was about engaging young people to reflect on the issues in solidarity, understanding the connections with their own situations rather than simply providing them with facts and figures about apartheid and South Africa's military interventions elsewhere. There were cross-references to a range of materials in these packages, including works of fiction, as well as a list of criteria for evaluating bias in textbooks for children.

This project was developed in response to Sheffield City Council's decision to declare that the city was an apartheid free zone in 1981 – the first council in Britain to make such a commitment. As an apartheid free zone, the council was committed to the AAM's policies on boycott and disinvestment, as well as being committed to encouraging positive teaching of the histories, cultures and struggles for self-determination of the South African peoples, and promoting public understanding of the situation in Southern Africa more widely. People in Sheffield needed to understand the links between the exploitation and degradation of apartheid and the problems that were being experienced within their own cities, towns and villages, argued David Blunkett, then leader of the city council. And this included the need to challenge racism in schools, colleges, libraries and adult education provision.

Reflecting on the reasons for Sheffield's principled stance, an active trade unionist referred to the significance of the trade union movement's support during this period, particularly the Amalgamated Engineering Union, which had strong international connections around the world, including connections with South Africa. The AAM had well-developed links with tenants' groups and community organisations locally too, as well as increasing support from the churches. Sheffield's internationalism was reinforced with support from Wortley Hall and Northern College, providers of adult, community and trade union education in the area. More of Northern College and Sheffield's internationalism in Chapter 7.

The trade union movement had not been comprehensively supportive of the struggle against apartheid, though. The Trades Union Congress (TUC) had had links with White trade unions in South Africa that had a history of supporting the exclusion of Black workers from specific jobs. And the TUC's International Department had initially supported the policy of 'constructive engagement' rather than the AAM's calls for boycotts and disinvestment. But there had also been challenges to the TUC on these issues (IDAF, 1974; AAM, 1982), with more trade unions becoming involved with the AAM as time went by. There had been examples of international solidarity, from the early days onwards in any case, whatever the TUC's formal stance – including Ruskin College students' involvement in disrupting South African sports tours.

By the final decade, in the 1980s, the AAM had become a mass movement, using a variety of approaches to build support for the campaign. Over 70,000 attended the Wembley concert to mark Nelson Mandela's forthcoming 70th birthday and to campaign for his release from prison, an event that was broadcast to more than 60 countries worldwide, raising further awareness on a global scale. The AAM was working in alliance with the United Democratic Front (UDF) by this time too – along with other anti-apartheid organisations and groups within South Africa – which takes the discussion on to the history of learning for freedom, racial equality and democratic transformation within South Africa itself.

Community education and development within apartheid South Africa: the Black Consciousness Movement

By the 1970s, resistance had been building up again within South Africa, despite the brutality of state repression and the gaps that had been left as a result of the banning of the ANC and other anti-apartheid organisations

(Bernstein, 1978). A new generation was finding its own way forward (Sikakane, 1977), with students taking leading roles in the development of the BCM. Seeing White students as tending to dominate in the non-racial National Union of South African Students, Black students had decided to set up their own organisation, the South African Students Organisation (SASO), officially launched in 1969. As Steve Biko, the first president, explained, 'white students had this problem, you know of superiority, and they tended to take us for granted' (Arnold, 1978: 8). SASO went on to become centrally important in the development of the BCM.

The BCM drew inspiration from the Black Power Movement in US, including the writings of Malcolm X and the consciousness that 'Black is beautiful'. This was an inclusive approach to the definition of Blackness in the South African context, applying the term to the different groups that the apartheid system had been separating – Indians and Coloured (mixed race) peoples as well as Black Africans. Other influences on the BCM included the works of Fanon, a writer whose contributions have already been identified in previous chapters, as well as those of Paulo Freire. These sources offered inspiration and guidance as to how to decolonise the minds of the oppressed, promoting critical consciousness, self-reliance, dignity and pride. Biko set these aims out himself when he gave evidence in support of activists accused of terrorism in 1976. 'The most potent weapon in the hands of the oppressor is the mind of the oppressed', he explained (Arnold, 1978: xix). Black consciousness was being promoted in a number of ways to challenge this, he continued, including via literacy projects through which '[w]e try to get Blacks in conscientization to grapple realistically with their problems, to attempt to find solutions to their problems, to develop what one might call an awareness, a physical awareness of their situation, to be able to analyze it, and to provide answers for themselves' and so build up their humanity (Arnold, 1978: 8) – Freirean approaches in practice, in other words.

Steve Biko went on to outline the range of community development initiatives that were being developed alongside these literacy programmes. There were clinics promoting preventative approaches towards health and well-being. There were leadership training programmes for women. And there were economic development projects promoting Black community businesses and co-operative initiatives in rural areas (Arnold, 1978) aiming to improve people's immediate conditions while facilitating the development of self-reliance for the future. Cultural initiatives featured too, including Black theatre, poetry and art. There would seem to be echoes here of some of the initiatives that had been explored in the US and in other African contexts, as outlined in the previous chapter.

By espousing a non-violent approach, the initial hope was that the BCM would be able to operate legally rather than having to work underground.

At first, the BCM's emphasis upon Black consciousness and its criticisms of White liberals might even have been perceived as consistent with apartheid's strategy for separate development, it has been suggested (Sikakane, 1977). It soon became clear that this was most certainly not the case, however. Steve Biko was absolutely opposed to apartheid, and he supported anti-colonial struggles internationally.

This was all too much for the government to tolerate, and the state moved against the BCM with violence. Steve Biko himself was subjected to a banning order. He was subsequently arrested and savagely beaten, dying in police custody as a result in 1977, an event that symbolises the horrors of the apartheid regime and the extraordinary courage of those who risked their lives opposing it (Bernstein, 1978).

Supporting civil society mobilisations against apartheid in Durban and Cape Town

By the 1980s, resistance to apartheid was mounting, building on the BCM's initiatives despite the brutality of governmental repression. This period has been described as marking a watershed in South African politics. There was an upsurge of civil society mobilisations with the growth of community-based organisations as well as non-governmental organisations (NGOs) concerned with struggles for democracy (Matiwana and Walters, 1986). Civic organisations in Black townships drew women into politics as well as men, building democratic traditions within grassroots organisations in the process (Walters and Butterwick, 2017).

There were several reasons for this proliferation, it has been suggested, including the fact that there was an increasing climate of political insecurity, with the advance of freedom from colonial rule in neighbouring Angola and Mozambique (1975) and the independence settlement in Zimbabwe (1980). White minority rule was beginning to seem less certain for the future. Meanwhile, the economic situation was becoming more challenging as South Africa became less attractive to foreign investors. This was partly as a result of trade union and community-based activism within South Africa, with spontaneous uprisings in the townships starting in 1984, and partly as the result of anti-apartheid mobilisations internationally.

There is not the space here to unpack the relative weights of different factors within the country and beyond, let alone to estimate the impact of interventions via the armed struggle. The point to emphasise is simply that resistance to the apartheid regime was building up, as was demonstrated by the development of the UDF, bringing together some 400 organisations, including trade unions, students' unions, women's organisations and church groups, linking trade union struggles in solidarity with struggles in the community. New spaces were opening up, including new spaces for learning for social transformation.

Durban was a major site for trade union mobilisations from the early 1970s, for example. Astrid von Kotze was actively involved in providing trade unionists with support in Durban by the early 1980s, supporting the development of workers' theatre and other forms of learning through creativity at this time (von Kotze, 1996). After so many years of colonialism and cultural imperialism, which had defined South African culture narrowly in terms of tribal art, culture was being recognised as a tool for liberation (von Kotze, 1988).

When she had been a student in Johannesburg, von Kotze had developed an interest in making critical plays about the situation in South Africa, part of a group that had set up a theatre company for the purpose. Although these students had all been White (universities having been segregated at the time, as it has already been explained), they had gone on to join forces with a Black theatre company, developing workers' theatre together in support of workers' struggles.

When she moved to Durban in the early 1980s, trade unions came to ask her and her partner to get involved in similar ways, making plays that would tell the stories of the big strikes that were being organised at the time – at the Dunlop factory, for example – building wider understanding and alliances between workplaces and communities in the process. There was much to be done at this time, characterised as it was by a groundswell of organising activities.

As time went on, more and more trade unions began to approach von Kotze and her partner for assistance. As these demands grew, it was decided that the way forward would be to run a course enabling trade unionists to learn how to do this for themselves, running workshops and promoting storytelling and other forms of creativity in support of their struggles. A two-year course on culture and working life was developed as a result.

Up to this point von Kotze hadn't really thought of these activities as adult education. But plays could also be – and were – educative as well as providing tools for mobilisation (von Kotze, 1988). Cultural struggles were becoming increasingly effective tools for learning as well as for mobilising, in fact. A lot of cultural activists were being locked up at this time, and activists were being murdered by vigilantes during the State of Emergency from 1985, von Kotze pointed out, demonstrating that you know when you are having an impact when you are getting a reaction from the powers that be.

Von Kotze has also reflected on the astonishing commitments of those involved in these struggles. For example, there had been civil unrest in KwaZulu Natal, which had made travelling extremely hazardous. Participants would come by public taxis as this was the only way to travel in these circumstances, and they would opt to work nightshifts so that they could participate by day. This was about a process of re-awakening through culture and creativity in everyday life, going way beyond more instrumental forms of learning in order to dream about alternative ways of being. Workers started negotiating spaces for rehearsals, giving cultural issues central importance in their struggles. Culture was too important to be left in the hands of the enemy, trade unionists explained (von Kotze, 1988).

This was an exhilarating time. Von Kotze had written the booklet *Organise and Act* (von Kotze, 1988), which was to be republished in time for the 40th anniversary of the Durban strikes. This re-publication was to commemorate the creative popular education work that had been developed in support of these strikes. Creativity and the importance of having hopeful visions for the future have constituted continuing themes in von Kotze's subsequent writings and practice in post-apartheid South Africa. The Durban Workers' Cultural Local had pioneered these creative approaches to building a democracy in which people could for the first time control their productive and creative power (von Kotze, 1988).

Von Kotze subsequently moved to the University of the Western Cape (UWC) in Cape Town. Here too, people were mobilising in communities and workplaces, coming together under one umbrella – their shared opposition to apartheid. Described as the University of the Left, UWC was intimately connected with these wider struggles, the place to be for those committed to supporting progressive movements – a significant exception, despite the wider context of higher education under the apartheid system. This brings the discussion on to the development of learning programmes for social transformation at UWC.

Learning to prepare for a democratic future

Following a study of the potential role of UWC in the field of adult education (Walters, 1989), the university decided to establish a chair in adult and continuing education. Jakes Gerwel, the Dean of Arts at that time and an activist-scholar within the democratic movement, supported the appointment of Shirley Walters in 1985 to lead this initiative. She had only recently completed her PhD, which had adopted a participatory research approach to the study of education for democracy within the progressive social movements (Walters, 1989).

Drawing upon Illich's writings on de-schooling, along with the theoretical contributions of Gramsci and Paulo Freire, this research linked theory with practice in the South African context. There were significant implications here for the development of participatory democracy and effective accountability within civil society for the future. Walters built upon these understandings as she developed adult learning and education programmes in support of a democratic future for a non-racial, non-sexist South Africa.

Reflecting on these programmes more recently, Walters described the Centre for Adult and Continuing Education's (CACE) two-year certificate programme as an illustration of their approach. It had been possible to obtain anti-apartheid funding for such progressive courses in the context of UWC at that time, promoting learning in flexible ways without the constraints of the more formal curricula that were then prevalent. This two-year certificate programme was targeted at the hundreds of activists who lived in rural areas and the urban periphery and had had typically little, if any, access to higher education to date.

The aim was to provide training for these activists to enable them to be maximally effective themselves as well as empowering them to support and train others in their turn. The course intersected with their lives, linking up with local initiatives in their areas as well as providing a sound theoretical basis for their work. The 'Contextual Studies' element was particularly significant in this respect, addressing issues of political economy. The programme was about taking learners' own experiences and concerns as the basis for moving on further, developing the wider knowledge and critical understanding that would be required to achieve a transformative future.

The programme was delivered via distance learning, with workbooks provided as learning materials along with support from local tutors. The distance learning elements were then supplemented with residential weekends every two months. These residentials were central elements of the programme. They brought students together to learn as a group and to share experiences (which also enabled them to build supportive networks for the future). An important aspect was that resources were made available for travel and accommodation so that students from beyond the city could participate in these residential elements.

The students were nominated via their local organisations. Their participation was validated by these organisations, and they were encouraged to develop projects that related to local concerns. But each student was also assessed as an individual in recognition of the value of the theoretical components of the programme. They were encouraged to take theory seriously as scholars, with particular emphasis upon theorists such as Gramsci, for example. These were students who hadn't generally expected to study at university, so this was seen as a great opportunity. The programme was clearly relevant to their lives in their communities as well as being significant and valuable in academic terms.

This was a highly effective model, developed in a very creative period, despite the challenges of apartheid constraints and the failures of higher education under apartheid more widely. There was a high level of resilience among the staff as well as the students involved. Some students were arrested, for instance. But ways were found to smuggle workbooks into their jail. As Walters concluded, this was possible because of the levels of commitment involved, part of a broader collective movement, the feeling that whatever people's differences (in terms of race, class, gender and geography, among other differences), those involved were 'all in this together' and struggling for a common cause.

Others have similarly stressed the importance of having this shared objective – the umbrella struggle to end apartheid – as the basis for building an inclusive, non-racial, non-sexist and democratic future. This didn't mean that there were no differences to be negotiated or tensions to be managed, however. Walters and Manicom's publication *Gender and Popular Education* identified a number of such challenges, taking account of race and gender along with other inequalities of power. There were knife-edge dilemmas to be negotiated, balancing the tensions between facilitation on the one hand and control by the facilitator on the other, for example, just as there were potential tensions between the processes and the outcomes that needed to be managed (Walters and Manicom, 1996). And there were tensions in terms of respecting other cultures, including traditional cultures, while still advancing feminist goals.

Developing leadership for the future, post-apartheid

The South African Development Programme (SADEP) provides another case study of adult learning at UWC which focused on social transformation in post-apartheid South Africa. Although the struggle for democracy was formally achieved by 1994, there were remaining challenges to be faced if South Africa was to move forward towards a more equitable non-racial future, as has already been suggested. The ANC had gained a wider membership since being unbanned, but this new membership did not necessarily share the movement's history of struggle. Nor did the new membership necessarily share an understanding of what needed to happen next in order to build a fully democratic state. So, there were plenty of challenges inherent in the post-1994 context.

Most importantly, in addition, there were legacies from South Africa's 'colonialism of a special type/colonialism within one country' to be challenged, legacies that dated back even before the formal establishment of apartheid in 1948, as SADEP's initiator Viviene Taylor explained (personal interview). The apartheid system that had been established from 1948 had re-enforced previously existing racialised divisions, bolstering the entrenchment of White supremacy rule. This had been underpinned by the apartheid education system that dictated who could study what and with what outcomes. This divided education system was central to the reproduction of entrenched differences in terms of race and class as well as gender and geography (between rural and urban areas) under the apartheid regime.

Most importantly too, transformative education needed to challenge the psychology of uncritical acceptance that the apartheid system had been re-enforcing – encouraging people to be challenging instead, to ask the right questions and to be unafraid of having different views. This was about facilitating critical thinking, in other words, giving people the confidence to make their voices heard, to be 'dissidents', to challenge the mentality of apartheid's tightly engineered past, with its legacy of not going against the norm. This was going to be incredibly important, but difficult to achieve, given that people had been so regularly punished for expressing challenging views during the apartheid years.

SADEP was launched at the beginning of the 1990s, when the liberation movements were unbanned, to address these challenges with the overall aim of developing learning for the creation of change, embedding constitutional democracy and social justice (Taylor, 2018). The programme was based at UWC, which was supportive from the very top. UWC has already been referred to as the University of the Left, an exceptional 'liberated zone' under the leadership of Professor Jakes Gerwel, an extraordinary educationalist who was very encouraging to SADEP throughout this period (1991–99). Prior to this there had also been discussions with Oliver Tambo, the ANC leader in exile, who had been keen for the project to go ahead.

This was an extraordinary period of preparing to govern, rethinking policies and processes – including education policies and processes – and developing political literacy and the abilities to promote change. SADEP was specifically targeted at activists and former combatants, setting out to equip them with the knowledge and skills, especially tools for critical analysis, that they would need to become effective leaders in post-apartheid South Africa. These were to include the specific policy development skills that they would need if they were to become parliamentarians and policy makers in the structures of governance.

There was momentum for SADEP, then, with enthusiasm for preparing for a non-racial, more equitable and more fully democratic future. Despite these initial advantages, though, there were inherent challenges, as Taylor reflected subsequently. It was important to remember that this was only one set of programmes working against powerful countervailing influences, including the knock-on effects of the apartheid education system and the legacies of previously established structures and approaches to development. These tended to be more individualistic, with correspondingly less emphasis on collective development, equity and distributive justice. That was what SADEP was fighting against, tensions that are still alive in post-apartheid South Africa two decades later.

Like the CACE programme that has already been outlined, SADEP drew upon the theoretical work of Gramsci along with the educational writings of Paulo Freire. The *Training for Transformation* manuals (Hope and Timmel, 2001) were also cited as very significant influences, translating Freire's methodology into locally relevant and practical materials for trainers and educators as programmes were developed elsewhere in Africa. These guides were incredibly useful, Taylor reflected: they gave educators the confidence to work in different ways, facilitating more active approaches to learning. The authors, Anne Hope and Sally Timmel, were both very supportive, also contributing to courses in person. They were enthusiastic about SADEP and subsequently worked together on its programmes.

Training for Transformation materials were also adapted to include wider resources on the critical analysis of political development processes. The focus was also upon policy processes and how to influence these in post-apartheid South Africa – how to make an impact while taking account of wider forces beyond local control, including the forces of neoliberal globalisation, financialisation and deindustrialisation. People needed to understand these wider forces and to learn about ways of addressing the challenges and locating the cracks despite the countervailing pressures from market forces and structural adjustment.

It was also important to get accreditation for SADEP courses. This gave trainers the confidence to develop courses that were going against the grain, using alternative pedagogical approaches with different outcomes and presenting critical materials in more learner-centred ways with participative forms of evaluation (Taylor and Conradie, 1997). Accreditation gave them the confidence to be different types of educators in terms of the methodologies that they were using as well as the content of their courses.

Taylor's own background had been in political studies rather than adult education, but she was very comfortable with this participative type of approach to teaching and learning. As a student in the 1970s, she had been in a study group that used the works of Paulo Freire and others. These had been key influences on the young student activists who had engaged with the BCM. Other sources that they had studied in the early 1970s included Saul Alinsky and Illich (on de-schooling) as well as writers on decolonisation including Fanon, Nkrumah and Nyerere. The BCM's community development work had also been influential and significant in the period before the banning of Steve Biko and others. There were thus important crossovers of influences, intertwined organically through many different streams of thinking about participative learning for decolonisation and sustainable development.

Taylor reflected on the number of returning exiles who became excited by these programmes. SADEP had provided a space for sharing thinking about what should change and how these changes could be implemented.

Many students had subsequently played key roles in government structures and the legislature. Taylor went on to establish a programme for leading policy makers, involving key academics and politicians such as Harold Wolpe, Rob Davies and Kadar Ismal. There were courses and seminars on wider issues in the context of globalisation too, gathering trade unionists as well as state officials.

These courses brought SADEP participants together with policy makers, enabling them to acquire knowledge and skills and to understand the levers that they needed to use in order to develop and implement strategies for progressive policy changes. These were very significant courses and seminars, then, whether they had been covering gender issues, constitutional issues, educational issues or other aspects of progressive policy developments at the time.

Sadly, however, SADEP courses are no longer running. Following Taylor's secondment to the United Nations to work with Amartya Sen, the university (the University of Cape Town by this time rather than UWC) did not sustain these initiatives. But there was still a need for such programmes as well as new ones on environmental concerns, in Taylor's view. Environmental issues have been directly linked to development issues, with the poorest, most vulnerable people being the most seriously affected by climate change. Although far from new, disasters such as drought and famine have been taking place on an unprecedented scale in the contemporary context. There continues to be a need for educational processes to explore the causes and to understand holistically the impacts of ecological disasters on people's health and well-being. The risks of further pandemics are increasing, Taylor has noted, a challenge that also needs to be understood and addressed with solidarity across the globe.

Challenges of the contemporary context

The challenges of the contemporary context have been as great if not even greater than ever – decolonisation as a continuing process, in other words. The prospect of fighting for a different future had been greeted with exhilaration and relief, as Walters reflected in parallel. But this wasn't quite how this had all turned out in practice. Social movements, including the trade union movement, had become weakened, and the resources available for anti-apartheid work had been drying up. Activists went into government, as has already been demonstrated, but radical politics began to be squeezed out as neoliberal approaches became increasingly influential.

There are potentially new sites of struggle and new spaces to be opened up, though, as Walters also went on to explain. These include spaces within parts of the structures of the state and indeed within the universities. Lifelong learning has been part of the radical tradition, for example, but this could still be presented in terms which could be acceptable from neoliberal perspectives as well as from the more radical perspectives of the past. So, for several years it was possible to maintain lifelong learning, continuing the radical traditions that had been supported at UWC. It was also possible to obtain accreditation for prior experiential learning (APEL), opening up opportunities and spaces for progressive adult educational agendas in the process. Radical traditions were maintained for several years in these ways, then, working through the paradoxes.

There have been several additional ways of developing and safeguarding spaces for progressive approaches, including the establishment of the annual Julius Nyerere lecture. There have been spaces for cultural practices too, including poetry, dance, song and contributions from progressive speakers, keeping the university's radical traditions alive.

Women's cross-campus breakfasts have provided another set of examples, opening up safe spaces in which women have been enabled to come together across race and class divisions, developing alternatives to the more formalised, bureaucratised practices that were becoming all too prevalent again in higher education. These breakfasts have become significant as in-between spaces. In a context in which 'social transformation' had been losing its political edge, it has become more important than ever to enable women to come together to identify and to utilise such in-between spaces.

Von Kotze also provided examples of how she had been facilitating learning for women's empowerment in post-apartheid South Africa in other ways. Street plays had been very powerful as a tool for engaging people in critical discussions, for example, unpacking the plays' implications afterwards. Most of the audience for the play about violence in the home had been women. But there had also been a few men in the audience on one occasion. Two of them apologised to their wives and mothers in a very moving recognition of the wrongfulness of their previous behaviour. While still recognising the unacceptability of domestic violence, the subsequent discussion explored the reasons for such behaviours, understanding the contributory factors when men came home tired, hungry and disappointed in their search for work, taking their frustrations out on their families.

Theatre provided safe spaces where such issues could be discussed and ways forward identified in the discussions that followed the play. Like Walters, von Kotze pointed to the spaces that could still be found for different types of learning, promoting critical understanding and solidarity despite the increasing inequalities of race, class and gender – and despite the fragmentation that was being experienced among social movements more generally in post-apartheid South Africa.

COVID-19: a potentially transformative opportunity

The COVID-19 pandemic might have provided another moment when people could come together in face of a common threat, as they had done under the umbrella of the common struggle during the apartheid years. Grassroots organisations in Cape Town did, in fact, come together very rapidly in 'Cape Town Together' following the outbreak of the COVID-19 pandemic, as von Kotze went on to explain. This was to promote a community-driven, collective response based on solidarity rather than charity: 'Your health is my health'. One of the key figures in this was a doctor who had worked in the context of Ebola outbreaks in West Africa, experiences which had convinced her of the importance of this type of approach.

Some 160 community action networks were set up with great speed in the Cape Town area. These were very diverse groups bringing together people from different backgrounds. The groups in the more affluent areas had also partnered with groups in poorer areas, raising funds for food and for other needs such as personal protective equipment.

There were weekly learning sessions where people had shared information, ideas and experiences, organising via Zoom. In this way, learning was at the centre. These sessions involved discussions on a range of related issues, including gender-based violence, as well as discussions on how to address immediately practical issues such as how to organise a soup kitchen. Some of these groups were still functioning – at least to some extent – at the time of our discussions in late 2022. But these responses to COVID-19 had not taken off in the ways in which anti-apartheid struggles had previously developed.

Von Kotze also reflected on her experiences of facilitating learning with different types of organisations through the COVID-19 pandemic. These included using role play with religious leaders, for example, to enable them to challenge the view that vaccinations were unnecessary because God just said 'no'. Rather than simply telling people that they were mistaken – that this was nonsense – this was about responding to people's misgivings about vaccinations through engaging them in processes of critical dialogue. There were still many myths to be challenged, including myths about health and nutrition more generally, and many gaps in people's knowledge about their health that Freirean approaches could address. Chapter 3 has already outlined some of the myths that were associated with HIV/AIDS, for instance, together with the mobilisations that the Treatment Action Campaign (TAC) developed in the campaign for effective treatments.

Reflecting on the continuing relevance of Freire's *Pedagogy of the Oppressed* more specifically, von Kotze has also written about her experiences of bringing her first copy across the border from Botswana concealed under a spare tyre because it was a banned book at that time. These ideas were still 'dangerous' in the sense that they were making the case for education as 'a process of conscientisation aimed at action for radical transformation' (von Kotze, 2018: 96). This was despite the risk that such ideas could become incorporated in 'neo-liberal speak and values' as they became mainstreamed within higher education syllabi (von Kotze, 2018: 97). Popular education was more necessary than ever, in fact, in the context of continuing inequalities of gender as well as of race, class and geography (rural areas still being particularly deprived). In addition, environmental issues needed to be addressed holistically along with the challenges that had emerged with the COVID-19 pandemic.

Ecofeminism

The importance of addressing the challenges of the climate crisis emerged as a key issue, building on the popular education initiatives for social transformation that had been developed both during and after the end of apartheid. Von Kotze's work with women and livelihoods had involved listening to nature, for example, learning from women and appreciating women's strength as they found ways to survive. She explained that it was only in the past five or six years or so that she had actually been using the term ecofeminism, but she had been using the concepts well before this. She and Walters had been sharing their thinking on feminism and environmental concerns, developing their approach to ecofeminism and the implications for adult learning over this period (Walters and von Kotze, 2021). For example, participatory learning activities could enable communities to manage risks and mitigate disasters, such as droughts, as effectively as possible (von Kotze and Holloway, 1996), disasters that were having the most impact on the most vulnerable people – including women – within the most vulnerable communities.

Walters' reflections on the development of her thinking on ecofeminism had also referred to the issue of drought, focusing upon the drought of 2017–18, which had been extreme (Walters, 2018). This had been a key moment in terms of people's mobilisations in response. People had very different experiences of drought depending on their circumstances – and very different forms of explanations. Poor people had always experienced problems with water supplies and knew about living with less water, for instance, whereas this was a very different shock for the middle classes, making them far more immediately aware of environmental issues. Organising in response to this drought had been a significant factor in Walters' engagement with ecofeminism, making the links between capitalism, class, gender, race and ecology.

As she went on to explain, environmental issues include so much else, providing a new umbrella which includes political economy as well focusing upon people's health, well-being and livelihoods, with both micro and macro dimensions. There is no one simple answer to the climate crisis (for example, recycling). There has to be a holistic response, such as the response offered by the Climate Justice Charter (https://cjcm.org.za/). We need to rethink how we live and who we are, Walters explained (personal interview). And we need to recognise both what we know and what we don't know, respectfully acknowledging the contributions of Indigenous knowledge. People in rich countries need to realise the urgency of climate change, von Kotze and Walters emphasise. All our backs are to the wall, so we need to learn to work in solidarity at every level, in their view, including collaborating with those who are prepared to work on these issues in structures of governance. Solidarity doesn't just happen, though, it has to be forged, they explain, as has already been emphasised (Walters and Butterwick, 2017).

Conclusions

Solidarity has been a continuing theme throughout this chapter. As ANC leader Oliver Tambo had reflected from exile in 1971, 'Our bedrock is unshakeable; it is international solidarity that so firmly rejects apartheid and race oppression' (quoted in Kasrils, 2021: 15). International solidarity played a significant part in supporting the struggle against apartheid within South Africa itself, promoting learning about the underlying connections between international capital and the supporters of the apartheid state.

Solidarity – based upon mutuality rather than charity – continues to be centrally important, as the development of the mutual aid groups that were established in response to the COVID-19 pandemic has illustrated. And solidarity continues to be centrally important in the context of the climate crisis, although this is not necessarily how this is presently being perceived or indeed experienced.

Solidarity has continuing significance too when it comes to the more personal dimensions of learning for social transformation. As Walters and Butterwick have pointed out, quoting an Australian Aboriginal woman's challenge, 'If you have come to help me, you are wasting your time. But if you have come because your liberation is bound up with mine, then let us work together' (Walters and Butterwick, 2017).

There are many implications here for community education and development, facilitating mutual learning across differences in terms of race, class and gender, and especially so in the context of the divisive and demeaning legacies of apartheid. There are wider implications here as well. As D'Arcangelis and Huntley have pointed out, based upon their experiences in Canada working with Indigenous women, there are deeply entrenched colonialist attitudes to be addressed; in other words, community educators need to be able to acknowledge their relative privilege without being paralysed by it (D'Arcangelis and Huntley, 2012).

Decolonisation was being re-affirmed as an ongoing process, then, as the South African experiences clearly illustrate. The free elections of 1994 marked the end of colonisation as it was embodied in the structures of the apartheid regime. But there were continuing legacies to be challenged, along with increasing inequalities in terms of social class as well as continuing inequalities in terms of race and gender. Early gains were being threatened by increasing marketisation, including within the higher education system and within adult learning more specifically – recolonisation by market forces, in other words. Meanwhile, there have been increasing challenges to be addressed in the context of the growing climate crisis, challenges which have their roots in the colonial past and its globalised model of racialised resource extraction (Kapoor et al, 2022), challenges that also need to be addressed on a global scale.

6

Co-creating knowledge and learning from labour movement histories

This chapter moves on to focus on education and participatory action research (PAR) within the trade union and labour movement. The three overarching themes of the book run through this chapter in parallel, with a particular focus on the role of ideas and the development of critical consciousness within social movements. This includes experiences of questioning whose knowledge counts and the implications for the promotion of knowledge democracy, re-examining social movements' own histories as the basis for developing more inclusive approaches and building solidarity for the future. The trade union movement has much to learn from its past engagements with colonialism as well as its past and more recent engagements with movements for decolonisation, as this chapter sets out to explore.

Trade unionism has been criticised for failing to challenge the legacies of slavery, colonialism and imperialism in Britain and the US in particular, with continuing inequalities of race within the movement itself as well as within the wider society (Marable, 1991; Ramdin, 2017). There have been very different histories too, however, as the previous chapter has already illustrated. Although there was evidence of trade union collusion with the racist regime, for example, there was also evidence of heroic mobilisations of solidarity against apartheid. While pulling no punches on the failings of trade unions in working against colonialism and racism more generally, trade unions have also made very real contributions (Davis et al, 2006).

The first part of this chapter summarises the competing approaches that have been identifiable within the history of trade union and labour movement education, with a particular focus on the implications for international solidarity and anti-racism. This sets the context for the discussion of specific approaches to trade union education and participatory research. The Unite History Project (UHP) co-produced six short volumes about the history of one of the two component parts of Unite: Amicus and the Transport and General Workers' Union, whose centenary would have been in 2022 had it not been for the merger, including materials produced via oral history interviews that were conducted by trade union educators and activists themselves (in order of publication Davis and Foster, 2021; Seifert, 2022; Mayo, 2022; Foster, 2022; Davis, 2023; Weir, 2023). The UHP's aim has been to develop learning materials for the contemporary context, evaluating previous successes as well as reflecting on the limitations of previous achievements. There are potentially relevant lessons here for the development for decolonising the community education and development curriculum.

Meanwhile, the Knowledge for Change project (K4C), has been promoting the development of PAR, drawing on international experiences of working for the democratisation of knowledge, experiences that Chapter 3 has already outlined. K4C's pilot project with Unite has also drawn on the UHP's experiences, illustrating ways in which such materials can be used more widely, including through the production of case studies for educational purposes.

The chapter concludes with further reflections on the scope for trade union and labour movement education and research, drawing on these approaches. However limited in themselves, and however pressured in the current context, these initiatives have potentially wider implications with particular relevance for the promotion of equalities and international solidarity within the labour and trade union movement and within communities more widely.

Contested approaches

The aims of workers' education have been contested ever since the 19th century, if not earlier. Across Europe, from the Scientific Revolution of the 17th century and the Enlightenment of the 18th century, there had been increasing recognition that knowledge could be harnessed for political change (Steele, 2010). 'Knowledge is power' is a slogan that predates Foucault's usage (Foucault, 1980) by more than a century. In fact, knowledge can be – and has been – acquired in the pursuit of differing agendas over time.

Education and training can be promoted to enable workers to improve their pay, conditions and employment prospects, for example, obtaining better jobs and so lifting themselves and their families out of poverty (Fieldhouse, 1998). This type of approach has already been described as learning to obtain 'useful knowledge' – enabling people to cope with their situations as effectively as possible, even if potentially diverting them from more radical pursuits (West, 2016).

'Really useful knowledge' in contrast, has already been characterised as learning to enable people to analyse the underlying causes of their problems as the basis for developing strategies for social change (Johnson, 1979). Previous chapters have outlined the contributions of adult educators who have been committed to the promotion of 'really useful' education for democratic participation and social justice. Popular education has been defined in just such terms in more recent times, drawing on Freirean commitments to learning for the promotion of critical consciousness and progressive social change (Crowther et al, 2005).

Case Study: Debates within and between Ruskin College, Oxford, the National Council of Labour Colleges and the Workers Educational Association

The history of debates within and between the Workers Educational Association (WEA), the National Council of Labour Colleges (NCLC) and Ruskin College, Oxford illustrate significant differences of approach, as they played out in practice in the previous century, as Chapter 4 has already pointed out. Founded in 1899, Ruskin College, Oxford aimed to provide opportunities for trade unionists and labour movement activists to study in a residential setting at a time when there were very few, if any, such educational opportunities elsewhere.

But how was this to be achieved and on what basis? 'Was it [the purpose of the college] to equip its students to challenge the existing social order and work to transform it', queried educational historian Brian Simon (Simon, 1992: 19). Or was the purpose more modest – 'to prepare students to function within the limitations set by existing [highly unequal] social relations?' (Simon, 1992: 19). This question underpinned a number of related debates as these played out in Ruskin and elsewhere. How should the college relate to the University of Oxford more specifically, for example – the university being seen by its critics as representing the ideology and material interests of the status quo (Simon, 1992) – although the history of the university's extra-mural work proved more complex in practice, as Chapter 4 has already illustrated? And how should workers' education be funded when state funding became more available, state funding being viewed with understandable suspicion because of the potential limitations that this could entail?

Following a student led strike in 1909, the predominantly Marxist 'Plebs League' split off from Ruskin to set up the Central Labour College (Craik, 1964; Pollins, 1984; Simon, 1992; Andrews, Kean and Thompson, J., eds. 1999). This went on to become part of the NCLC, which was seen to represent the more radical strands within workers' education.

Founded in 1903, the WEA, in contrast, had close links with Christian Socialist approaches within the university extension movement. The NCLC has been quoted as viewing the WEA – along with Ruskin to a lesser extent – as supporting the existing economic and social system in the guise of 'neutral education' (Pollins, 1984). And the WEA was critical of the NCLC in its turn, dismissing the NCLC approach as 'mere class-war propaganda and not education at all' (Pollins, 1984: 19). There were differences over the form as well as the content of workers' education. The WEA argued that 'the Labour Colleges teach what to think, the WEA teaches how to think' (McIlroy, 1980). And there were differences over whether to accept state funding when this became possible.

Despite their political differences, however, each made significant contributions to working-class education. Between them the NCLC, Ruskin and the WEA provided learning opportunities for many students over the years. Nor were their approaches always mutually exclusive in practice. The WEA included progressive adult educators among its tutors, despite its more 'neutral' reputation, tutors such as Raymond Williams and Thomas Hodgkin, for instance, as previous chapters have already illustrated. And the Workers Education Trade Union Committee (WETUC), which was established by the WEA in 1919, drew upon the expertise of Marxist intellectuals such as Raymond Postgate, Emile Burns, Maurice Dobb, Palme Dutt and Robin Page Arnot (Corfield, 1969). Unsurprisingly, there were lively debates between Marxists and social democrats across workers' educational provision during this period.

There were international contributions too, in addition to these varied contributions to trade union and labour movement education in Britain. Ruskin's alumni included activists from Britain's former colonies, some of whom went on to play leading roles in their countries' struggles for independence. The extent to which they went on to work for social transformation – or to become members of post-colonial elites – is a question that is beyond the scope of this particular chapter.

Ruskin was also seen as a potential model that could be transplanted to post-colonial contexts, as Chapter 4 has already outlined. Julius Nyerere himself was very clear about the type of education that Kivukoni College was to promote in what was then Tanganyika – socialist adult education for collective approaches to development from the bottom up rather than adult education for individual advancement. Given the shortage of professionally trained personnel in the country, such debates may not have seemed particularly relevant at that time, although they certainly became more relevant subsequently, as demonstrated in Chapter 4.

Meanwhile, the WETUC and the NCLC became integrated within the Trades Union Congress's (TUC's) provision in 1965. TUC courses became the predominant form for trade union and labour movement education, with developing opportunities for state funding. On the plus side, it has been argued, trade union education increased and active participatory approaches to learning were encouraged. But the emphasis was upon role education, learning how to be maximally effective as a trade union representative. Critics have argued that this meant 'the virtual elimination of politics from the curriculum' (Fisher, 2005: 227). These overall weaknesses were similarly identifiable in the lack of critical analysis of racism and its roots.

This didn't mean that the spaces for political education were entirely eliminated, of course; trade union educators did identify and utilise such spaces within TUC courses, including spaces to address racism, taking account of racism's historical roots in slavery and colonialism. There were informal opportunities for political education as well, through gatherings, reading groups and one-off events.

The reality has been more complex, then, just as the impact of learning itself has been more complex and unpredictable. The title of Fisher's history of TGWU education *Bread on the Waters* makes precisely this point. It was Arthur Deakin, General Secretary of the TGWU in the 1950s, who used this phrase; recognising the difficulties of predicting educational outcomes, whatever his own preferences (for education outcomes that would keep the union safe from 'agitators', especially Marxist agitators) (Fisher, 2005). There would seem to be parallels with the British Colonial Office's attitudes more generally, to forestall agitation and to promote 'responsible trade unionism rather than riots' (Ramdin, 2017: 256) – domestication as the aim, in other words, if not necessarily so readily achievable in practice.

With the impacts of Thatcherism from the 1980s, parts of the T&G most closely associated with the progressive Broad Left in the union realised that education for its members with an explicit political content was necessary. The London Region of the union launched its Political Weekend School from 1991, held at the union's residential centre in Eastbourne and taught by John Fisher and Pat Hayes (Fisher, 2005: 230–231). None of the material used on these courses (which ran for a decade) has survived; suffice it to say that a Marxist element was apparent in the Friday evening and Saturday sessions, with the Sunday morning given over to mobilising support for the Labour Party. These courses were paid for by the union (using its political fund), with no support from public monies at all.

At the same time, the London Region also launched its Labour History Weekend School (Fisher, 2005: 285), taught by Mike Hayes and Adrian Weir – not with an explicitly decolonised curriculum but certainly promoting equalities throughout. Here too, this course was provided outside of the functional skills requirements that were eligible for public funding and so was directly paid for by the union itself.

Since then, state funding has been cut right back, limiting the scope for trade union education still further. Ruskin College no longer exists in its previous form as a centre for trade union and labour movement learning and research, and the WEA has been experiencing major restructuring and cuts as state funding has become increasingly focused on meeting the needs of the economy. State funding might have had its problems, as its critics have so forcefully argued – a 'Faustian Pact', providing education for thousands of workplace representatives over the years but 'disabling educators from engaging in political and economic analysis' (McGrath, 2017: 102). But changes in state funding, along with increasing marketisation, have been posing further problems of their own, exacerbating these challenges still further.

In summary, then, workers' education has been a site of struggle, education for domestication, education for coping as effectively as possible within the confines of the status quo and education for the development of critical consciousness and social transformation. Far from attempting a comprehensive history of workers' education, the discussion so far has simply illustrated some of these underlying tensions – challenges from the past with some continuing resonance in more recent times. Trade union education needs to include some account of these histories, it has been argued – the backstory that can enable representatives and members to appreciate that 'the struggle for progressive values has been a long time in the making' (McGrath, 2017: 104), along with an appreciation of the possibilities for alternative futures.

How far do these contested histories matter more specifically, then, when it comes to tackling the legacies of slavery and colonialism? Marable's *Race, Reform and Rebellion* (1991) was explicit about the importance of history for young Black people, who needed to learn about past experiences of segregation in order to understand the background to continuing disadvantages of race, class and gender. 'History's greatest dangers are waiting for those who fail to learn its lessons. Any oppressed people who abandon their own protest history, or who fail to analyze its lessons, will only perpetuate their domination by others' he argued (Marable, 1991: xi). Marable went on to give examples of discriminatory practices within many unions in US in the post-war period. It was Black workers themselves, influenced by the Black Power Movement, who began to fight union racism, he argued, forming their own unions in some cases. This illustrated the importance of self-organisation, in his view, a continuing theme in the history of strategies to combat racism within the trade union movement itself as well as within the wider society.

The TUC's report *Working against Racism* includes recognition of precisely this, along with the importance of understanding peoples' varying histories. As the report points out, 'Those black workers who came from the Caribbean and other former British colonies to the UK were active trade unionists in their countries of origin', experiences that also needed recognition (Davis et al, 2006: 20). This was part of a wider discussion about the importance of history within trade union education strategies to promote anti-racist agendas, including the importance of trade union activism within struggles for freedom in Britain's colonies in the past (Ramdin, 2017). In summary, the report concluded, trade unions should:

> ensure that there is an anti-racist component within all union education programmes in order to build confidence among activists in challenging and combatting it in the union and in their workplace. This should include an explanation of the roots and nature of racism and why such a divisive ideology is contrary to the interests of ALL workers, black and white. (Davis et al, 2006: 23, emphasis in original)

Britain's imperial past has particular relevance here, setting the context for the history of Unite that follows (Davis and Foster, 2021).

Beyond functionalism: the Unite History Project

When the T&G came together with Amicus to form Unite the Union (Unite) in 2007, new traditions and structures were developed to meet the needs of the combined membership of over a million trade unionists across private, public and voluntary sectors, including manufacturing, public services, transport, food, finance and construction. These developments included a guide for tutors explaining the union's educational approach. 'Beyond Functionalism' started by recognising past educational achievements, with 'its student centred pedagogy combined with often first rate learning materials equipping participants to undertake their representational and organising roles in the workplace' (Unite, 2009: 3), useful knowledge to enable them to function effectively within their existing contexts. So far, so good. But the pursuit of the union's three pillars – organising, politics and internationalism – required more than this, it was argued: going beyond functionalism, in other words.

> Given the current crisis of capitalism and the sustained nature of our elite's attacks on working people', the report continued, 'our educational provision must provide our Reps with the understandings necessary to organise and argue for the translation of our values into [a] viable and realistic alternative to a system which advantages the few at the expense of the many. A functionalist approach cannot achieve this on its own. Through skills and knowledge development must be added real political understanding of what stands in the way of achieving a fairer, more just world and what we must do to achieve it. (Unite, 2009: 3)

The study of history would be a significant component, exploring past experiences and struggles with contemporary resonance for individuals as well as for the trade union movement more widely, in Britain and beyond. As the sociologist C. Wright Mills had already pointed out, the report continued:

> past and present, public and private combine to create understanding of the fact that ... every individual lives, from one generation to the next, in some society ... lives out a biography ... lives it out within some historical sequence ... and that this conjuncture presents ... as minute points of the intersections of biography and history within society. (quoted in Unite, 2009: 27)

Tutors were encouraged to help participants to make these connections between their own experiences and the wider context, in different times and varying places, building international understanding and solidarity in the process.

This was the framework within which the UHP was developed, aiming to co-produce knowledge and critical understandings and providing learning materials for the coming period. In his foreword to the first volume, Len McCluskey, then the union's General Secretary, explained the project's aims and approach. The T&G's history was to be documented from its beginnings and official launch in 1922 through to the formation of Unite in 2007. This was to be co-researched and co-produced by teams of trade union education officers and activists working alongside academics via the Marx Memorial Library and Workers School (MML) on the basis of their shared research (Davis and Foster, 2021). Together they would produce political education resources, 'building on experiences of political education in the past, focusing on histories of collective action, within a national framework' (Davis and Foster, 2021: xi). The outputs would include both web-based resources and six accessible volumes covering different periods within the project's overall framework. Each volume could be read as a stand-alone account of the period in question, but each would also focus on the following common themes reflecting on:

- (p)ast experiences of class struggles including experiences of international solidarity and of solidarity with communities and public service users;
- struggles for democracy and equalities for women, Black, Asian and Minority Ethnic (BAME) communities and LGBT people, both within the trade union and Labour movement and within the wider social context; and
- relationships between trade unions, employers and the state, with a particular focus on relationships with the Labour Party.

The project would draw 'lessons from past achievements and mistakes to apply these critically to contemporary challenges, recognising past shortcomings as well as celebrating past achievements' (Davis and Foster, 2021: xi).

International solidarity and anti-racism

International solidarity and equalities were central concerns, then, themes that ran through the union's history from the late 19th century onwards, set in the context of Britain's imperial past. Volume 1 starts from precisely this context, setting the scene for the spread of trade unionism to previously unorganised workers and the revival of socialist activity in the 1880s. 'However, this period [the last quarter of the nineteenth century] was one of adjustment rather than breakdown, in which the old labour-capital consensus, although shaken, was ultimately renewed', Davis and Foster explained (Davis and Foster, 2021: 3), going on to add that 'the material basis for the capitalist state's ability to adjust was due to the massive expansion of the British Empire in the last quarter of the nineteenth century' (2021: 3).

Imperial expansion continued to have an impact as a key element in the context for industrial relations, as Davis and Foster went on to explain. After Germany's defeat in the First World War, her colonies were divided between Britain and France, with the result that 'the British Empire increased in size to cover a quarter of the World's surface and population' (Davis and Foster, 2021: 17). 'Providing as it did a lucrative return on the export of capital, imperial expansion also served to mask Britain's manufacturing decline', Davis and Foster continued. There were inherent tensions here, including tensions between the interests of finance capital and industrial capital, skewing the British economy for the longer term, as subsequent volumes go on demonstrate. Colonialism was inherently contradictory, in other words, entailing costs as well as benefits, enabling the capitalist state to manage working-class militancy, exacerbating divisions by providing upper sections of the working class with short-term gains, while storing up problems for the British economy in the longer term. Lenin's writings on imperialism explored just such contradictions and their effects on class struggles in Britain in particular, given its history as a major colonial power (Lenin, 2010).

Volume 2 (Seifert, 2022) takes up these contradictory themes as they impacted on the trade union and labour movement in the 1930s. 'Colonialism was backed by the TGWU leadership as strong supporters of Empire', Seifert explains, 'but they were also aware of the hardships of black workers in the UK and in the colonies' (Seifert, 2022: 20). As General Secretary from 1922, 'Bevin [a proud supporter of Empire in principle] exhibited ambiguous attitudes towards colonial peoples and their rights', Seifert continues, which 'hampered the TGWU's solidarity with liberation movements, limited its ability to reconfigure economic policy away from imperial benefits' and created 'a disastrous lack of clarity in relation to government policies', in his view. Indian independence was supported by the union in the 1930s, but the coverage of Indian trade unionism was 'a mixture of support and somewhat patronising efforts to offer a helping hand from those that know best' (Seifert, 2022: 20), precisely the types of attitudes that Steve Biko and other Black students had found so unacceptable, deciding to self-organise and form their own South African Students Organisation, as outlined in Chapter 5.

Both TGWU leaders and activists were united in their opposition to fascism in the 1930s. But there were differences here too. The official line was 'also strongly anti-racist, and deplored outbreaks of anti-Semitism among its

London taxicab members' (Seifert, 2022: 67). The leadership was somewhat tardy and hesitant, however, when it came to supporting the republican side fighting the fascists in the Spanish Civil War (1936–38). And TGWU leaders refused to join the United and Popular Front anti-fascist coalitions. 'This mattered and further divided the TGWU membership with regard to fighting the fascists in the streets and on the battlefields of Spain', Seifert explained (Seifert, 2022: 67–68), although there were activists throughout the union who used their positions to promote working-class unity, 'solidarity-building that stretched for some as far as the colonies' (Seifert, 2022: 76). Anti-racism, anti-Semitism, anti-colonialism and international solidarity remained contested within the union, in other words, representing continuing sites of struggle.

Seifert summarised the situation by describing Bevin's imperialism as 'the usual medley of superiority of the white man, bringing civilisation to the world, benefits to his members from preferential trade and market, and onward Christian soldiers' (Seifert, 2022: 77). Overall, the TGWU tended to support the empire under Bevin's leadership at this period, he pointed out, although there was also evidence of support for the plight of workers in the colonies – in India and the West Indies, for example. Bevin was not alone in such attitudes. Other labour movement leaders shared similar views. But there was also 'a substantial group of those fighting for an end to Empire, for national self-determination, and clear on racial equality' (2022: 77).

Volume 3 picks up on these themes in the post-World War Two period (1945–1960). This was the volume with which I was most directly involved (Mayo, 2022), hence my particular interest in this part of the story. This was an especially significant period in any case, though, with striking parallels with contemporary debates on immigration, race and the legacies of the colonial past.

Given the time frame for this volume, there was very limited scope for oral history interviews. Few of the key protagonists had lived long enough to be interviewed, although the volume did include a limited number of interviews with women and men who had been involved in the 1959 print strike as very young workers. So, Volume 3 had to rely upon written sources in the main, including newspapers and pamphlets as well as the T&G's own records of this formative period and the struggles for progressive approaches within the union and beyond (see the T&G records at the Modern Records Centre at the University of Warwick, 1953).

Britain had emerged victorious from the Second World War in 1945, the leader of a global empire. Prime Minister Winston Churchill expected that the country would continue to play a leading role internationally, with a 'seat at the top table' alongside its wartime allies, the US and the USSR. The reality turned out to be far more problematic, however. Britain was effectively bankrupt and increasingly dependent on the US, while relationships with the USSR soon deteriorated with the advent of the Cold War. So, Britain became the junior partner of the US in this post-war context, despite its glorious/inglorious imperial past as a global power in its own right. Reflecting on these changing relationships, Macmillan (Conservative politician and Prime Minister from 1957 to 1963) referred to the times when Britain had been on an equal footing with the US as a respected ally during the war, contrasting this with the situation that developed subsequently when Britain was being treated with 'a mixture of patronising pity and contempt' (quoted in Barr, 2018: 150). These changes have had and continue to have significant implications for the ways in which Britain's global role has been (mis)understood and (mis)recognised, along with the legacies of its colonial past.

Britain's position in the world was most certainly not what it had been, as previous chapters have also recognised, whether or not politicians and colonial officials were prepared to accept this. And decolonisation was on the agenda, however fiercely this was to be contested. Indian independence had been widely accepted as a necessity in 1947, for instance, but this was by no means a unanimous view. Former T&G leader turned Labour Foreign Secretary Bevin had argued against what he described as the 'scuttle' from India, believing that there could be continuing partnerships between Britain and its colonies for 'mutual benefit' (or at least that was what he argued; the colonised might well have had very different views about the supposed mutuality of these benefits). Bevin's views on Britain's future role as a world power alongside the US, though, were shared by a number of leading trade unionists at the time, including Bevin's successor as General Secretary of the T&G, Arthur Deakin. Others took very different positions, however, supporting the case for colonial freedoms and racial equality.

These differences were played out through the history of the World Federation of Trade Unions (WFTU) in the post-war period, with major implications for the development of trade union internationalism. The WFTU set out to build an all-inclusive federation of national federations, united in their aims to protect workers' rights. By 1947 there were 71 affiliated centres representing some 70 million workers worldwide, including workers who were engaged in struggles for colonial freedom, as well as workers in Britain and other colonial powers.

The WFTU took stands on workers' rights in colonial contexts, along with stands against racial discrimination. The organisation's pamphlet *Discrimination against Coloured People* provides illustrations of this as it challenged differential pay and conditions in countries such as Kenya, Tanganyika, South Africa, Australia, the Belgian Congo and Indonesia, for example. Colonial exploitation was an essential feature of capitalism, the report concluded (Yeates, 1950).

There were differing views within the WFTU, though, differences that related to widening divisions as a result of the Cold War. The British Foreign Office engaged in secret discussions with Bevin as Foreign Secretary at the time, along with Arthur Deakin from the T&G, fearing the WFTU's support for colonial peoples could undermine Western democracies and facilitate the propagation of communism in the colonies and former colonies. In the event, Deakin organised a walkout in 1947 along with others, including representatives from the US and the Netherlands, leading to a split which seriously weakened the WFTU. Western federations then went on to form the International Confederation of Free Trade Unions (ICFTU) with the backing of the US, thereby reinforcing Cold War differences within the trade union movement internationally.

Although the T&G leadership had played such a regressive role globally, in the immediate post-war period it was all change by the time that Frank Cousins became General Secretary in 1956. There had been pressures for change building up before this, however, as Cousins himself recognised, pointing out that he was only giving voice to views that already existed among the membership, including views about international solidarity and support for movements for colonial freedom.

The Movement for Colonial Freedom (MCF, now Liberty) was founded in 1954, bringing trade unionists and labour movement supporters together in solidarity with trade union and national liberation activists in a range of contexts. MCF opposed colonial authorities' restrictions on trade union activities, mobilising support against particular atrocities, which were all too numerous. Trade unionists were arrested, and their federation banned in Malaya in 1948, for example. These moves were followed by detention without trial and the 'resettlement' (that is, displacement) of some 600,000 Malaysians to undermine support for those who were engaged in armed struggle against the colonial regime. There were atrocities in Kenya between 1953 and 1955, in particular, leading to hundreds of deaths, crimes that the colonial authorities initially attempted to cover up, as previous chapters have also indicated. And the British government sent troops into what was then British Guiana in 1953, on the very day that a Labour Relations Bill was being put together to promote trade union rights – on the spurious grounds that the colony's ruling Peoples Progressive Party, under the leadership of Cheddi Jagan, was in the pay of Moscow (no evidence to support this allegation was ever found). Sadly, the British TUC and the Labour Party supported these moves, although there were, of course, objections from progressives in the wider trade union and labour movement.

Racism and anti-Semitism were similarly contested within the trade union and labour movement in the post-war period. Despite the defeat of the Nazis, Oswald Mosley's fascist gangs still continued to harass Jewish communities in London and elsewhere, proclaiming anti-Semitic slogans such as 'Not enough Jews were burnt at Belsen'. A group of Jewish veterans, the 43 Group, mobilised opposition to such outrages, whether through heckling fascists at their meetings or confronting them directly on the streets (Beckman, 2013). Trade union activists were involved in these anti-fascist mobilisations, including a number of taxi drivers, many of whom would have been members of the T&G. In contrast with the taxi drivers who had been deplored for their anti-Semitism in the pre-war period, these cabbies provided support in a number of ways, including being on hand to drive activists to safety if confrontations with the fascists became too threatening. As one of the UHP team, Danny Freeman, regional education and development organiser for the London and Eastern Region of Unite, had discovered when he had previously researched this subject, it was difficult to obtain detailed information about these courageous activists (the cabbies would have risked losing their taxi drivers' badges, and so their livelihoods, if they had been publicly identified; Freeman, 2014). But their contributions were crucially important, along with the contributions of other sections of the Left.

Meanwhile, the Far Right's attention was moving on to focus on race and immigration from the colonies. In 1948 the Attlee government had passed the British Nationality Act, encouraging migration from the Commonwealth in order to provide the skilled labour that was so badly needed for post-war reconstruction. There had been more specific attempts to recruit labour in the Caribbean as well, with that arch-racist Enoch Powell recruiting nurses to come from Barbados to fill staffing gaps in the newly formed NHS. As Volume 3 reflects, to describe the policy context as ambivalent would be something of an understatement. Chapter 4 has already outlined some of the background to this situation.

The T&G's biennial conferences provided the UHP with illustrations of these competing approaches. The conference in 1953 passed a motion condemning the colour bar, for example, along with a motion re-affirming the union's belief in the universal brotherhood of man, endorsing the UN Human Rights Charter and describing discrimination on the grounds of race or colour as 'unchristian and contrary to trade union principles' (Modern Records Centre, University of Warwick, 1953). That same conference also passed a motion expressing concern about migration, however, calling for the government to work with the TUC to control it, a motion that was passed unanimously. There were clearly anxieties about the possible effects of migration on jobs, pay and conditions, concerns that could be played upon to exacerbate divisions within the labour force in particular contexts. In contrast, there was also evidence of anti-racism and solidarity, with illustrations from within the T&G and the wider trade union and labour movement.

Case Study: The Bristol Bus Boycott

The Bristol Bus Boycott provides one of the best-known examples of such struggles. The origins date back to the 1950s, although the Bristol Bus Boycott itself took place in 1963, as Volume 4 explains (Dresser, 1986; Foster, 2022). Bus transport had been one of the sectors in which newly arrived migrants had found employment in the 1950s, but in some towns there seem to have been quotas, imposed by informal agreements between managers and the union. These were very contentious issues within the union. In 1955 there had been a ballot of busmen in the Passenger (transport) Group of the T&G in Bristol, for example. And a majority had voted against the employment of Black bus crews. But the maintenance section had voted the other way.

Meanwhile, management stirred the situation further, pursuing a strategy of divide and rule by announcing that they were fine with employing Black crews. It was the T&G that was not, a statement that was contested in its turn, the regional officer explaining that the union was not at all opposed to the employment of Black workers – there was no colour bar in the T&G. Anti-racists criticised the regional secretary for not taking a firmer stand, however, and relations between the West Indian Development Council and the local branch of the T&G deteriorated into a bitter war of words in the local media, culminating in a libel case which found against the T&G, which was also condemned by the Bristol Trades Council.

This is to jump ahead, however. It was the decisive campaigning of the West Indian Development Committee that resolved the issue, with support from the wider community, including the local MP, Tony Benn, among other prominent progressives across the colour divide. In 1963 the Bristol Bus Boycott was launched, drawing upon experiences of bus boycotts in the US during the Civil Rights Movement in the 1950s. When the company announced that it would reverse its discriminatory policies three months later, the victory was celebrated with the delivery of Martin Luther King's 'I have a dream' speech, setting the campaign firmly within this wider international context. Three weeks later the company recruited two West Indians, one Sikh and two drivers from Pakistan.

This was a seriously unhappy episode for the union, demonstrating the persistence of racism despite the T&G's formal opposition to racial discrimination within its ranks. The Bristol Bus Boycott dispute was only finally resolved in 2013 when Unite issued an apology for its predecessor's handling of the matter. These have been ongoing struggles within the union, then, just as they have been within wider society. Volume 4 and subsequent volumes provide further examples of T&G struggles against racism along with examples of international solidarity within the T&G, from solidarity with Chilean trade unionists following the military coup in 1973 to solidarity with the anti-apartheid movement more recently, as Chapter 5 has outlined.

Volume 5 picks up on these themes, responding to pressures from members themselves as well as from movements for Women's Liberation and Black Liberation. There were, in addition, pressures to recruit more widely in the face of declining trade union membership. As Davis explains, in relation to the recruitment and active engagement of Black trade unionists, however, 'it also became increasingly clear that there was little appetite among many in the white trade union leadership to deal with the racism that black workers faced from their white workmates – often fellow trade union members – or from their employer'. As she went on to explain, 'This led black workers to fall back on what they knew from their history of resisting slavery and colonialism – that collectively organising as black workers could bring results' (Davis, 2023: 99).

Varying forms of Black self-organisation began to emerge in the early 1980s. The TUC adopted its charter *Black Workers: A TUC Charter for Equality of Opportunity* (1981). And the issues were raised within the T&G, including calls for the union to put its own house in order, at the union's 1987 conference. It was essential to eradicate some of the racist attitudes that were still prevalent, a delegate at this conference pointed out, while others referred to the need to do more than to simply pass resolutions. Racism still prevailed and the trouble was that a lot of people did not recognise it in themselves (Davis, 2023). National and Regional Advisory Committees were established in 1989 to address these challenges systematically, and equalities was included as a core subject in the union's education programmes, marking the recognition of how much more needed to be done within the T&G and within the trade union and labour movement more widely.

A major rule change was passed in 1998 to address these continuing challenges by requiring that positive steps be taken to redress the under-representation of women as workplace representatives on workplace committees and branch committees and as Regional Industrial Organisers. These requirements were also to be applied to Black, Asian and Minority Ethnic (BAME) members, requirements that entailed the need for the development of monitoring systems if they were to be effectively implemented. There was, in addition, recognition from the National Women's Committee and the National Race Equality Committee that BAME members needed encouragement and support, with union education courses to address these needs.

The final volume in the series (Weir, 2023) also discusses the T&G's international solidarity and commitment to peace and, marking a change from the past, an international policy more likely to be allied with anti-imperialism. In the last years of the T&G, the union was firmly identified with the struggle of the Palestinian people and against Bush and Blair's war in Iraq. The union also committed itself to liberation struggles in Latin America, from support for Cuba to support for social movement activists in Colombia often facing serious threats to their lives.

The later volumes have provided more scope for the inclusion of oral history–based materials. These bring the past to life, highlighting the learning to be shared from previous struggles against racism, along with the learning from previous expressions of solidarity with international struggles for freedom and equalities. Recounting their stories, the activists who were involved in solidarity with Chilean trade unionists recorded their pride, for instance, as they reflected on their refusal to work on repairing Chilean weapons of war, weapons that had been used to attack the opponents of the military coup in 1973. And they recalled the support that had been demonstrated in local communities, opening their hearts and welcoming Chilean refugees into their homes (Foster, 2022: 110–113). These accounts have been sources of pride for those recalling them from the past, as well as providing inspirational sources of learning for contemporary activists. More of the welcomes that were extended to Chilean refugees and the contributions of communities and local authorities in Chapter 7.

Drawing on the Unite History Project via 'Knowledge for Change'

Chapter 3 has already outlined the Knowledge for Change Consortium's contributions to the development of knowledge democracy, building civil society organisations' research capacity through training in PAR. Based in 23 hubs in 16 different countries, the UNESCO-supported programme has been delivering online learning together with a week's residential course, providing participants with the tools to go on to train others in their turn. An additional pilot hub was also developed to explore the possibilities of collaborating with a trade union organisation, Unite, and aiming to work in partnership with Ruskin College, Oxford to provide academic support.

The core workbook for this pilot began with an introduction expressing support from the General Secretary, followed by some introductory words from the National Education Office explaining that the course was designed to help participants to create really useful knowledge focusing on the issues of concern in their workplaces as well as supporting the union's overarching pillars of organising and political influence. And it would build the union's capacity to promote fairness and equalities in the context of agendas for international solidarity. This was to be delivered in two blocks of five weekly sessions each, with group projects between these two blocks researching the issues that the participants themselves identified in their workplaces. Those who successfully completed the course would gain an accredited qualification (a diploma at Level 2).

The core workbook provided a variety of materials on the union itself in its international context as well as providing materials on research methodologies, including the use of creative approaches to participatory research such as poetry, photography, storytelling and oral history. Research ethics was built into the course. And there was a strong emphasis on tackling discrimination and promoting equalities. The core workbook also drew upon UHP materials and experiences in a number of ways.

Overall, this was a very successful pilot project, demonstrating ways in which participatory research could be promoted to further the union's agendas, organising for fairness, equalities and social justice agendas in the workplace and beyond. Sadly, as it turned out, resources to build upon these experiences were not available. Trade unions have been subject to financial pressures too, limiting the scope for co-creating really useful knowledge and constructing learning resources for moving beyond functionalism.

UHP resources are still being used elsewhere, however. MML courses draw upon them, for example, sharing their analysis of the underlying causes of exploitation, discrimination and oppression, rooted as these have been in the histories of slavery, colonialism and imperialism. This builds upon MML's long history of organising courses on imperialism and past struggles for colonial freedom, as well as providing learning materials on ways of tackling racism and sexism within the movement itself, as well as within the wider society.

Conclusions

The trade union movement had some 6 million members in Britain at the time of writing. Although the movement is far smaller than it was at its height in the 1970s, before the effects of massive deindustrialisation along with the impacts of draconian anti-trade union legislation, this is still by far the largest civil society movement in the country. Trade union education really matters, in other words. Of course, trade unionists need to have access to useful knowledge in order to be effective in their current situations. But they also need to have access to political education in order to gain really useful knowledge, going beyond functionalism to be as effective as possible, promoting equalities and international solidarity.

The initiatives that have been outlined in this chapter have been small in themselves. But they do offer examples of what can be achieved, co-producing knowledge and developing skills within the trade union movement, with particular relevance for decolonisation and anti-racist struggles. As Marable (1991) and Ramdin (1987) have already been quoted as demonstrating, it is essential that each generation has critical understandings of the legacies of slavery and colonialism and their impacts. These legacies form the context for contemporary struggles against racism and sexism within the trade union movement itself, as well as within the wider society. 'We are here because you were there', as the interconnections between colonialism, racism and immigration in post-colonial Britain have been so aptly summarised. The impacts of 'divide and rule' strategies continue to have to be contested, centrally important as these strategies have been – and continue to be – in the wider battle of ideas, building critical consciousness in the contemporary context.

The reality, however, is that the spaces for political education have been squeezed. Austerity constraints have been accompanied by increasing marketisation, impacting on public services, including educational provision, as previous chapters have already illustrated. Finding such spaces presents increasing challenges, although much can still be achieved, as Chapter 7 sets out to explore in the context of progressive municipalities as they have been engaging with trade unions and communities to promote equalities and international solidarity.

7

Communities, social movements and municipal strategies for equalities and solidarity

This chapter explores the ways in which the book's three overarching themes weave through comparative experiences of municipal strategies in Britain and the US that work with communities and social movements to tackle the legacies of slavery and colonialism (Blunkett and Jackson, 1987; Mackintosh and Wainwright, 1987; Jackson, 2021). These experiences illustrate some of the challenges involved in the promotion of decolonisation as an ongoing process, questioning predominantly held ideas – the prevailing 'common-sense' of neoliberal globalisation – and providing the basis for promoting more inclusive policies and practices. Building on the experiences of community development programmes from the late 1960s, social movements began to engage with municipal authorities to respond to these challenges by developing strategies for equalities and international solidarity.

Whatever their inherent contradictions, programmes such as the US War on Poverty and the UK Community Development and Urban Programmes had promoted community participation, strengthening social movements in a number of contexts, as Chapter 4 has already outlined. There were positive legacies here as well as negative ones, providing the basis for neighbourhoods, communities and social movements to work with – as well as against – the local state, finding spaces for the pursuit of progressive agendas. This was despite the increasing predominance of neoliberal policies at national levels during the Reagan/Thatcher years of the 1980s.

A number of towns and cities reacted progressively when faced with these pressures and challenges. Together they developed a range of alternative economic, social and political strategies, working in collaboration with the trade union movement along with community-based organisations and social movement campaigns (Blunkett and Jackson, 1987; Mackintosh and Wainwright, 1987; Newman, 2014; Jackson, 2021). This is in no way to suggest that such collaborations were without their own inherent tensions and conflicts. They were not. But there were possibilities for progressive collaborations all the same, with examples from Britain and the US for illustration, demonstrating the scope for alternatives to neoliberalism as developed by the new urban Left. These alternatives focused on the promotion of equalities and social solidarity rather individualism and hostility to the 'other', whether the 'other' was being characterised as the 'enemy within' – such as striking miners – or the enemy without – the refugees and migrants who were supposed to be threatening to 'swamp' Thatcher's Britain.

Rather than attempting a comprehensive review, this chapter starts by focusing on municipal strategies that set out to tackle the racial discrimination that constituted such a persistent legacy of slavery and colonialism. Adult education and training initiatives were promoted to enable Black and ethnic minority communities and women to access employment, for example, along with initiatives to improve the quality and inclusivity of services for communities. There have also been strategies to tackle structural inequalities and to improve the quality of jobs through the promotion of fair trade internationally, including strategies to improve the quality of jobs in Britain's former colonies in West Africa. And there have been initiatives to promote international solidarity through establishing Cities of Sanctuary in order to welcome and provide support for asylum seekers and refugees. Here too, there are illustrations from cities in the US as well as from cities and regions in Britain, challenging national government strategies to create hostile environments instead of welcoming those in urgent need of protection from discrimination and violence, which themselves are too often legacies of the colonial past or the neo-colonial, imperialist present. The chapter concludes by reflecting on these experiences and their potential value, despite their inherent limitations, while spaces for these types of strategies have been shrinking in the contemporary policy context.

Progressive cities in the US

As national policies shifted to the Right with the growth of neoliberalism during the Reagan years, a number of US cities began to develop alternative approaches towards urban development. City planning had tended to focus on the promotion of economic growth in the post-war period, enabling property developers to profit from lucrative downtown initiatives. The planners' role in the US was typically envisaged as facilitating these processes rather than attempting to intervene in the operations of the private property market (Clavel, 1986). This may have worked well enough for the developers, if considerably less well for the tenants and residents of more disadvantaged neighbourhoods. But this all began to change from the 1960s onwards, as Clavel and others have demonstrated.

The contexts for these developments in US cities had been changing, as Chapter 4 has already explained, with the migration of Black populations from the rural South in search of a better life. Industrial jobs were beginning to decline, however, with growing concentrations of poverty and deprivation. And these problems were especially concentrated among Black communities in the neighbourhoods. Racial injustice was centrally important in divided cities such as Chicago, for example – a potentially explosive issue, as urban uprisings in the late 1960s had all too clearly demonstrated.

Social movements had been strengthened, though, as neighbourhoods had been gaining resources from the community development programmes that had been supported by the federal government's War on Poverty. Although the overall level of federal funding had been reduced by the mid-1970s, some resources were still available via Community Development Block Grants, mainly targeted towards projects to promote self-reliance, such as co-operative development schemes. However limited, though, such initiatives did facilitate the development of community organisations. New leaderships were emerging as a result, including new leaderships within Black communities. The Civil Rights Movement and the Black Power Movement had been important influences here, even if these neighbourhood community development organisations had tended to focus on less transformative goals in practice – improving access to jobs, affordable housing, education and health care, for example.

Meanwhile, social movements had also been impacting on a whole new generation of politicians and professionals. In addition to the Civil Rights Movement and the Black Power Movement, these politicians and professionals had also been affected by the student movement, the women's liberation movement and the movement against the Vietnam war. Chapter 2 has already referred to some of those who had represented key influences in the 1960s, such as Marcuse, who was quoted as reflecting on the conflicts that were taking place in Vietnam, the Congo and South Africa as well as within the 'affluent society' in Mississippi, Alabama and Harlem (Marcuse, 1966: xiii). These were revolts against 'the intolerable heritage of colonialism and its prolongation by neo-colonialism', in his view, with revolts in the US expressing solidarity with 'the wretched of the earth' (the title of Fanon's influential publication, as outlined in Chapter 2).

Clavel's study of progressive cities identified a number of politicians and professionals who had been in some way influenced by the zeitgeist of those times. These included Bernie Sanders, for example, the radical mayor of Burlington, Vermont, who made news in more recent times with his bid for the Democratic Party nomination to stand for election as US president in 2016. Bernie Sanders had been actively involved in the Civil Rights Movement and the Anti-Vietnam War Movement. These had been the key influences which had shaped his subsequent thinking when he became mayor of Burlington in 1981.

Citizen participation was central to progressive strategies in cities such as Burlington, where neighbourhood organising had been emerging in response to the challenges of the time. Jobs had been disappearing, as they had in many other cities, and there were increasing housing pressures in the wake of market-driven development strategies. In addition, there were problems with access to education and healthcare, exacerbating feelings of frustration within deprived communities.

Progressive mayors set out to engage with communities, especially Black communities whose voices had not been so effectively heard, aiming to build coalitions of support for their strategies to address these inequalities. Bernie Sanders established Neighbourhood Planning Assemblies, for example (Clavel, 1986). There were cities that developed collaborations with universities and other agencies too, providing critical analyses and support for community development initiatives in the neighbourhoods. In Cleveland, for instance, there were links with Cleveland State University's Center for Neighbourhood Development. Neighbourhood discussion groups had also been organised in Cleveland through the Commission on Catholic Community Action, with a strategic focus on empowerment rather than simply prioritising organising per se – the more pragmatic approach that had been developed by Saul Alinsky in Chicago via the Industrial Areas Foundation (Clavel, 1986).

Strategies to strengthen citizen participation and empowerment brought their own inherent tensions too, of course. Relationships between neighbourhood organisations and city halls were not always constructive, to say the least. Nor were alliances between different interest groups necessarily harmonious. There were inherent tensions, including tensions based upon differences of social class within Black communities, for instance, as well as tensions based upon wider racial differences.

Reflecting on the experiences of these cities overall, however, Clavel concluded that citizen participation initiatives had demonstrated the potential for constructing mass bases, building support for progressive planning policies and addressing social inequalities rather than simply facilitating the pursuit of the interests of the property development growth machine.

Harold Washington and the Chicago neighbourhoods

Harold Washington's time as Chicago's first African American mayor illustrates these possibilities in practice, along with their inherent tensions. He was an iconic figure, inspiring devoted loyalty among his many supporters. Alton Miller, who had been Washington's press secretary (and was presumably firmly on board with his agenda), described him as giving the city to the Black people, going on to suggest that he was opening up a new era, building a rainbow coalition in support of his vision of Chicago as the city that works together (Miller, 1987). Washington was something of a legend in his time.

Harold Washington was born in 1922 in Bronzeville, described as a vibrant Black neighbourhood in Chicago. His forbears had been slaves. Having served in the army in the Second World War, he graduated from Roosevelt University before going on to obtain a law degree from Northwestern

Law School – the only Black person in his class. He practised as a lawyer in Chicago before going into politics, serving in the Illinois House of Representatives (1965–76), the Illinois Senate (1976–80) and the US House of Representatives (1980–83). By the time he stood for mayor in 1983, then, he was already an experienced politician with clear ideas on what needed to change in Chicago.

The machine politics of city patronage had to be challenged. Racial disadvantages had to be tackled in this very divided city (Biles, 2018). And economic development had to be promoted to meet the needs of communities in disadvantaged neighbourhoods rather than fuelling the profits of property developers in the city centre. Harold Washington himself described the issues as being about 'money and power and morality' (Biles, 2018: 6) – taking on the powerful in order to promote equalities and social justice agendas.

Like several other US cities, Chicago had been experiencing major changes. Industrial jobs had been disappearing in the context of industrial restructuring, while federal funds had been shrinking, trends that were exacerbated by the neoliberal policies of the Reagan era. While the effects were being experienced most acutely in the neighbourhoods where Black, Hispanic and poor White communities struggled to make a living, property developers were enjoying new opportunities for making profits in the city centre. In parallel with this trend, there were also major political changes during this period, with the need for new coalitions in response to growing pressures from social movements, including pressures from the Black Power Movement (Clavel and Wiewel, 1991). Chicago already had a long history of community organising in any case, stimulated by the work of Saul Alinsky (Alinsky, 1971), whose approach to mobilising around single, winnable issues (whatever the criticism of its limitations) had been and continued to be influential in the politics of the city during the Harold Washington years.

Harold Washington was not short of challenges, then, when he was elected mayor in 1983 following a successful voter registration campaign. He faced problems within City Hall, for a start, with a majority of White aldermen in opposition. And he lacked effective powers and resources in key areas (Biles, 2018). But he had already built a support base within Black community neighbourhoods. The next step was to widen this support base further, developing what became described as a rainbow coalition of interests, including poor Latinos and poor Whites as well as reform-minded Jewish interests and Black business elites (Gills, 1991). Trade union interests had tended to support the patronage-style machine politics of previous incumbents, such as Irish American Mayor Daley. But Mayor Washington did also manage to gain some support from trade unionists, enabling him to develop his own, very different, approach.

The Chicago Workshop for Economic Development (CWED) shifted the whole approach away from market-driven redevelopment schemes, for example. Instead, the CWED focused on schemes that prioritised job retention (slowing down plant closures) and job creation schemes in the neighbourhoods. And there was a focus on using the city's purchasing power to ensure that contractors provided quality jobs that were accessible on an equal basis.

These local economic development strategies were part of wider attempts to tackle poverty and racism. Washington was not anti-business per se, but he did believe that development could be promoted in ways that could benefit poorer neighbourhoods and that power could be decentralised, at least to some extent. Access to decision-making processes could be widened, resulting in fairer allocations of resources and better services. And equalities could be promoted through contract compliance along with targeted education and training initiatives. Although he himself was Black, he was not a Black nationalist; poor Hispanics and poor Whites were included in the broad coalition that constituted the mass base in support of his approach.

Under Washington, it has been argued, the machine politics of the past were dead, with a development of politics from the bottom up. But machine politics may have been re-emerging in new guises, it has also been suggested (Gills, 1991). One of the criticisms that has been levelled at Harold Washington's approach is that activists gained links into City Hall, with some obtaining jobs there. There were concerns about the incorporation of protest as a result, along with concerns that new forms of machine politics might be emerging in place of the former structures of patronage (Clavel and Wiewel, 1991; Gills, 1991). Washington's Political Education Project may have seemed consistent with such criticisms – described as an initiative to strengthen his voter base rather than to promote political education in more participative ways.

Despite the limitations of Washington's mayoralty, however, there was, according to Gills, 'something beautiful about it and something that brought the dead to life' (Gills, 1991: 60). Gills was not entirely disinterested in his views, as he himself explained, being on the board of the CWED, which he had helped to found. But Gills was not uncritical overall, which makes these reflections all the more credible.

There was further evidence of Washington's impact from the circumstances surrounding his untimely death. When he died of a sudden heart attack soon after his re-election in 1987, there were extraordinarily emotional expressions of grief, testifying to his amazing popularity across the city. He was revered for demonstrating the possibilities for promoting alternative and more equitable approaches to city government based on community participation from the bottom up.

There would seem to be parallels as well as differences between the experiences of progressive cities such as Chicago and those of municipal authorities in Britain over a similar timescale. The 1980s were a period of industrial restructuring increasingly dominated by the neoliberal policy agendas of Thatcher and Reagan. Despite the pressures that these agendas generated, however, there were municipal and regional authorities that responded by developing alternative approaches, working with trade unions, communities and social movement organisations to promote equalities and international solidarity.

Municipal socialism in Britain

While progressive cities such as Chicago addressed the long-term effects of slavery in the context of neoliberal policy agendas, municipal socialist cities and regions in Britain addressed the legacies of both slavery and colonialism in the context of neoliberal globalisation – legacies with political as well as socio-economic implications. Blunkett and Jackson's analysis started from the proposition that democracy was in crisis. Faced with profound economic and social change, parliamentarians had failed to address people's fears and anxieties in an increasingly uncertain and seriously unequal world (Blunkett and Jackson, 1987). Local government and local political action could not solve unemployment in an era dominated by giant transnational corporations, they accepted. Nor could local authorities provide major redistributions of resources on their own without national support. But they *could* still make a difference, they believed. Most importantly, they could strengthen democracy through the promotion of active citizenship. And communities could be empowered to engage in building alternatives to neoliberal narratives based on fear and prejudice.

Britain had particular issues to address here in the face of the contemporary challenges of neoliberal globalisation. 'For over 200 years', Blunkett and Jackson pointed out, 'a British sense of wellbeing and material prosperity has depended on the possession of an empire' (Blunkett and Jackson, 1987: 9). Other nations that had possessed and then lost empires, like Japan, had 'moved on to create a new political and economic role in the world' – for better or worse – in their view (Blunkett and Jackson, 1987: 9). But Britain had been hanging on to its imperial legacy, with serious consequences, helping to create poverty and social divisions both at home and overseas. (There are parallels with Gilroy's analysis here, as outlined in Chapter 2.) Blunkett and Jackson went on to quote Walter Rodney's analysis of the exploitative roles of imperial powers in the present as well as in the colonial past (Rodney, 1976), built, as colonialism and capitalism had been, upon piracy, conquest and slavery (Blunkett and Jackson, 1987: 43). While far less extreme, the legacies of imperialism were also being experienced in Britain, with economic policy dominated and distorted by the requirements of finance capital in the City of London.

The divisive social effects of empire were no less damaging, in Blunkett and Jackson's view. The end of empire could have offered an opportunity for developing 'cooperation between black and white, who had been torn apart by imperialism' (Blunkett and Jackson, 1987: 34). But, as the need for their labour became seen as less acute, they argued, 'successive governments have regarded black people as a problem, an embarrassing relic of Empire', with racist and fascist groups explicitly linking 'the causes of Britain's present discontents with the "loss of Empire"'. Although *Democracy in Crisis* was published over three decades ago, the analysis is still strikingly relevant to contemporary discussions on decolonisation and the roles that local and regional authorities could be playing in response to these challenges.

Tackling racial disadvantage and promoting international solidarity

Democracy in Crisis went on to provide a range of examples to illustrate the ways in which some local authorities were pursuing alternative strategies to meet local needs in an increasingly cold climate. The provision of free, or at least genuinely affordable, public transport formed part of local and regional authority approaches in London and South Yorkshire, for instance. There were strategies to safeguard jobs where possible and to promote socially useful alternatives where this was more appropriate (as with the case of jobs in the defence sector, for instance). They were also concerned to provide support for voluntary, community and trade union organisations – including tenants' and residents' organisations, women's groups and trade union advice and campaign centres – as part of strategies to promote decentralisation and community participation in decision-making processes.

Rather than attempting to provide a comprehensive account of these types of interventions, this chapter focuses on local authority strategies to address racial inequalities more specifically, as well as to promote international solidarity and development. There were programmes to tackle discrimination, including anti-racist education and training, and others to provide education and training to widen Black and minority ethnic communities' access to employment. And there were initiatives to support the development of Black and ethnic minority businesses. In parallel, international solidarity was being promoted through support for struggles against apartheid (as Chapter 5 has illustrated), along with the establishment of twinning arrangements and support for the development of fair trade schemes. There have also been examples of schemes to support refugees and asylum seekers – schemes that have been becoming increasingly significant with the growth of hostile environments in Britain and the US in more recent years.

South Yorkshire County Council was one of several progressive metropolitan authorities that played key roles in the early 1980s in these respects, along with the Greater London Council (GLC). Both councils were abolished by the Conservative Thatcher government in 1986. Between them, along with several of the local authorities within their regions, they challenged Thatcher's reactionary agendas in a number of ways, with implications for tackling racism and for promoting solidarity and development internationally.

One of the initiatives that has been described as 'constantly cropping up' in the development of South Yorkshire's history during this period was the founding of Northern College, established to provide residential adult education in 1978. The college had been founded through the initiative of the labour movement in South Yorkshire, influenced by the Black Power and consciousness movements as well as by the women's liberation movement. Northern College went on to play what has been described as 'a key role in developing awareness of the importance of race and gender as well as class within socialism' (Jackson, 2021: 60).

Although the college has often been identified as the 'Ruskin of the North', there were differences as well as similarities in its approaches to the provision of adult and community-based learning for working-class adults. Northern College was more collectivist in its approach, for example, providing short courses that delivered political education for community organisations and social movements as well as longer learning programmes to enable individual learners to gain access to higher education. The first principal, Michael Barratt Brown, was the son of a former principal of Ruskin College, Oxford, Alfred Barratt Brown. Like his father before him, Michael Barratt Brown was a distinguished scholar. He had a track record of extra-mural work at the University of Sheffield and elsewhere – more of Michael Barratt Brown subsequently. The college set out to achieve its educational goals with an equal balance between women and men in its student body, as well as reaching out to Black and minority ethnic communities and immigrant communities across South Yorkshire.

Northern College succeeded in maintaining this commitment to equalities over the years and in differing contexts. By the beginning of the 21st century, it was clear that South Yorkshire was undergoing rapid changes as manufacturing jobs continued to decline while public services continued to struggle to meet increasing social needs, a situation that has been described as fostering anxieties and resentments, with growing support for the Far Right. This was the context within which Northern College developed a programme of anti-racist popular education specifically aiming to promote 'really useful knowledge' and critical consciousness (Grayson, 2010), creatively finding the resources to do this from a government-sponsored programme to promote active citizenship (Grayson, 2010). Between 2003 and 2006 a series of residential short courses was organised to develop anti-racist working and solidarity. The programme included 'Kicking Out Racism in Your Community', for example, and 'Divided We Fall: Resolving Conflict in Communities', along with a course for refugees on how to self-organise refugee organisations (Grayson, 2010). In addition, Northern

College organised 'Teach-Ins' for college students, community activists and community organisations in South Yorkshire, drawing on the analyses and experiences of those with first-hand knowledge of these issues, such as Zimbabwean and Congolese refugees.

Grayson concluded by reflecting on the achievements of popular anti-racist adult education at Northern College, finding the spaces for radical approaches within the framework of public funding programmes. Rather than seeing these opportunities as spaces, however, he suggested that they felt more like 'holding pens', waiting for their demise as government funding was being reduced. Northern College itself was being seriously (perhaps terminally) injured in this climate, in his view, 'having to turn to new marketized skills-based and vocational programmes' (Grayson, 2010: 166). There are many parallels with the recent history of adult education, community development and community-based research elsewhere, as previous chapters have already identified.

There were similar pressures on Sheffield City Council's initiatives to promote alternative approaches from the bottom up, working with trade unions, communities and social movements to promote equalities, including via the improvement of access to jobs and training within the Council's own workforce. The Council had developed a Race Equality Unit to tackle racism as well as establishing an Afro Caribbean Enterprise project to provide training opportunities, for example. The city already had a strong tradition of campaigning against racism, with contributions from the trade unions and the Sheffield Campaign Against Racism. Trade union support was absolutely crucial in these respects, in fact. There had been, in addition, a well-established tradition of supporting international struggles, including the struggle against apartheid in South Africa, as Chapter 5 has also illustrated.

Helen Jackson's political memoir provides both personal and political examples of international solidarity during her time as an activist, as a Sheffield city councillor and then as a Member of Parliament. Back in 1975, she recounts, a Chilean refugee came to live with her family, having suffered imprisonment and torture following the overthrow of Allende's progressive government in 1973 with US foreknowledge, as more recently declassified documents demonstrate (Bartlett, 2023). Pinochet's dictatorship had then gone on to install neoliberal economists from the US as advisers, promoting precisely the type of neoliberal free market–dominated strategies that came to characterise the governments of Margaret Thatcher and Ronald Reagan. Chile had provided a test run, in other words, undermining trade unions and communities alike through their promotion of industrial restructuring accompanied by legislation to restrict the scope for organised resistance.

Events in Chile provided the basis for international solidarity here, and the labour movement in Sheffield rallied in response, working with the Chile Solidarity Campaign to provide support. Pedro and his family were among a number of Chileans who found refuge with Helen Jackson and many other Sheffield trade unionists and families over the following years. 'Political aspirations and international solidarity became part of our home environment and social activities', she explained (Jackson, 2021: 90). And the Chilean community reciprocated in their turn, with Chilean miners organising support for the miners' strike in Britain in 1984–85.

Along with Women Against Pit Closures, Chilean women were also influential in shaping Sheffield's subsequent decision to twin with Esteli, Nicaragua's second city. This was in support of the Sandinista government which had overthrown Somoza's US-backed regime. On a study tour at the invitation of the Nicaraguan Solidarity Movement in 1987, Helen Jackson was able to include conversations with community development workers and adult educators, noting the parallels between their approaches to popular education and the approaches that had been applied in short-course programmes at Northern College.

Much had been achieved, then. But there had been growing pressures, resulting in aggressive national policies and diminishing resources. The *People's Republic of South Yorkshire* reflected that 'the bold emphasis on people-led progress towards a fairer society, driven by the belief that what was good for social progress and equal opportunity would help the local economy thrive and vice versa, became more hesitant and muted' (Jackson, 2021: 257). The Council began to explore opportunities for partnerships with the private sector, striving to make the best of an increasingly challenging situation. The title of a report to the Labour Group in 1986 had already summarised this as follows: *Furthering Socialism in a Cold Climate* (Jackson, 2021: 251).

Even so, the *People's Republic of South Yorkshire* ends on a positive note, re-affirming the importance of internationalism in a world of global interdependence. And the book emphasises the importance of community development and lifelong learning. Northern College's contributions were to be celebrated, especially their achievements in opening up opportunities for women and responding to the needs of refugees and immigrant communities in South Yorkshire.

The Greater London Council and the Greater London Enterprise Board

There are parallels between these developments in South Yorkshire and the approaches that were being adopted by the GLC and the Greater London Enterprise Board (GLEB), established in 1982 to implement the GLC's industrial strategy. There were regular exchanges between the GLC and South Yorkshire, as well as exchanges with several other local and regional authorities. Between them they shared a number of concerns, responding and developing alternatives to the strategies of the Thatcher government.

For a start, equalities was central to the GLC's agenda, focusing on addressing inequalities of gender and disabilities as well as of race – set out in terms of the legacies of Britain's imperial past. As the relevant chapter of the London Labour Plan – the labour market companion of the London Industrial Strategy – explained, 'The fact that black workers proportionately have worse jobs than white people and their level of unemployment is higher is not something that they have brought upon themselves. It is the result of white racism which has its roots in Britain's colonial past' – a legacy which was being exacerbated by immigration and nationality acts which were effectively racist (London Labour Plan, 1986: 103). Black people were mostly coming from Britain's former colonies and other Third World countries that had been systematically under-developed, the report went on to explain, going on to experience discrimination at work, in housing and in education in the so-called 'mother country'. These experiences of racism had their roots in the slave trade and the colonial past as well as the post-colonial present, the report continued.

The GLC's strategies in response to racial discrimination included the provision of support for the development of Black businesses and co-operatives as well as the provision of support for training. Equal opportunities were also being promoted throughout the GLC's own workforce as well as through contract compliance – building equalities considerations into contracts when purchasing goods and services from other organisations and agencies. In addition, equalities requirements were embedded in agreements to invest in businesses and co-operatives as part of the GLC's strategic approach to safeguarding and improving jobs in the local economy.

The London Industrial Strategy (LIS) was the most ambitious of local authority programmes to promote economic development, *restructuring for labour* rather than restructuring for capital. In his forward to the LIS, Michael Ward explained that the strategy set out to 'replace the anarchy of the market economy with justice and fairness' (GLC, 1985: vii). 'The uniqueness of the London Industrial Strategy is that we show how this can be done in the interests of the people who live and work in London, and in ways which involve working people in the process of planning and restructuring', he continued. Working with employers, trade unions and consumer groups, municipal authorities could invest and otherwise intervene to safeguard existing jobs and create new jobs while improving working conditions. This was about the promotion of industrial democracy, in other words, part of the GLC's wider brief to promote democratic participation, popular planning and community engagement, building a rainbow coalition in support of strategies to promote equalities and social justice from the bottom up. The banners that were displayed from County Hall, across the river from Parliament, proclaimed these values for all to see, fundamentally challenging the Thatcher government's mantra that there was no alternative to their policies. On the contrary, as Michael Ward had already maintained in an earlier pamphlet titled *Job Creation and the Council: Local Government and the Struggle for Full Employment*, there was an alternative based on the rational, democratic planning of public resources from the bottom up (Ward, 1981).

The GLC's strategy was ambitious, to say the least. There was evidently more scope for exerting influence on small and medium-sized businesses and co-operatives than there was when it came to large transnational enterprises, whether this was about promoting agendas for equalities or promoting agendas for industrial democracy, or both (Mackintosh and Wainwright, 1987). Cochrane's collection of essays *Developing Local Economic Strategies* came to similar conclusions about the challenges of implementing the GLC's wider social goals, while recognising the potential value of the planning agreements that the GLEB developed when negotiating support for private enterprises (Cochrane, 1987). There was also recognition that the GLC's social objectives – for the promotion of equalities, for instance – were difficult to monitor effectively, although the GLEB did reflect on these challenges and adjusted their approaches accordingly (Massey, 1987).

Critics have also questioned the extent to which Black people were involved with the GLC directly (Hatherley, 2020) – although there was evidence that some, at least, *were* engaging, just as there was evidence that some communities were engaging in processes of popular planning. But engaging with communities takes time, and time was not on the GLC's side. Reflecting on the popular planning process that produced the People's Plan for the Royal Docks, one of those who had been involved wrote of the 'hopefulness and naivety' of attempting to reach out to engage those who were not already directly involved within what was effectively a four-month period (Brownhill, 1988: 16). Given these constraints, it seems remarkable that there were as many achievements as there were, then, before the GLC's untimely abolition in 1986.

International solidarity and the promotion of fair trade

The most relevant legacies of the GLC's efforts, for the focus of this chapter, were its policies to promote international solidarity and sustainable development. There was support for collaborations between trade unionists across national boundaries, sharing strategies to save and improve jobs in transnational enterprises such as Kodak, for example. And there was support for challenging the ways in which global trade systems were contributing to uneven development, widening gaps within and between the First and Third Worlds. The fair trade movement has roots in the GLC's strategies to secure a better deal for farmers and workers on a global scale.

The key figure here was Michael Barratt Brown, the innovative academic and adult educator who has already emerged in this chapter as one of the founders and first principal of Northern College. Michael Barratt Brown had previously written on empire and its aftermath. As he explained at the beginning of his first major contribution on this subject, *After Imperialism*, the book was built upon lectures that he had given over more than ten years under the auspices of Technical Colleges, the Workers Educational Association and University Extra-Mural Departments (Barratt Brown, 1963). The starting point for *After Imperialism* was the great divide between rich and poor within as well as between states across the First and Third Worlds. The role of imperialism was central to his analysis, emphasising that this was not just about empire in terms of the political control of one country by another. This was about fundamentally unequal and exploitative economic relationships. As he went on to point out, countries can indeed gain political independence and still be subjected to political interference, in order to ensure that their governments remain sympathetic to the underlying interests of the former colonisers and their allies (as Britain, among other formal colonial powers, has so amply demonstrated). These were economic relationships within the context of contemporary capitalism, although they had been underpinned by ideological 'justifications', as he went on to explain – ideas about racial superiority and the supposedly civilising mission of the Whites.

The British working class may have enjoyed some benefits from the fruits of empire, in Barratt Brown's view. But he firmly rejected the argument that 'the interests of workers in the rich nations are antagonistic to those of peasants and workers in the poor nations' (Barratt Brown, 1972: 75). On the contrary, the costs of uneven development outweighed the benefits for workers in the developed nations, in his view. Colonisation was ultimately detrimental for the working class in developed countries, leading to distorted patterns of private investment (the predominance of the financial sector in the City of London at the expense of manufacturing industry and jobs) as well as leading to distorted patterns of government spending on the military rather than on the provision of public services. In addition, Barratt Brown argued – somewhat ahead of the curve at this time – developed nations were actually becoming over-developed, using up the world's resources in unsustainable ways. There needed to be a new framework for international trade and sustainable development, working out in the interests of the working class in the developed as well as the under-developed economies.

Barratt Brown's usages of the terms 'developed' versus 'under-developed' economies might seem less familiar in the contemporary context. But he was pointing to vitally important connections here. 'Under-development' was not an accident of history or indeed an accident of geography, let alone the result of racial inferiority, as White supremacists had been arguing. On the contrary, 'under-development' resulted from structural inequalities that were inherent within capitalism. Addressing these structural inequalities involved challenging the interests of both transnational corporations and national bourgeoisies, in Barratt Brown's view – making the case for a very different approach while taking account of environmental considerations in the development process.

Barratt Brown had been part of the New Left that had emerged in the post-war period, a grouping that had been strongly critical of Soviet-style centralised planning. So, this was absolutely not the type of system that he had in mind for the future. While he recognised that some forms of planning would be required, in his alternative scenario he was committed to the development of democratic planning from the bottom up – industrial democracy both within and between economies internationally.

This was the thinking that underpinned the development of initiatives to promote fair trade in partnership with the GLC, with its overarching aim of 'replacing the anarchy of the market economy with justice and fairness' (GLC,1985: vii). Michael Barratt Brown had made contact with his old friend Robin Murray, the development economist who was Chief Economic Adviser to the GLC at that time (1981–86), knowing that they both shared similar concerns. The two had, in fact, known each other since Robin Murray had been a baby, their families having a shared background as Quakers. Together, Barratt Brown and Murray set up a conference which led to the establishment of the Third World Information Network (TWIN), with a trading company to promote fair trade principles in practice (Michael Barratt Brown interviewed by Louise Brodie, British Library).

As Barratt Brown explained subsequently, the dominant trade system was fundamentally unfair (Barratt Brown, 1993). Plunder and slavery had been followed by colonialism and the development of capitalism, which had expanded in fundamentally unequal ways – with deeply unequal trading relationships dominated by giant transnational corporations. *Fair Trade* had set out to provide a better deal for small farmers and rural workers in the Global South while providing high-quality, sustainably produced goods for consumers in the Global North. Although this was a small start, it could be argued, the ultimate aim was to contribute to the development of a new international order based upon justice and environmental sustainability for the longer term.

The initial emphasis had been on developing trade relationships with Vietnam, Cuba and Nicaragua, moving on to focus upon getting produce into the supermarkets, starting with an agreement with Safeway to sell Mexican coffee. The Co-op was then involved, followed by Sainsbury's and Waitrose. The requirements were tough in terms of quality control. And there were tough requirements about work conditions and bans on child labour in developing countries (even if these conditions were challenging to monitor in practice). Through its support for TWIN then, the GLC contributed to the promotion of international solidarity in innovative ways, developing significant legacies for the future.

TWIN Trading operated successfully for 30 years. But in 2019 TWIN went into administration (although parts of the operation were subsequently acquired by a US ethical trading organisation). These were indeed challenging initiatives to sustain over time. As Michael Ward has subsequently reflected (personal communication, 2023), this illustrates the difficulties of the GLC's attempts to combine commercial, social and ethical objectives – not a reason for not trying them but a reason for not over-claiming success. These were extremely ambitious aims, after all, as Michael Barratt Brown himself had previously explained (Barratt Brown, 1993). TWIN didn't transform trade relations, as he subsequently reflected, although he added that 'a beginning has been made' (Barratt Brown, 2013: 193).

Still, the fair trade movement has grown exponentially in more recent times, with hundreds of fair trade towns, schools, universities, faith groups and supporters across the country and beyond, according to the Fairtrade Foundation (https:/www.fairtrade.org.uk/). Set up in 1992 by CAFOD (the Catholic Agency for Overseas Development), Christian Aid, Oxfam, Traidcraft, Global Justice Now and Women's Institutes, the Fairtrade Foundation licenses the use of the FAIRTRADE Mark in the UK, helping to increase the demand for fair trade products while empowering producers and their organisations and networks. The movement is also concerned with political education in the UK and elsewhere, raising public awareness about the need for fairer trade and how to make trade more equitable. The Foundation is the UK member of Fairtrade International, which brings more than 20 labelling initiatives together across Europe, Japan, North America, Mexico and Australia/New Zealand, as well as supporting networks of producer organisations from Asia, Africa, Latin America and the Caribbean.

Alternative legacies of survival and resistance

There are several other ways in which Sheffield, the GLC and other local authorities set about safeguarding their legacies. Among these was the formation of the Centre for Local Economic Strategies (CLES) in 1986. Based in Manchester, CLES developed an action research focus, drawing on evidence from local authorities, publishing reports and facilitating the exchange of experiences. CLES soon built up its membership, facilitating mutual support processes as local authorities struggled to maintain economic development initiatives, prioritising the needs of women and those living in disadvantaged communities and so most directly affected by public spending constraints. As John Shutt, a subsequent deputy director and research manager, reflected decades later, CLES adapted and survived over the years, pioneering new forms of intervention in local economies and challenging inequalities of race as well as of gender (Jackson, 2021: 283).

In more recent times CLES has also emphasised its contributions in terms of curating the Community Wealth Building Movement. This approach to economic development sets out to change the way that local economies function, retaining more wealth and opportunities for the benefit of local people. Preston has been quoted as a model in this respect, along with a number of other cities and combined authorities, including Birmingham, Manchester and North Tyneside (Brown and Jones, 2001). The focus has been upon the promotion of democratically controlled initiatives such as co-operatives and community land trusts, along with the preservation of anchor organisations and businesses with the capacity for purchasing locally. This has been about enhancing the local economy in the interests of local communities, taking account of equalities and environmental considerations in the process – strategies for survival and sustainability in climates that have been becoming politically even colder.

There have been more directly challenging legacies as well. The notion of Cities of Sanctuary has developed on both sides of the Atlantic, with Sheffield leading the way in Britain, recognising the plight of refugees and offering them support. This network started from the need to provide an alternative approach to the Conservative government's policies to promote a 'hostile environment', policies that were deliberately making it harder for refugees and asylum seekers to settle in Britain. Those who could not prove their right to remain in Britain were also affected, including the Windrush Generation (those who had come from Britain's former colonies in the Caribbean, when they had still been colonies, to meet the needs of the colonial power for their labour, as previously outlined). The hostile environment was, of course, also targeting those who were fleeing from more recent British interventions in the affairs of other states in the pursuit of Britain's own interests.

The Cities of Sanctuary movement's commitment was to a very different approach, working in solidarity with others in towns and cities across the country. This was also about involving local people and partner organisations, fostering solidarity between receiving communities and those seeking sanctuary from elsewhere. The Cities of Sanctuary network has been growing as more and more local authorities commit to challenging the government's hostile policies.

There have also been similar developments in the US. Although Berkeley, California was the first city to pass a sanctuary resolution back in 1971, the movement didn't really take off until more recent times, with widespread mobilisations in response to the Trump Government's policies of deportations and the victimisation of undocumented migrants. These mobilisations have been very controversial and strongly contested. Despite government attempts to prevent states that were supporting the Cities of Sanctuary movement from receiving federal funds, there have been states, such as California, that have responded with defiance.

There is not the space here to explore the contributions and challenges of Cities and Boroughs of Sanctuary further, whether in the US or in Britain. Rather, the point is simply to note the continuing scope for social movements to work with – as well as against – local authorities, challenging national government policies in the process and promoting alternative approaches, despite their inherent limitations, in the contemporary context.

Community and social movement organisations can and do, of course, pursue their own ways of expressing international solidarity. There have been, and continue to be, mobilisations of resistance to manifestations of street violence from the Far Right, for example. And there have been, and continue to be, mobilisations to resist state violence in the form of forcible deportations. As Brewis reflected on the mobilisations that took place in Kenmure Street, Glasgow, for instance, this had been 'a day that went beyond race, religion, gender, ideas of left vs right, or even ideology; it was community, and it was strength, and through this came victory'. The battle was won', Brewis concluded, 'but the war continues' (Brewis, 2023: 106).

Conclusions

Social movements have impacted on local authorities in a variety of ways, just as progressive local authorities have impacted on social movements in their turn. While there have been, and continue to be, tensions between them, there have been, and continue to be, possibilities for working together in pursuit of common causes, including in response to the challenges of decolonisation. Progressive cities have responded to the legacies of slavery, addressing the continuing challenges of racial inequalities in the US, just as local authorities have responded to the legacies of slavery and colonialism in Britain. The reaction of Bristol City Council to the toppling of the statue of slave trader Edward Colston is a case in point, as Chapter 3 has already flagged up, putting the statue on display accompanied by an explanation of its provenance in order to provide public education about slavery as the source of so much wealth in Bristol and elsewhere in Britain. Most significantly, in addition, local authorities have responded to unequal trade systems in the context of neoliberal globalisation, as the history of the fair trade movement illustrates.

The limitations of such alliances have been only too clear – they have been no more than small steps in the direction of a fairer, more environmentally sustainable future. As a number of those who have been involved have also reflected, the spaces for developing alternative strategies have been shrinking in the meantime. These have been described as years of trauma for local government, struggling in the face of market fundamentalism (Newman, 2014). Local authorities such as Sheffield have been striving to make the best of an increasingly challenging situation, then, 'furthering socialism in a cold climate'. The spaces for progressive, anti-racist adult education at Northern College were described in similar terms – feeling more like 'holding pens' as government funding was being reduced and the college was struggling to survive without jeopardising its original mission. Meanwhile, the GLC and South Yorkshire authorities have long since been abolished.

Despite the pressures on local authorities in Britain – the loss of powers, the commodification of public services and the decimation of resources – they do still have some agency, however (Newman, 2014). And they do still have some possibilities for working alongside communities and social movements in empowering ways, challenging regressive policies and practices at wider levels and remaining committed to the development of fairer, more inclusive and more sustainable futures. If more powers and resources were to be decentralised, the scope for such forms of collaboration could be correspondingly increased.

8

Learning through the arts: cultural strategies for decolonisation

This chapter returns to the first theme – cultures and culture wars – and questions as to whose knowledge counts. Here the focus is on cultural strategies for engaging with experiential forms of knowledge, engaging with people's emotions and building empathetic understandings through the arts. The focus is upon learning about slavery, colonisation and decolonisation in this chapter, understanding exploitation and oppression in different ways, touching our emotions and stimulating our abilities to imagine alternative futures.

Chapter 2 explored the contested notion of culture itself, 'one of the two or three most complicated words in the English language', according to Raymond Williams (Williams, 1988: 87) – cultures as whole ways of life, linked to societies' productive bases but not in crudely determinist ways. Cultures reflect social relationships and structures of feeling, as Williams went on to explain, with working-class values of mutual aid and co-operation standing in contrast with the hegemonic ideas that Gramsci identified as the prevailing 'common sense' (Gramsci, 1968). Previous chapters have questioned these 'common sense' assumptions about the status quo and the assumed superiority of the 'free' market, along with 'common sense' assumptions about the nature of knowledge and whose ideas really count.

This chapter moves on to focus on culture in terms of the arts more specifically too, including museums and galleries. Cultural strategies have been promoted to re-enforce the prevailing common sense, just as they have been promoted to challenge existing norms and values, offering different ways of thinking about the past, as illustrated in the previous chapter's discussion of the display of slave trader Edward Colston's statue. Most importantly, the arts can also stimulate new ways of imagining alternative futures. There have been significant implications here for community education and development, exploring the contributions of the arts, including the visual arts, poetry, drama and song, raising awareness and strengthening solidarity in the pursuit of equalities and social justice during the apartheid years, as outlined in Chapter 5.

Decolonising museums and galleries

Museums and galleries provide illustrations of just such cultural strategies and challenges, testifying to the violence of Britain's supposedly 'civilising' mission and the resistance that this has provoked, along with the backlash that has followed in its turn. Battles have been, and are still being, waged over Britain's cultural heritage. Museums and galleries have particular contributions to make here through their community education and outreach programmes, contributions that have especial relevance for decolonisation.

The contested history of public museums has been dated back to the late 18th and 19th centuries, coinciding with the spread of Britain's empire and the growth of capitalism. Private collections had been accumulated by aristocrats on their European grand tours. But public museums and galleries were very different entities, established as part of Britain's imperial mission to 'civilise primitive peoples', it has been argued, while bringing culture back home to the masses (Bennett, 1995; Keith, 2011). Rather than carousing in the pubs, where they were feared to be spending their leisure time, the popular masses were to be encouraged to behave in orderly ways, becoming civilised by learning how to appreciate the superiority of British culture, as contrasted with the cultures of the 'others', as Bennett has summarised these aims. This was about the representation of colonised people and the authorisation of the practices of colonialism (Bennett, 1995), portraying 'primitive peoples' as part of this supposedly evolutionary story, culminating in the cultural achievements of the British Empire (Bennett, 1995: 78–79).

The proceeds of slavery underpinned these initiatives, the wealth that enabled collectors such as Henry Tate to build their collections and then to donate them to the nation, forming the basis of the Tate Galleries as we know them today. Tate was not a slave owner himself, nor was he directly involved in the slave trade, which had been abolished before he was born. But he was involved in the sugar industry that had been developed in Jamaica and elsewhere, an industry that had been developed on precisely this basis. Slavery and colonialism have been central to the development of Britain's cultural heritage, then, whether these connections are being recognised or contested in the context of contemporary culture wars.

The violence of slavery and colonialism has already been referenced in previous chapters (Elkins, 2005, 2022). The story of the Benin Bronzes provides yet more evidence of the contradictions inherent in colonialism's so-called 'civilising mission' (Hicks, 2021). These bronzes were plundered in 1897 as part of a brutal mission of reprisals perpetrated by a British expeditionary force. The spoils were then passed on to Queen Victoria, the British Museum and other collections in Britain and beyond. The restitution of the Benin Bronzes remains a work in progress, just as the case for the restitution of the Parthenon sculptures – the so-called Elgin Marbles – remains contested, despite the spaces that await them in the Acropolis Museum in Athens.

Museums can – and increasingly do – provide education about the past in different ways, though, as part of cultural strategies for decolonisation. For example, the Victoria and Albert Museum's website refers to broadening and deepening our understanding of the legacy of empire and slavery in the context of the museum's ongoing commitment to addressing the colonial heritage. Museums and galleries have displayed the works of Black artists representing their own realities, including their own experiences of racism. Existing collections have been revisited and curated in more critical terms, pointing to their connections with slavery and colonialism. And there have been celebrations of the contributions of contemporary artists. Tate Britain's exhibition of Isaac Julien's films included reflections on the contributions of the Harlem Renaissance poet, novelist and playwright Langston Hughes, for example (in 'What Freedom Is to Me'). Another film in this exhibition reflected on the abolitionist Frederick Douglass' visit to Scotland, Ireland and England to campaign against slavery between 1845 and 1847. And the exhibition included a film reflecting on migrations in small boats, a film with very particular contemporary resonance.

Tate Modern's exhibition of contemporary African photography ('A World in Common') posed challenging questions about the ways in which Africans have been represented and the ways in which they have chosen to represent themselves. And the Victoria and Albert Museum's Africa Fashion exhibition demonstrated ways in which African designers had been developing their own creative approaches in the context of post-colonial freedoms (Victoria and Albert Museum, 2022). Incidentally, this exhibition included an African dress that had been donated by Lalage Bown, the adult educator whose contributions to decolonisation were referenced in Chapter 4.

In summary, then, museums and galleries have been developing their own strategies for learning for decolonisation. These strategies have involved their own challenges (Keith, 2011). And they have been strongly contested, contestations that have included impassioned debates about the restitution of items which had previously been plundered. There are many issues of relevance for community education and development in the context of these debates.

Many opportunities for learning through the arts arise in other ways, too, of course, whether from the visual or the performing arts, including poetry, drama, song and dance. Rather than attempting to offer a comprehensive review, this chapter focuses on a limited number of examples from works of literature and film to illustrate different aspects of learning about decolonisation, including emotional learning about:

- the injustices and violence inherent in slavery and colonialism;
- their subsequent legacies;
- stories of resilience and resistance, despite the continuing challenges.

Learning about slavery through novels and film

Slavery has been represented in varying ways in novels and films. Margaret Mitchell's novel *Gone with the Wind* (Mitchell, 2020, first released 1936) was turned into an extremely popular film, for example. This film was not intended to be pro slavery. But critics such as C.L.R. James still felt that the film was offensive for portraying the Black characters in stereotypical ways. In addition, there were criticisms of the ways in which Black actors were treated, both during the filming process and afterwards. For example, Hattie McDaniel won an Oscar for best supporting actress for her role as Mammy, the loyal Black servant, but she had to sit at a separate table from the White actors at the Academy Awards ceremony in 1940 (Taylor, 2019).

There are echoes here of some of the criticisms of Harriet Beecher Stowe's novel *Uncle Tom's Cabin*, published in serial form between 1851 and 1852. While the novel was to be taken up by abolitionists, providing evidence for their campaigns against the inhumanity of slavery, subsequent writers, including James Baldwin, have nevertheless criticised the novel for being racist and patronising, portraying Black people as subservient and effectively complicit in White supremacy, as the term 'Uncle Tom' has subsequently come to imply.

In more recent times, however, Black writers and filmmakers have been telling their own stories, providing counter-narratives for themselves. Alex Haley's *Roots: The Saga of an American Family* (2001, first published in 1976) traces his family's roots back to his forebear Kunta Kinte, who was captured by slavers in the Gambia in the second half of the 18th century. The book recounts the violence of slavery and its aftermath, both the physical violence of the beatings and the mutilations and the psychological violences involved in the attempted destruction of Africans' cultural heritage. Kunta Kinte suffered beatings because he resisted being called by a new name, slavery entailing the loss of his identity as well as the loss of his physical freedom.

Roots was made into a television series the year after the book's publication, going on to win a number of awards. This raised a stir at the time, increasing awareness of slavery's destructive violence and promoting increasing awareness of alternative understandings of African American histories and cultures.

Steve McQueen's *Twelve Years a Slave* (2013) provides a more recent example. This film was based on a true story, documented by Solomon Northrup in the autobiography that he published in 1853. He had been living what had seemed to be a relatively comfortable life with his wife and children when the story begins, set in the state of New York where Solomon's free status was recognised. Tricked into travelling south to Washington DC in 1851, he was captured by slavers who put him in chains, falsely claiming that he was a runaway slave from the state of Georgia.

No one believed his claims to the contrary, so he ended up being transported to a slave market where men, women and children were being stripped and prodded by potential buyers, treated like animals – or worse. He watched a woman being forcibly separated from her child, weeping incessantly as she and her child were dragged apart. Solomon himself was renamed – as Pratt – despite his resistance to this particular assault on his identity. But he refused to despair, despite all such attempts to rob him of his humanity. His first owner actually recognised that slaves were human beings – and gifted human beings at that, in Solomon's case, since he was a musician who could play the violin for White folks' parties. But gruesome forms of mistreatment were still taking place on his plantation, culminating in Solomon's near-death experience by hanging.

Solomon's subsequent experiences were even more appalling. He was sold on to a psychopath who treated his slaves with pathological cruelty – and pathological lust when it came to his female slaves. There are scenes that are unbearably upsetting to watch, lynchings and floggings, including floggings that slaves were forced to inflict upon each other. Meanwhile, religion was being used to instil the acceptance of slavery as Black people's lot in life, a level of hypocrisy that doesn't pass unnoticed in the film. Slaves had their own approaches to religion and culture, though, as evidenced through their use of song, singing as they worked together as well as when they were required to sing for the Whites.

Eventually Solomon managed to persuade a White Canadian to write a letter on his behalf, enabling him to contact those who could vouch for his status as a free man. He was eventually reunited with his family as a result, meeting his baby grandson for the first time in an emotional scene back home in the North. So far, so good, in terms of happy endings?

Well, not entirely. He subsequently failed to obtain any form of legal redress for his sufferings, as the film goes on to explain. And slavery continued to exist in the slave states of the South. But Solomon Northrup didn't forget the plight of those he had left behind. He became active as an anti-slavery campaigner, lecturing on the evils of slavery and supporting the Underground Railroad of slaves fleeing North in search of freedom. Meanwhile, however, others were still being kidnapped and enslaved, with few being as fortunate as Northrup in terms of eventually regaining their freedom.

This was a film with extraordinary emotional impact. The violence was horrifying, although never gratuitous. 'The peculiar institution' (as slavery has been termed) was also psychologically destructive, involving the systematic denial of slaves' humanity, the ultimate 'othering' of the oppressed. The characters were only too believable as they responded to this in their different ways, with Solomon as the man who managed to maintain some sort of hope for the future, despite every attempt to beat him into submission.

This was a film that engaged the senses as well as the emotions. It was visually stunning – unsurprisingly perhaps, given Steve McQueen's own background in the fine arts and his continuing work as a visual artist (Kim and Moran, 2020). The beauty of the photography contrasted sharply with the horrors that were being portrayed. As McQueen has been quoted as explaining, the most horrific things sometimes happen in the most beautiful places (Kim, 2020).

This was a film that was also extremely thought provoking. McQueen has been quoted as commenting that if the film's confrontation with the past starts a conversation, then wonderful. Rather than appealing to the realms of the emotions and the senses *or* to the realms of rationality, *Twelve Years a Slave* was making its appeal to both. The film raises many questions for further discussions. What have we learnt and how have we reacted when presented with such an extraordinary story?

The unfairness of Solomon's enslavement is only too evident. What about those who were born into slavery, though, and the injustices of their situations? How does the audience feel when slaves are forced to inflict violence on each other? How does the film deal with the differences between the two slave owners – and their womenfolk – and the variety of ways in which they abused their power and attempted to justify their behaviour to others? More of Steve McQueen later in this chapter, with his portrayal of Black experiences in Britain in the latter part of the 20th century, drawing on his own experiences as an artist and filmmaker of African Caribbean heritage.

Learning about colonialism and its legacies

There are many works of art from which to choose when it comes to learning about the violence and injustices inherent in colonialism and their legacies. Conrad's *Heart of Darkness* paints the most appalling picture of the violence of Belgian colonialism in what was then the Congo, for example (Conrad, 1983). But the novel has also been strongly criticised by African writers, such as the Nigerian Chinua Achebe, for the ways in which the book portrays and – in his view – dehumanises Africans.

Achebe has made a particularly important contribution to the development of African writing, providing inspiration and support to a number of African writers of his own generation as well as providing a role model for subsequent authors, including Chimamanda Ngozi Adichie, who has acknowledged the extent of her debt to him. Her novel *Half of a Yellow Sun*, set in the context of the Biafran war, was described as the Nigerian answer to *Gone with the Wind* by Thandie Newton, the lead actor when it was turned into a film.

Achebe's own writings have explored the ways in which colonialism undermined traditional cultures as well perpetrating extreme forms of physical violence on those who resisted colonial rule. His first novel, *Things Fall Apart* (Achebe, 2001b), first published in 1958, was very successful, leading the publishers, Heinemann, to decide to establish its African Writers

Series, with Achebe as editorial adviser from 1962 to 1972. He has played a very significant role through his promotion of the work of other African writers as well through his own writings as a novelist.

Between 1962 and 2003 (when the series was discontinued before being relaunched in 2021) the Heinemann series published more than 350 books, mainly novels, but also poetry, short stories and dramas, some of them translated from African languages. Nadine Gordimer, the Nobel-winning South African writer, has described Achebe as the father of modern African literature. Steve Biko was among the many authors whose works were published through this series, along with many others who had engaged with colonialism and its destructive legacies.

Things Fall Apart forms part of Achebe's own Nigerian trilogy. The Igbo community in which the novel is set was far from idyllic (especially for women). But it did have its own culture and its own mechanisms for managing conflicts. Things started to fall apart, though, when the missionaries arrived, along with the British colonisers. Okonkwo, the patriarch at the centre of the story, was horrified when his son joined the missionaries. But this was far from being the end of his troubles as the situation deteriorated. The novel ends with Okonkwo's suicide, hanging himself after killing one of the colonisers' messengers – a crime as well as a violation of traditional cultural norms, suicide being an offence against the earth according to local customs.

The next novel, *No Longer at Ease* (published in 1963), takes up the story of Okonkwo's family, focusing on his grandson, Obi. Having obtained a Western education in Nigeria, Obi is sponsored to go to England before returning to gain employment in the colonial government service. This turns out to be a somewhat mixed blessing, however. On his first day, Mr Green, the White manager, explains that his job is 'to do what you are told', not to think (Achebe, 2010: 52), subsequently commenting that Africans have too many privileges rather than thinking of the good of their country first. 'And you tell me you want to govern yourselves', Mr Green concludes (Achebe, 2010: 122), demonstrating his complete lack of understanding or refusal to understand the nature of colonialism and colonial self-interest. Ironically, though, it is Obi, not the colonisers, who ends up being found guilty, having succumbed to the temptation to take a bribe in order to cope with meeting traditional cultural obligations while maintaining a quasi-European lifestyle.

The roots of corruption emerge in the colonial context, then, a theme that resurfaces in Achebe's subsequent novel, *Anthills of the Savannah* (published in 1987). This is a dystopian account of life under military dictatorship in an unidentified African country (Achebe, 2001a). The destructive legacies of colonialism are only too clear, although the novels seem to be concerned to understand this without in any way seeking to exonerate the corruption and violence and the elitism that Achebe's novels explore in the context of post-colonial Nigeria.

These themes also emerge in the writings of several of the writers who were encouraged and inspired by Achebe, including the Kenyan Ngugi wa Thiong'o. There are particular parallels in their concerns with the cultural effects of colonialism, leading to the disintegration of African communities and the seduction of would-be African elites. There are also differences, though, including differences in their attitudes to the use of language itself. Achebe chose to write in English in order to reach the widest possible audience, although he drew upon local storytelling traditions and speech patterns in his novels. Like Achebe, who encouraged him with the publication of his first novels, *Weep Not Child* (Ngugi wa Thiong'o, 1964) and *The River Between* (Ngugi wa Thiong'o, 1965), Ngugi wa Thiong'o also began by writing in English. But he came to rethink this as he engaged with radical thinking from the Black Power Movement in the US along with the writings of anti-colonial thinkers such as Nkrumah (Nkrumah, 1965) and Fanon (Fanon, 2021). Rejecting the use of the colonisers' language was central to the decolonisation of the mind (inspiring the title of one of his publications, *Decolonising the Mind*; Ngugi wa Thiong'o, 1986). In his view, as expressed in an interview more recently, he has also reflected that 'When I wrote my first book, I wrote it in a language my mother couldn't access. I rewarded her for taking me to school by writing in a language she can't read or write' (Baraka, 2023: 6).

The play that he developed with Ngugi wa Mirii, *I Will Marry When I Want* (Ngugi wa Thiong'o and Ngugi wa Mirii (1982 translation), was first written in Gikuyu, engaging with local audiences to great effect. The play built upon Ngugi wa Mirii's cultural community development work in the area, tapping into local concerns through the use of drama and song. This was powerful stuff. The play's criticisms of the new elite were particularly disturbing – for the new elite. The theatre was dismantled, Ngugi wa Thiong'o was subsequently detained, and Ngugi wa Mirii went into exile in Zimbabwe.

The new elite were subjected to such criticisms because of the ways in which they had benefitted from the legacies of colonialism and colonial violence, violence that they were continuing to perpetrate. Ngugi wa Thiong'o had experienced colonial violence only too directly himself, as his subsequent writings demonstrate. One of his brothers had been detained, a half-brother had been killed, and his village had been burned to the ground during the Mau Mau/Kenya Land and Freedom Army period (Newman, 2016). Estimates of those killed during the 'Emergency' measures that the British announced in 1952 have varied from between tens of thousands to hundreds of thousands, despite attempts to cover up British violations of Kenyans' human rights (Elkins, 2005).

Ngugi's novels address these brutalities and their impacts along with their varying interpretations. Ngugi himself firmly rejects the colonial forces' portrayal of the Mau Mau as savages with bestial impulses. But he doesn't portray traditional societies in idealised ways either, exploring the impacts of the tradition of female genital mutilation, for example, a tradition with potentially lethal consequences (Newman, 2016). Nor does he portray post-colonial Kenya as an exemplar of decolonisation – on the contrary, in fact. National independence represented no more than the very beginning of that process.

Indian experiences

Kenyan experiences of colonial violence were extreme but by no means unique. The violence that was inherent in colonialism could – and did – take different forms in varying contexts. There were deaths caused by troops firing on peacefully protesting civilians, as happened in 1919 at Jallianwala Bagh, in India, also known as the Massacre of Amritsar. But there were deaths caused in less direct ways too. Satyajit Ray's *Distant Thunder* uses film to explore the deaths of some five million Indians during the Bengal Famine of 1943–44, raising disturbing questions in the process, including questions about Indian society and the need for change.

Distant Thunder was made in 1973, some three decades after the Bengal Famine took place, but it drew upon an earlier novel by Bibhutibhusen Banerjee, published soon after the events in question. Ray himself had memories of starving refugees pouring into Calcutta (Cardullo, 2007). Yet this was primarily a rural rather than an urban catastrophe, perhaps attracting less attention as a result. Ray was concerned that young Bengalis should be educated to know about this disaster and, most importantly, that they should come to understand the causes of the famine.

The film opens with Ananga, a beautiful young Brahmin wife, enjoying a bathe. The scene is idyllic, it seems, despite a number of 'flying ships' passing overhead, signalling the war that is going to have such an impact on their lives. Ray's use of photography is stunning, and so is his use of music (which he composed, being a composer and visual artist as well as a filmmaker). Like *Twelve Years a Slave*, this is a film that appeals to the senses as well as to the emotions while raising many questions for further discussion.

Ananga and her husband, Gangacharan, have recently arrived in their village. He has plans to use his status as a Brahmin to open a school as well as to perform priestly functions, which is a traditional setup. The villagers look up to Gangacharan. They send their children to his school and seek his advice and his remedies for their ailments, although it soon transpires that he actually knows very little more than they do. When villagers come from a neighbouring village where cholera has broken out, for example, he surreptitiously looks up advice from a text on basic hygiene before passing this advice on as his own words of wisdom – in return for saris for his wife. And when news arrives that the British have failed to hold onto Singapore, he is unable to explain where Singapore is. He is effectively living off his position in the caste system, then, an exploitative situation that he comes to recognise as unjustifiable as the famine progresses, putting unbearable strains on traditional social relationships.

Meanwhile, the effects of the shortages of rice and kerosene soon become apparent. The planes continue to fly overhead as rice is diverted for the war effort. The price of rice rockets accordingly. And people begin to suffer from starvation.

People respond in different ways. Traders try to make money from hoarding rice, while local women demonstrate their resilience, digging for roots and making curries from pond snails. And norms begin to break down. Ananga starts to work, husking rice, despite her husband's disapproval of her working for lower-caste people. One of the women gets rice in exchange for sex, ultimately leaving the village because she doesn't want to die of hunger in the countryside. Meanwhile, robbers have beaten up the local trader who is suspected of hoarding hidden rice. And the price of rice continues to soar.

Caste barriers remain powerful, but they are beginning to break down by this point as well. A dying woman refuses to let Ananga touch her because she is untouchable. But when she dies, Gangacharan does actually touch the body because he cannot bring himself to leave it lying there without cremation. The famine has brought him face to face with the injustices of the status quo. As he explains at one point to Ananga, what is really wrong is that the peasants do all the work while they live off them. Things need to change. The colonisers' war efforts are seen as to blame for the famine, diverting food to the war effort and refusing to intervene in market forces to control the price of rice. But the causes are multiply intertwined – unfettered market forces and colonial agendas combined alongside the inequalities that have been so deeply rooted within Indian society itself.

Subsequent Ray films provide further evidence of the complexity of his attitudes toward colonialism and its impacts. He appreciated aspects of British culture while being only too aware of colonialism's darker sides. Nor was pre-colonial India without its shortcomings. As Julius Nyerere has already been quoted as reflecting in Chapter 4, pre-colonial Africa had not been an ideal place where noble savages had lived idyllic existences either (Nyerere, 1969). But colonialism had fundamentally undermined traditional cultures with long-term effects, including on the nature of resistance movements. Ray has been seen as somewhat apolitical, in a party-political sense. But he was deeply critical of British colonialism, just as he was deeply critical of social hierarchies, including inequalities of caste and women's oppression. And he was deeply critical of bourgeois nationalism (Cooper, 2000). This emerged very powerfully from *The Home and the World*, the film that Ray made in 1984.

The film was based upon a novel by Rabindranath Tagore, whose writings had been influential in the development of the Indian Independence Movement. Ray had himself attended the educational centre that Tagore had founded at Santiniketan ('Abode of Peace'), a centre for adult learning and community development. This has been established to promote experimental, learner-focused approaches to education, involving environmental as well as aesthetic considerations. Most importantly in this particular context, Tagore had also been concerned to draw upon different cultures, religions and traditions. He has been seen as introducing Indian culture to the West – and vice versa – while being strongly opposed to the violence of British colonialism. (He gave back his knighthood in disgust following the massacre at Jallianwala Bagh in 1919.)

Tagore's novel was set at the beginning of the 20th century, when Lord Curzon was engaged in the partition of Bengal between East and West and between Muslim and Hindu, part of the British strategy to divide and rule the colonised. The Swadeshi movement that arose in response called for resistance through the boycott of Western goods. While there were non-violent strands in the developing movement for independence, there were less peaceful elements too, as the novel and the film go on to explore.

The novel and Ray's film both focus on a love triangle, the relationships between a Westernised young man, Nikhil, his wife, Bimala, and his friend Sandip, an activist in the Swadeshi movement. Nikhil wants his wife to become emancipated, encouraging her to come out of seclusion to meet Sandip when he comes to visit. Bimala is anxious about adopting Western cultural ways at first. But she becomes attracted by Sandip and his fervour for the Swadeshi movement, eventually selling her jewellery for the cause (at least she believes that this is for the cause, although it subsequently emerges that this is not exactly so, as Sandip is keeping some of the money to spend on himself).

Meanwhile, Sandip is using her as a conduit to Nikhil, trying to persuade him to stop the market in his area from selling foreign goods (although they are cheaper and so more readily purchased by the poor). There are very contentious issues here, raising concerns about religious divisions (many of the traders are Muslim) as well as concerns about poverty and class, along with questions about women's emancipation. And there are dilemmas about different strategies for independence too, such as the extent to which the ends can justify the means (including violent means).

Violence does eventually break out despite Nikhil's pleas for tolerance. Nikhil finally tells Sandip that he has to leave because he is causing trouble, setting fire to peasants' houses and oppressing Muslim traders (whose livelihoods are being threatened by the boycott). Bimala comes to see that there are problems with Sandip and his ways of working – something that Nikhil had decided that she had needed to work out for herself rather than simply being given orders by her husband. She and her sister-in-law are sent to Calcutta for their safety in the final scenes of the film. But Nikhil goes out to try to quell the riots, with tragic consequences.

Like *Distant Thunder* and *Twelve Years a Slave*, *The Home and the World* is a very beautiful film. The deep colours are sensational. But it is also a very disturbing film, posing many questions for further discussion, as has already been suggested. These include questions about the impact of the colonial past and the divide and rule tactics that were being pursued by the British – who were described as having actually welcomed the riots because of their divisive effects, effectively ending the whole Swadeshi movement (Robinson, 1982). The violence that erupted between Hindu nationalists and Muslim communities seemed grimly prescient of more contemporary conflicts – legacies that were continuing to be exploited in too many post-colonial contexts.

Although Satyajit Ray himself described the film as a love story rather than a particularly political film (Malcolm, 1982), this was a love story set against a strong political background. In an interview with filmmaker Lindsay Anderson, Ray explained that 'I don't provide answers [to social problems]'. But he did 'like to make the audience aware of certain things and to clarify certain things' (Anderson, 1979: 107). He distrusted propaganda and doubted the extent to which films could produce social change. But he did believe that it was important to make his audiences aware of what had happened in the past – including the ways in which political leaders had fomented trouble between Hindu and Muslim communities, not considering Muslims as part of India at all. The film poses many questions about colonialism and decolonisation, then, along with questions about the interconnections between exploitation, discrimination and oppression, whether according to race, class, caste, religion or gender.

Resilience and resistance

Many novels and films can be drawn upon to explore resilience and resistance in the face of discrimination and oppression in the context of cultural differences. The Heinemann African series included very few women writers in the early days, but there were a few, such as Buchi Emecheta, whose first novel, *In the Ditch* (first published in 1972), exemplified these themes as lived through the experiences of migrants from the colonies and former colonies on their arrival in the so-called 'mother country'.

Emecheta (1944–2017) was evidently extraordinarily gifted as well as extremely determined. Arriving in Britain from Nigeria in the 1960s, she struggled with the challenges of racism and poverty in London as a single parent with five young children. But she succeeded in obtaining a degree in sociology and then earning a living as a youth and community worker while writing successful novels and children's books. This could be read as the story of an individual's triumph over adversity – pulling oneself up by one's own bootstraps – making a successful career for herself through her own determination and resilience (Emecheta went on to receive a number of literary awards and accolades). But she was only too aware of the structural problems of racism, sexism and poverty, along with the ways in which the poor were being stereotyped and stigmatised more generally.

These themes run through the novel. Adah, the young mother at the centre of the story, finds life in Britain bewildering, starting from the casual racism that she encounters from her neighbours. What does a remark like 'Look I don't mind your colour' really mean, she wonders, what colour was he talking about. It takes her a minute or two to realise that this is actually about the colour of her skin.

Adah demonstrates determination and courage as she addresses these challenges, finding friendship and mutual support while she navigates the contradictions of the welfare system. She holds on to her ambitions for a very different future for herself and her children, whatever the obstacles in her way. And she resists negative stereotyping from officials, responding with humour as she points to the absurdities of some of their comments, such as their disparagement of people who have large families. What about the royal family? she asks, refusing to be put down in this way. This is a story of survival against the odds, then – resilience in the face of structural inequalities.

These themes of resilience and struggle resonate through the writings of many authors, particularly women authors, both in Britain and the US. Monica Ali's *Brick Lane* (Ali, 2023), for example, tells the story of a young woman from what is now Bangladesh who finds ways to survive despite the challenges that she faces as a Muslim woman, adjusting to life in a very different and rapidly changing cultural context during a period of increasing racial tension. The novel was subsequently made into a film, reaching wider audiences as a result, although not without controversy. Some Bangladeshis felt that this was presenting negative stereotypes of their community, thus raising a number of questions for further discussion.

Andrea Levy's *Small Island* (Levy, 2004) provides another example of novels about resilience and resistance, exploring Caribbeans' experiences during and after the Second World War, along with the experiences of the landlady who faces racism when she takes in Jamaican lodgers. In one memorable scene, Gilbert, a Jamaican airman who has volunteered to fight for the 'mother country', goes to the cinema to watch *Gone with the Wind* in the company of a White woman and her father-in-law, only to find that White GIs (American soldiers) refuse to allow him into their section of the cinema. Gilbert stands his ground, rejecting their attempts to impose Jim

Crow segregation laws in Britain, an act of resistance that leads to a fight. Although he has support from others at the time, including support from White Britons, there seems to be less in the way of solidarity once the war is over, when Gilbert returns as a civilian. *Small Island* tells the central characters' stories from their own perspectives, and the novel also reached wider audiences as a two-part television series made in 2009.

These and other writings explore the experiences of migrants from Britain's former colonies coping with racism and many other challenges in the so-called 'mother country'. They came 'in the wake of a dream', as the title of Donald Hinds' account of the lives of the Windrush generation explains, summarising their feelings about their situations and coping with their disappointments with humour and resilience (Hinds, 2014).

Migration features in the experiences of US writers too, with a focus on internal migration within the US to escape the racism of the Southern states. This was the writer Zora Neale Hurston's own background, for example, all four of her grandparents having been born into slavery in the South. She grew up in Eatonville, Florida, one of the first all-Black towns to be incorporated in the US, free of the overt racism that surrounded the town, although not without its own hierarchies, as described in her 1937 novel *Their Eyes Were Watching God* (Hurston, 2007). By that time, though, she had left the South, becoming a well-known figure in the Harlem Renaissance, the cultural centre for Black writers, artists, photographers, dancers and musicians of that period.

Hurston did not see herself as focusing upon racism per se, but the effects of slavery provide the starting point for *Their Eyes Were Watching God*. Janie, the protagonist, was brought up by her grandmother, Nanny, a woman who had lived under slavery and was only too well aware of racial and sexual hierarchies in the South, where 'de white man is the ruler of everything as fur as Ah been able tuh find out'. And the 'n***** woman is de mule uh de world' (Hurston, 2007: 19). So, she organises a marriage for young Janie, choosing a relatively comfortably off farmer with 60 acres of his own land as the best way to protect her for the future. But Janie refuses to accept this state of affairs. Her first two marriages are deeply frustrating because she resists traditional definitions of her place in the social hierarchy. Leaving her first husband, she sets off for Eatonville with her second husband, Joe, where he successfully establishes himself in business. His views about the position of women are not that different from her previous husband's, though, as he explains: he has to think for Janie because women 'sho don't think none themselves' (Hurston, 2007: 95). Over the years, this second marriage is described as having taken all the fight out of Janie's face. But she turns out to be a survivor of determination and strength after all.

While Janie is particularly concerned to survive the effects of sexual inequality, she is only too aware of the hierarchies of class and colour within

Black communities, as well as between White and Black people. Eatonville is described as an all-Black town where African Americans could live as they chose without White bosses, an island within the wider racist society. But within Eatonville there are also differences of wealth and power, differences that she is expected to appreciate as the wife of Joe, the successful businessman who becomes mayor. Yet these privileges prove constricting; Joe is jealous as well as being concerned for his status, refusing to let Janie socialise with others, as she would have preferred. When Joe dies, she leaves Eatonville with 'Tea Cake', despite the disapproval of those who think that he is socially beneath her. It is only with this third husband, a younger man who treats her as an equal, that she finds love. But even he beats her on one occasion, asserting himself to demonstrate his masculine power.

There are hierarchies of colour within Black communities too, another reason for people to disapprove of Janie's marriage to Tea Cake. Mrs Turner, their landlady, is enchanted with Janie's coffee-and-cream complexion and her luxurious hair, finding it unforgiveable that she should marry such a dark man as Tea Cake. The race should be lightened up, according to Mrs Turner, the unattainable goal of Caucasian characteristics for all, as Hurston summarises these views.

Mrs Turner has strong views about Booker T. Washington as well – the controversial founder of Tuskegee whose contributions to adult education and community development have already emerged in Chapter 4. Despite her admiration for all things Caucasian, she refers to him as a White folks' n***** who talks about work when 'de race ain't done nothin' else' (Hurston, 2007: 190). Janie's response is simply that she has been brought up with the notion that he was a great man; Hurston leaves the reader to draw their own conclusions. *Their Eyes Were Watching God* is an ambivalent text in some ways, then, raising questions for discussion rather than presenting definitive answers for the future. Janie is strong and resilient. Yet her return to Eatonville after Tea Cake's death doesn't offer a conventionally happy ending.

Hurston seems to have held a mixture of views herself. She was an anthropologist as well as an author and filmmaker, researching African American and Caribbean folklore and folk music with anthropologist Franz Boas, among others, valuing different cultures in their own right rather than seeing cultures in terms of a hierarchy that culminated in Western European civilisation as the summit of human achievement. This could be taken to imply that there was a case for separate development rather than integration, however, which was the position that Hurston took in relation to the integration of schools in the US. Black schools could be just as good as White schools, in her view, so why press for integration – a controversial opinion, to say the least, in the context of the Civil Rights Movement.

Hurston's decision to use dialect for direct speech was also controversial. Critics felt that this was demeaning, re-enforcing White stereotypes of

African Americans as uneducated folk. The beauty of her writing style, including this use of dialect, has been appreciated by others, though, including the author Zadie Smith, who wrote an introduction to the 2007 edition. Smith reflected that 'My resistance to dialogue (encouraged by Nabokov, whom I idolised) struggled and then tumbled before Hurston's ear for black colloquial speech. In the mouths of unlettered people, she finds the bliss of quotidian metaphor', going on to celebrate the ways in which Hurston conveyed 'wisdom lightly worn' along with her ability to reveal individual personalities swiftly and accurately through this use of dialogue (Smith, 2007: x).

Zora Neale Hurston's writings had become less available by the time of her death in 1969. But she became appreciated once again subsequently when African American writer Alice Walker rediscovered her, publishing an article in *MS* magazine in 1975, 'In search of Zora Neale Hurston' (Walker, 1975). Walker saw *Their Eyes Were Watching God* as empowering through the challenges that the novel poses to patriarchy. The book was adapted for television in 2005, and for BBC radio in 2011.

One of the television series that I have found particularly striking in terms of resistance to racism in Britain has been Steve McQueen's *Small Axe*, named after a Bob Marley song that states a small axe can fell a big tree. *Mangrove*, the first film in the series, was premiered in 2020. The story starts in the late 1960s in London's Notting Hill area, where racism was rife, as local graffiti so clearly illustrate in the film ('W★★★ go home', for example). The Mangrove restaurant became a vibrant cultural haven where African Caribbeans could eat, drink and dance together in safety, away from the threats posed by Enoch Powell's racist pronouncements, warnings of rivers of blood flowing in our street. Except that the Mangrove wasn't at all safe once the police involved themselves.

The film provides chilling illustrations of the racism that was prevalent among the local police at the time: 'The Black man has got to know his place', and 'we all look after each other here', as one office explained to a newcomer, covering for each other when accused of racist violence. The Mangrove was subjected to a series of police raids – and thus became a centre of Black resistance. As one of the leading figures, Darcus Howe, explained, it was no good Black people relying on White structures to defend themselves from racial discrimination and violence; they needed to self-organise.

Following a protest march against police racism, the group of activists who became known as the Mangrove Nine were put on trial. The group included Darcus Howe himself and the US Black Panther leader, Althea Jones-Lecointe, both of whom decided to represent themselves in court, which they did with determination, humour and aplomb. Darcus Howe exposed the fabrications behind the police evidence, holding the police up to ridicule to great effect. He went on to argue that history was on the side of those resisting the injustices that linked back to the stench of British colonialism.

Together the defendants presented an effective united front. Although four of the accused were found guilty on less serious charges, they were found not guilty on the most serious charge of conspiracy to incite a riot. The rest were found not guilty on all charges. The battle had been won, then – but not the war. The Mangrove suffered further harassment for another 18 years before it was closed down in 1992.

Mangrove was followed by four further films: a film celebrating reggae music and dance, a film recounting the experiences of a Black police officer who joined the force in order to try to challenge police racism from within, a film about a Black author who was imprisoned following the Brixton disturbances of 1981, and a film about Black children's experiences of being stereotyped and labelled as educationally sub-normal. This was reminiscent of Steve McQueen's own experiences in the school system as a child of African Caribbean heritage. Together, then, these *Small Axe* films tell the story of racism and resistance in Britain from the late 1960s to the mid-1980s, raising issues that are still only too relevant today in the wake of George Floyd's death and the Black Lives Matter movement, with continuing evidence of institutional racism on both sides of the Atlantic.

Reflecting on the series in discussion with Steve McQueen, David Olusoga opined that the stories were told 'in a way that you can't intellectualise, in a way that's deeply emotional' (Olusoga, 2020: 26). The films indeed aroused strong feelings, as well as raising many issues for further discussion. When asked about his own hopes for the catalytic effect of the series, McQueen replied that he hoped for an awakening: 'People must understand that there are other histories that make up the history of our nation' (Olusoga, 2020: 35).

Bringing it all together

Novels and films can stimulate empathic understandings of slavery and colonialism and their toxic legacies in deeply emotional ways, as the previous examples illustrate, reaching the parts of our beings that other approaches fail to reach. But the same examples also show that they can stimulate critical discussions, of course, bringing different types of knowledge together to develop more holistic understandings of the implications for decolonisation. This is why they have such potential as tools to promote critical understanding – knowledge for social change.

Many of these examples have given voice to those from communities that have been enslaved or colonised in the past, people whose voices have so often been silenced or simply ignored as a result. Decolonisation strategies need to reverse these processes of cultural domination.

Between them, these examples raise many questions about cultures and cultural struggles. How to portray different cultural heritages without re-enforcing cultural stereotypes or freezing traditional cultures – being photographed in traditional costumes or choosing to be photographed in the clothing of the colonisers, for example? Do photographs of 19th-century Africans in Victorian dress provide evidence of mental colonisation, or did they challenge prevailing images of the African in the West (Cumming, 2023: 23)? How to reach target audiences, in Western languages or in local languages and dialects? These were the dilemmas that featured in debates between Chinua Achebe and Ngugi wa Thiong'o, for example, or the debates that surrounded Zora Neale Hurston's use of dialect. And most importantly, how can cultural insights contribute to an understanding of the interconnections between different forms of exploitation, discrimination and oppression and the legacies of racism, sexism, religious intolerance, caste oppression and class exploitation in contemporary times? There are many questions here, whether these relate to cultural issues in terms of the arts, or whether they relate to cultural issues in their wider sense – Raymond Williams' definition of cultures as whole ways of life.

Meanwhile, culture wars continue to be waged in both senses of the term, along with cultural strategies for resistance, as the concluding chapter explores.

9

Conclusions: Bringing it all together again

The motivation to write this book started from my increasing concern with contemporary 'culture wars', as Chapter 1 explained. There were fundamental challenges for community education and development here, challenges to their theoretical underpinnings, challenges to a critical understanding of their histories and challenges to the very basis of their practices. Key theorists were being dismissed as 'cultural Marxists'. And the histories of community education and development continue to be at risk of distortion by cultural warriors' refusals to recognise, let alone to engage with, the legacies of slavery and colonialism.

Most importantly, cultural warriors focus on blaming 'the other', especially migrants and refugees, along with their 'woke' supporters, such as 'lefty lawyers' and bleeding-heart liberals. Those who have been characterised as 'woke' are supposed to be responsible for the challenges of the day. It is in this way that cultural warriors aim to divert attention from the underlying causes of increasing polarisation, discrimination, poverty and xenophobia, along with increasing threats to the very future of the planet. Cultural warriors' methods represent the very antithesis of. community-based approaches that start from communities' own experiences and feelings, taking them as the basis for critical but respectful processes of dialogue while aiming to contribute towards democratic processes of social change for the longer term.

In contrast, cultural warriors focus on stirring feelings of resentment and fear, fanning divisions within and between communities as a result. Far from disappearing, manifestations of such toxic divisions have been continuing, and indeed increasing, as I have been writing this book. For example, the previous UK Home Secretary, Suella Braverman, has been strongly criticised for her incendiary statements about migrants and refugees, including her unfounded allegations about their supposed criminality – statements than could, and too often have, encouraged violent mobilisations from the Far Right. There have been community mobilisations, such as in Llanelli in 2023, when a protest camp was set up outside a hotel where asylum seekers were to be housed. This has been described as bringing a deluge of hate to a previously peaceful Welsh town (Chakrabortty, 2023). Such mobilisations provide chilling illustrations of the effects of these divisive strategies, potentially aggravated by more recent statements warning of a hurricane of migrants arriving on British shores.

There have, of course, been counterdemonstrations welcoming asylum seekers and refugees. And there have been mobilisations in support of asylum seekers and resisting unfair deportations, as Chapter 7 has also illustrated (Brewis, 2023). But the potential violence that can be unleashed when politicians play upon feelings of resentment and fear remains deeply disturbing. At the time of writing, there does not seem to be much, if indeed any, evidence to suggest that culture wars are on the wane, whether in Britain or internationally.

Decolonisation as the continuing thread

Decolonisation has been a continuing thread from the very start, a theme that has proved to be even more relevant than originally anticipated. Revisiting the past through a decolonising lens has been an extraordinarily revealing process as I have reflected on previous understandings and experiences. As I read and reread materials and watched and rewatched films through a decolonising lens, I became aware of just how many more connections there were to be made, and just how many more assumptions there were to be revisited and challenged. The histories of adult and community education were far more directly linked – and far more contested – than I had previously appreciated, with their varying, and sometimes deeply contested, connections with movements for colonial freedom, international solidarity and social justice.

I have also been struck by the extent to which professionals and activists have been influenced by the same sources, whether in movements for colonial freedom or in movements for civil rights and equalities in the US, UK and elsewhere. The examples of W.E.B. Du Bois, Franz Fanon, Kwame Nkrumah and Julius Nyerere come to mind, for a start, along with the influences of Antonio Gramsci and Paulo Freire. There are many threads that interconnect, here, including the ties between movements for colonial freedom and movements for civil rights in the US and elsewhere, as illustrated by the attendance of Martin Luther King and others at the celebrations for Ghanaian independence in 1957 (Williams, 2021). There are interconnections in both theory and in practice, then, along with interconnections through the development of public policies and processes.

The interconnections between US and British policies – in relation to community-based programmes to tackle the problems of poverty, inequality and racial disadvantage in the inner cities – had already been clear. I was also reminded of the interconnections between them and their varying histories of slavery and colonialism. British analysts of the Government's Community Development Programme included those with experience of community development in the former colonies too, just as those involved in the US War on Poverty included those who had been involved in the Civil Rights

Movement. And both sets of programmes had included contributions from those with previous involvements in movements for international solidarity. There were lessons to be drawn from such initiatives, rooted as they were in the political economy of poverty and deprivation, lessons that fed into the development of programmes for progressive cities in the US and for municipal socialism in Britain (see Chapter 7). These programmes focused on tackling the legacies of slavery and colonialism more explicitly, with particular emphasis on finding ways of addressing racial disadvantage. And they included a focus on addressing the underlying causes of continuing inequalities on an international scale – through the Greater London Council's promotion of 'fair trade', for example.

The issue of 'fair trade' raises further connections too, as the writings of Michael Barratt Brown, adult educator and first principal of Northern College, so clearly illustrate. The role of imperialism was central to his analysis. But this was not just about the political control of one country by another under colonialism, important though that had been. Rather, he was focusing on the fundamentally unequal and exploitative relationships that persisted *within as well as between* countries within the context of contemporary capitalism. Although the British working class may have reaped some benefits from the fruits of empire, then, the costs far outweighed the benefits in the longer term, in his view. There have been and continue to be possibilities for developing solidarity across national boundaries, which is particularly important in the context of contemporary environmental challenges. Hence the case for a new framework for international trade and sustainable development – although Barratt Brown didn't in any way underestimate the barriers that would have to be overcome in order to make progress towards achieving this goal.

Decolonisation as an ongoing process

The attainment of political independence has represented no more than the first step in the process of decolonisation. Former colonial powers can continue to exert influence for their own ends post-independence, as Nkrumah identified a long time ago through his exploration of neo-colonialism (Nkrumah, 1965). Local elites can and too often do collaborate in these processes of economic exploitation, just as they can borrow the former colonisers' tactics to divide and rule. Meanwhile, the rich may prosper and the poor may not, as Fanon also forcibly argued (Fanon, 2001). And market forces have continued to impact more generally in the context of neoliberal globalisation accompanied by increasing financialisation across national divides. The effects have been only too clear, whether in terms of the extraction of raw materials, the distortion of local economies or the reduction of resources for public services, all in the interests of private profitability.

Previous chapters have also included references to processes of recolonisation by market forces. The marketisation of higher education in South Africa provides an example here, illustrative of wider trends in Britain and elsewhere, as public services, including educational services, have been distorted and undermined as a result. Previous chapters have also highlighted the importance of understanding the interconnections between race, class and gender in the context of neoliberal globalisation. Racism emerged in its varying forms just as slavery and colonialism developed in the past. Decolonisation needs to be understood in precisely these terms too – understanding the interconnections and their implications for the development of solidarity between those experiencing exploitation, oppression and discrimination in the contemporary context. This is the case for community education and development for social transformation.

Continuing battles of ideas

Meanwhile, 'culture wars' continue to be waged, attempting to divert attention from the processes of polarisation that are gathering momentum. The wealthiest 1 per cent of the population has continued to flourish, enjoying state support since the economic crisis of 2007–08 and the COVID-19 pandemic despite neoliberal ideological objections to state intervention more generally (Mohun, 2022). Meanwhile, the rest of the population has continued to suffer from the effects of austerity and the cost-of-living crisis, patterns that have been particularly marked in, although by no means confined to, Britain. The neoliberal state has signally failed to address these challenges, let alone to respond to the environmental crisis for the future (Mohun, 2022). No wonder that Far Right governments resort to 'cultural wars' and the demonisation of 'the other', diverting attention elsewhere while economic polarisation erodes the political centre ground, opening up spaces for them to promote their divisive ideologies.

There are continuing battles of ideas to be waged, then, drawing on the contributions of theorists such as Antonio Gramsci and Paulo Freire, whose ideas have been centrally important to the development of community education and development. Previous chapters have already referred to their approaches to the development of critical consciousness – challenging 'common sense' notions and stereotypes, enabling people to unpack the underlying causes of their problems as the basis for building alliances for democratic change.

Critical consciousness can be stimulated by cultural strategies in a variety of ways too, including via the arts, as Chapter 8 demonstrated. Novels and films can stimulate empathetic understandings, for example, just as they can stimulate critical discussions, bringing together different ways of knowing holistically rather than posing one against the other. There is much to learn from these different approaches.

Learning from the past: community education and development in practice

There is much to learn from the past in relation to community-based practice too. There have always been tensions to be managed and dilemmas to be faced. The following examples explore some of the ways in which such issues have been addressed in different contexts over time, recognising the complexity of some of challenges involved rather than suggesting that there might have been any one set of 'right' answers out there. The point here is to explore – and to learn from – previous approaches.

The potential tension between theory and practice provides one such illustration, a tension with a long history in community education and development debates. Booker T. Washington's approach to learning at Tuskegee was at the practical end of the spectrum, learning key skills in order to enable communities to become more self-reliant. This stood in sharp contrast to W.E.B. Du Bois' emphasis on the importance of wider, more theoretical approaches to learning. But this did not have to be an 'either/or' choice between two competing approaches, as Washington and Du Bois both came to recognise eventually.

The case study chapters provide further illustration of this. South African adult educators such as Shirley Walters have similarly emphasised the importance of theory, as well as recognising the necessity of providing access to more practical forms of knowledge and skills. Both approaches were essential if communities were to contribute most effectively to the construction of a multi-racial democracy for the future.

Trade union educators came to similar conclusions when making the case for going 'beyond functionalism'. Of course, trade union representatives needed specific knowledge and skills in order to be effective on behalf of their members. But trade unionists also needed wider knowledge and critical understanding if they were to challenge exploitation, oppression and discrimination for the longer term, including challenging racial discrimination within the movement as well as within the wider society – a key aim of the Unite History Project. Both forms of knowledge were essential here too. This was about developing strategic approaches to both rather than opting for *either* one *or* the other as mutually exclusive choices.

This links into the next illustration, the question of the balance to be struck between the promotion of self-organisation and self-reliance, on the one hand, and the promotion of wider agendas for social change and social solidarity, on the other. The Black Consciousness Movement in South Africa was very clearly committed to doing both, promoting self-organisation and self-reliance within communities while promoting critical consciousness and solidarity, both within the country and beyond. Nyerere's approach to building African Socialism was similarly concerned to promote self-reliance within the Ujamaa villages programme as part of the development of a decolonised future, a Tanzania without exploitation, whether locally or globally (although neither aim was eventually achieved in practice, of course, as explained in Chapter 4).

Municipal strategies have similarly ranged from the most immediately achievable, such as the promotion of training opportunities for minority communities, through to the promotion of fair trade on an international scale. The ultimate aim here, according to Michael Barratt Brown, was to contribute to the development of a new international order based on justice and environmental sustainability for the longer term – extremely ambitious goals, to say the least, as Barratt Brown clearly recognised at the time. But a beginning had been made, starting with the promotion of fair trade coffee in supermarkets. These approaches did not have to be mutually exclusive either, then.

Chapter 7 provides a further illustration of the challenges inherent in striving to strike a balance between maintaining independence, on the one hand, while working with policy makers and statutory providers, on the other, including working *within* the structures of governance. Fears about incorporation can be traced throughout the histories of community education and development. Would public funding distort the scope and purpose of trade union and community education, for example? What about community–university partnerships or community–local authority partnerships? Would these end up as top-down initiatives reflecting the inherent power imbalances involved, diverting communities from pursuing their own agendas, incorporating activists and undermining the possibilities for independent strategies for social change?

The case studies confirm that there most certainly have been tensions and challenges to be faced in these regards. But there are also examples that demonstrate human resilience and creativity, of people finding the spaces to work effectively for social transformation from within the confines of inherently contradictory pressures. Adult educators such as Thomas Hodgkin developed learning for decolonisation within the context of British colonial policies, for example, just as municipal socialists have worked within as well as against national government policy frameworks, including the so-called 'hostile environment' towards asylum seekers and refugees.

None of this is to suggest that there were universally applicable answers or ready-made solutions to the dilemmas of community-based practice, though. On the contrary, such tensions have been only too challenging in the past and potentially even more challenging in the contemporary context, requiring greater creativity and resilience in response. But the evidence does suggest that posing such questions as dichotomies, requiring 'either/or' types of answers, can be less than helpful. Community education can be *both* functional *and* theoretical. These are not necessarily mutually exclusive approaches. Just as community development strategies *can* address communities' immediate concerns *while also* supporting wider movements for social justice. Which brings the discussion on to the implications for learning for the future.

Learning for the future

Cultural warriors have been continuing to challenge the theoretical bases for community education and development, potentially undermining their contributions to the development of critical consciousness in the process. Community educators and development professionals and activists have much to learn as they engage with these theoretical debates. This includes learning about the inherent biases in our knowledge systems and our understanding about whose knowledge counts – biases that have been challenged in many ways, including via the development of participatory action research. Decolonising the curriculum involves critically engaging with these questions too without simply jettisoning Enlightenment thinking in the process.

The decolonisation of the curriculum can also contribute to enhanced understandings of history. Slavery and colonialism have been central to the development of capitalism in Europe and elsewhere, with long-term impacts both within and between communities in the contemporary context. There are toxic legacies of racism and xenophobia here, along with toxic legacies of exploitation and oppression in terms of class, caste, gender, sexuality, religion, ability and age. These interconnections need to be unpacked and understood in relation to their historical roots if they are to be effectively challenged via community education and development policies and practices. As Marable (1991) and Ramdin (1987) have already been quoted as demonstrating, each generation needs to develop its own understandings of the legacies of slavery and colonialism and their impacts. This is particularly essential for young Black people, providing the basis for them to self-organise and to pursue equalities agendas within their workplaces as well as within their communities.

Previous chapters have also provided illustrations of the ways in which international solidarity can be promoted. Community education and development have contributed to building connections between social movements across local, national and international levels. There are examples from the past, as Chapter 5 demonstrated, along with examples of communities working for international solidarity and justice alongside local and regional government authorities in more recent times (see Chapter 7).

Building connections between the local and the global would seem more urgent than ever in the context of the climate crisis, as previous chapters have argued. The impacts of climate change bear disproportionately harshly on the most vulnerable within communities, as well as displacing those forced to move in search of more sustainable livelihoods. Community education and development have contributions to make to wider strategies for environmental justice and sustainable development for the future, just as they have contributions to make to more local strategies, developing ways of making refugees and asylum seekers more welcome.

Finding the spaces for progressive approaches?

The spaces for alternative approaches have been shrinking, however, as previous chapters have emphasised. Despite pressures to the contrary, adult educators, community professionals and activists have been continuing to find spaces, whether in higher education, trade union education or local government community development contexts. Meanwhile, the arts continue to pose challenges in their own ways, stimulating critical thinking as well as engaging people's emotions and empathy.

There is much to celebrate here, whatever the remaining challenges. Community education and development have inherently limited contributions to make as part of broader struggles for justice, solidarity and social transformation. They cannot, of course, resolve deep structural inequalities by themselves, let alone tackle the root causes of exploitation and oppression, either within or indeed across international borders. But they *can begin* to make a difference, facilitating the development of critical thinking, enabling communities to develop more collaborative, rather than more divisive, strategies to address their shared concerns.

Decolonisation is centrally important to these processes of conscientisation. As James Baldwin was quoted at the beginning of Chapter 1, *not everything that is faced can be changed, but nothing can be changed until it is faced.* The histories of slavery and colonisation need to be faced, then, along with their continuing legacies, if contemporary culture wars are to be challenged both within and between communities and at different levels. Whatever their inherent limitations, community education and development have contributions to make.

Conversely, without such contributions, the basis for challenging the divisive strategies of the Far Right – let alone for building broad democratic movements for social and environmental justice and racial equality – would seem to be considerably undermined. On the contrary, in fact, there are disturbing indications that confidence in democracy itself may be at risk. Concerns about democracy are far from new. Chapter 7 quoted from Blunkett and Jackson's book *Democracy in Crisis*, published over three decades ago (Blunkett and Jackson, 1987). Since then, such concerns would seem to have been increasing with the spread of Far Right populism, exacerbating people's anxieties for the future. Such concerns may have been levelling off somewhat since the Brexit referendum, when distrust in politicians seemed to have reached a peak. Popular distrust may have levelled off further, of course, by the time that this book is published. And the political landscape may have shifted significantly in parallel. But such possibilities seem less than likely in the current context, on the contrary in fact.

Young people seemed to be particularly dubious about the prospects for democratic ways of addressing the problems of the cost-of-living crisis, crumbling public services and precarious futures, along with the increasingly evident challenges that have been arising, and can be expected to continue to arise, as the result of climate change. While the problems of poverty, polarisation and precarity have become increasingly visible in Britain, these are problems with global dimensions too. UN leaders have come to recognise that far from being on track to reach the organisation's sustainable development goals, 'hunger and malnutrition are becoming more prevalent, humanitarian needs are rising, and the impacts of climate change are more pronounced. This has led to increased inequality exacerbated by weakened international solidarity and a shortfall of trust to jointly overcome these crises' (quoted by Wintour, 2023: 23).

A recent international survey (carried out across 30 countries by the Open Society Foundation) confirmed this shortfall, finding that only 30 per cent of those questioned had trust in their national politicians (a figure which fell to 20 per cent in UK) (Henley, 2023). Scepticism about the scope for democratic solutions to contemporary problems was even more pronounced among young people. Only just over a half of those aged 18 to 35 felt that democracy was preferable to any other form of governance, while over a third of this age group felt that a strong leader would be a good way to get things done, even if this leader didn't consult parliament or call elections. These findings have been described as both sobering and alarming (Henley, 2023). It seems unlikely, then, to say the least, that faith in democratic solutions will revive spontaneously. Nor does it seem likely that spaces for progressive alternatives will expand of their own accord. Doing nothing does not seem to be a very constructive option, in other words.

This would seem especially problematic if politicians and social media pundits continue to try to divert blame onto 'the other' rather than addressing the causes of poverty and inequalities in an increasingly unsustainable world. The Open Society Foundation has itself been blamed – by Twitter/X's former CEO, Elon Musk, for example – for appearing to want 'nothing less than the destruction of western civilization'. The Foundation has been particularly criticised for its support for civil society groups working on issues affecting the well-being of migrants, refugees and asylum seekers, making it a regular target of the Far Right (Farah, 2023: 26). Are there echoes of White supremacy here? All this makes the case for education for democratic citizenship all the more pressing – promoting decolonised approaches to community education and development while finding the spaces for confronting the past and its legacies as the basis for strengthening movements for more hopeful alternatives.

There are potential lessons here, perhaps, from previous attempts to build popular fronts in a number of European countries in order to resist the rise of fascism in the 1930s. This is in no way to suggest that the present situation has direct parallels with that time, let alone to suggest that the rise of fascism is an imminent prospect, whether in Britain or elsewhere. But the importance of building more effective alliances in solidarity and in response to such threats from authoritarian populism does have continuing relevance, along with the importance of building support for more hopeful futures.

Reflections from Paulo Freire have relevance here, emphasising the importance of practices that can unmask what he then described as the dominant lies (Freire, 1996). The lies being perpetrated through contemporary culture wars would seem to be particularly apposite here, along with their divisive effects. What was also needed, Freire continued, was hope – not just hope, though, but critical hope, reflecting on the lessons of the past in order to contribute to the fierce struggle for a better world for the future (Freire, 1996; Mayo, 2020). These conclusions seem more relevant than ever in the contemporary context.

References

AAM (1982) Report of the Anti-Apartheid Movement Trade Union Conference held on 27 November 1982

ABCA (1945) *Handbook*, ABCA

Abdul, G. (2022) 'Warsi hits out at culture wars in Jo Cox memorial lecture', *The Guardian*, Tuesday 17 May 2022

Abel-Smith, B. and Townsend, P. (1965) *The Poor and the Poorest*, London: Bell

Achebe, C. (2001a) *Anthills of the Savannah*, London: Penguin Books

Achebe, C. (2001b) *Things Fall Apart*, London: Penguin Books

Achebe, C. (2010) *No Longer at Ease*, London: Penguin Books

Aiello, T. (2016) *The Battle for the Souls of Black Folk*, Santa Barbara, CA: Praeger

Ali, M. (2023 edn) *Brick Lane*, London: Penguin Books

Alinsky, S. (1971) *Rules for Radicals*, New York: Random House

Anderson, L. (1979) 'Conversations with Satyajit Ray' in B. Cardullo (ed) (2007) *Satyajit Ray Interviews*, Jackson, MS: University of Mississippi Press, pp 94–114

Andrews, G., Kean, H. and Thompson, J. (eds) (1999) *Ruskin College: Contesting Knowledge, Dissenting Politics*, London: Lawrence and Wishart

Arday, J., Stennet, L., Kennedy, L. and Thompson, B. (eds) (2020) *The Black Curriculum: Black British History in the National Curriculum*, London: The Back Curriculum

Arnold, M. (ed) (1978) *Steve Biko: Black Consciousness in Africa*, New York: Random House

Atkinson, H., Bardgett, S., Budd, A., Finn, M., Kissane, C., Qureshi, S. et al (2018) *Race, Ethnicity and Equality in UK History: A Report and Resource for Change*, London: Royal Historical Society

Baatjes, I. and Mathe, K. (2004) 'Adult basic education and social change in South Africa, 1994 to 2003' in L. Chisholm (ed), *Changing Class: Education and Social Change in Post-Apartheid South Africa*, London: Zed Books, pp 393–420

Banks, S., Hart, A. and Ward, P. (eds) (2019) *Co-Producing Research: A Community Development Approach*, Bristol: Policy Press

Baraka, C. (2023) 'Ngugi wa Thiong'o: three days with a giant of African literature', *The Guardian*, Tuesday 13 June, The Long Read, pp 5–8

Barr, J. (2018) *Lords of the Desert*, London: Simon and Shuster

Barratt Brown, M. (1963) *After Imperialism*, London: Heinemann

Barratt Brown, M. (1972) *Essays on Imperialism*, Nottingham: Spokesman

Barratt Brown, M. (1993) Fair *Trade*, London: Zed Books

Barratt Brown, M. (2013) *Seekers: A Twentieth Century Life*, Nottingham: Spokesman

Bartlett, J. (2023) '*Papers reveal Nixon briefing on US-backed Chile coup in 1973*' *The Guardian*, Monday 28 August

Beckman, M. (2013) *The 43 Group*, Cheltenham: The History Press

Beecher Stowe, H. (1852, 1999 edn) *Uncle Tom's Cabin*, Ware, Hertfordshire: Wordsworth Classics

Begum, N. and Saini, R. (2019) 'Decolonising the curriculum', Political Studies Review, 17(2): 196–201

Bennett, T. (1995) *The Birth of the Museum*, London: Routledge

Bernstein, H. (1978) *Steve Biko*, London: IDAF

Bhattacharyya, G. (2015) *Crisis, Austerity and Everyday Life*, Basingstoke: Palgrave Macmillan

Bhattacharyya, G., Elliott-Cooper, A., Balani, S., Nişancıoğlu, K., Koram, K., Gebrial, D. et al (2021) *Empire's Endgame: Racism and the British State*, London: Pluto

Bieze, M. and Gasman, M. (2012) *Booker T. Washington Rediscovered*, Baltimore, MD: John Hopkins University Press

Biles, R. (2018) *Mayor Harold Washington*, Champaign, IL: University of Illinois Press

Blunkett, D. and Jackson, K. (1987) *Democracy in Crisis: The Town Halls Respond*, London: Hogarth

Bottomore, T. (1984) *The Frankfurt School*, London: Tavistock

Bown, L. and Tomori, S. (eds) (1979) *Handbook of Adult Education for West Africa*, London: Hutchinson

Brayne, F. (1945) *Better Villages*, Bombay: Oxford University Press

Brewis, G. (2023) 'The Kenmure Street protests: a community against the state', *Theory and Struggle*, 124(1): 98–107

Brokensha, D. and Hodge, P. (1969) *Community Development: An Interpretation*, New York: Chandler

Brown, M. and Jones, R. (2001) *How Preston Took Back Control and Your Town Can Too*, London: Repeater Books

Brownhill, S. (1988) 'The people's plan for the Royal Docks: some contradictions in popular planning', *Planning Practice and Research*, 2(4): 15–21

Bullough, O. (2022) *Butler to the World: How Britain Became the Servant of Tycoons, Tax Dodgers, Kleptocrats and Criminals*, London: Profile Books

Cardullo, B. (2007) 'Introduction', in B. Cardullo (ed), *Satyajit Ray Interviews*, Jackson, MI: University of Mississippi Press, pp vii–xx

Caute, D. (1970) *Fanon*, London: Fontana/Collins

CDP (1976) *The Costs of Industrial Change*, London: Community Development Project Inter-Project Editorial Team

CDP (1977) *Gilding the Ghetto: The State and the Poverty Experiments*, London: Community Development Project Inter-Project Editorial Team

Centre for Contemporary Cultural Studies (1982) *The Empire Strikes Back: Race and Racism in 70s Britain*, London: Hutchinson

Chakrabortty, A. (2023) 'A far-right backlash against the Home Secretary's asylum policy has brought a deluge of hate to a peaceful Welsh town' *The Guardian*, Thursday 24 August

Chambers, R. (1983) *Rural Development*, Harlow: Longman

Chisholm, L. (ed) *Changing Class*, London: Zed Books

Clavel, P. (1986) *The Progressive City*, New Brunswick, NJ: Rutgers University Press

Clavel, P. and Wiewel, W. (eds) (1991) *Harold Washington and the Neighbourhoods*, New Brunswick, NJ: Rutgers University Press

Clover, D. and Sanford, K. (eds) (2013) *Lifelong Learning, the Arts and Community Cultural Engagement in the Contemporary University*, Manchester: Manchester University Press

Clover, D. and Stalker, J. (eds) (2007) *The Arts and Social Justice*, Leicester: NIACE

Cochrane, A. (ed) (1987) *Developing Local Economic Strategies*, Milton Keynes: Open University Press

Collini, S. (2017) *Speaking of Universities*, London: Verso

Conrad, J. (1983 edn) *Heart of Darkness*, Harmondsworth: Penguin Books

Cooper, D. (2000) *The Cinema of Satyajit Ray*, Cambridge: Cambridge University Press

Corfield, A. (1969) *Epochs in Workers' Education*, London: WEA

Craig, G., Cole, B. and Ali, N. with Qureshi, I. (2019) *The Missing Dimension: Where Is 'Race' in Social Policy Teaching and Learning?* London: Social Policy Association

Craig, G., Mayo, M., Popple, K., Shaw, M. and Taylor, M. (eds) (2011) *The Community Development Reader*, Bristol: Policy Press

Craik, W. (1964) *The Central Labour College*, London: Lawrence and Wishart

Crowther, J., Galloway, V. and Martin, I. (eds) (2005) *Popular Education: Engaging the Academy*, Leicester: NIACE

Cumming, L. (2023) 'Africa through its own lens' *The Observer*, 9 July

D'Arcangelis, C.L. and Huntley, A. (2012) 'No more silence', in L. Manicom and S. Walters (eds), *Feminist Popular Education in Transnational Debates*, Basingstoke: Palgrave Macmillan, pp 41–58

Davis, M. (2023) *UNITE History Volume 5 (1974–1992)*, Liverpool: Liverpool University Press

Davis, M. and Foster, J. (2021) *UNITE History Volume 1 (1880–1931)* Liverpool: Liverpool University Press

Davis, M., McKenzie, R. and Sullivan, W. (2006) *Working against Racism: The Role of Trade Unions in Britain*, London: TUC

Day, A., Lee, L., Thomas, D. and Spickard, J. (eds) (2022) *Diversity, Inclusion and Decolonization*, Policy Press: Bristol

de Figueiredo-Cowen, M. and Gastaldo, D. (eds) (1995) *Paulo Freire at the Institute*, London: Institute of Education

Dorling, D. (2018) *Peak Inequality*, Bristol: Policy Press
Dresser, M. (1986) *Black and White on the Buses*, Bristol: Bristol Broadsides
Du Bois, W.E.B. (1971 edn) *The Seventh Son*, New York: Vintage
Du Bois, W.E.B. (1975 edn) *Dusk of Dawn*, Millwood, NY: Kraus-Thomson
Du Bois, W.E.B. (2017 edn) *The Souls of Black Folk*, New York: Restless Books
Du Sautoy, P. (1958) *Community Development in Ghana*, Oxford: Oxford University Press
Dworkin, D. (1997) *Cultural Marxism*, Durham, NC: Duke University Press
Elkins, C. (2022) *Legacy of Violence: A History of the British Empire*, London: Bodley Head
Elkins, C. (2005) *Britain's Gulag: The Brutal End of Empire in Kenya*, London: Jonathan Cape
Emecheta, B. (2023 edn) *In the Ditch*, London: Penguin Classics
English, L. and Irving, C. (2015) *Feminism in Community: Rotterdam:* Sense Publishers
Evans, R., Kurantowicz, E. and Lucio-Villegas, E. (2022) 'Introduction: Remaking Communities and Adult Learning' in R. Evans, E. Kurantowicz and E. Lucio-Villegas (eds), *Remaking Communities and Adult Learning*, Leiden: Brill, pp 1–15
Fals-Borda, O. and Rahman, M. (eds) (1991) *Action and Knowledge: Breaking the Monopoly with Participatory Action Research*, London: Intermediate Technology
Fanon, F. (2001 edn) Th*e Wretched of the Earth*, London: Penguin
Fanon, F. (2020 edn) *Black Skins, White Masks*, London: Penguin
Fanon, F. (2021 edn) *The Wretched of the Earth*, London: Penguin
Farah, H. (2023) 'Musk suggests Soros foundation seeking to "destroy civilisation"', *The Guardian*, Tuesday 19 September
Fieldhouse, R. (2005) *Anti-Apartheid*, London: Merlin
Fieldhouse, R. (2013) 'Thompson the adult educator', in R. Fieldhouse and R. Taylor (eds), *E.P. Thompson and English Radicalism*, Manchester: Manchester University Press, pp 25–47
Fieldhouse, R. and Associates (1998) *A History of Modern British Adult Education*, Leicester: NIACE
Fieldhouse, R., Koditschek, T. and Taylor, R. (2013) 'E.P. Thompson: a short introduction', in R. Fieldhouse and R. Taylor (eds), *E.P. Thompson and English Radicalism*, Manchester: Manchester University Press, pp 1–22
Finlayson, A., Kelly, A. and Topinka, R. (2022) 'Digital culture wars: understanding the far right's online powerbase', *Soundings*, 22(81): 43–64
Fisher, J. (2005) *Bread on the Waters: A History of TGWU Education 1922–2000* London: Lawrence and Wishart
Fisher, J. (2017) 'History and context of UK trade union education' in M. Seal (ed), *Trade Union Education: Transforming the World*, Workable Books: New Internationalist, pp 52–63

Fitch, B. and Oppenheimer, M. (1966) *Ghana: End of an illusion*, New York: Monthly Review Press

Foley, G. (1999) *Learning in Social Action*, Leicester: NIACE

Foster, J. (2022) *UNITE History Volume 4 (1960–1974)*, Liverpool: Liverpool University Press

Foucault, M. (1980) *Power/Knowledge: Selected Interviews and Other Writings, 1972–77*, Brighton: Harvester

Fraser, N. (2002) 'What's critical about critical theory? The case of Habermas and gender', in D. Rasmussen and J. Swindal (eds), *Jurgen Habermas*, London: Sage, pp 55–84

Freeman, D. (2014) *'Never again': The 43 Group and the Role of the London Taxi Trade*, MA thesis, London Metropolitan University

Freire, P. (1972) *Pedagogy of the Oppressed*, Harmondsworth: Penguin

Freire, P. (1996) *Pedagogy of Hope*, London: Bloomsbury

Fryer, P. (1984) *Staying Power*, London: Pluto Press

Giddens, A. (1976) 'Classical social theory and the origins of modern sociology', *American Journal of Sociology*, 81(4): 703–29

Gills, D. (1991) 'Chicago politics and community development: a social movement in perspective', in P. Clavel and W. Wiewel (eds), *Harold Washington and the Neighbourhoods*, New Brunswick, NJ: Rutgers University Press, pp 34–63

Gilroy, P. (2004) *After Empire*, London: Routledge

Gilroy, P. (2016) 'Foreword', in S. Ponzanesi and G. Colpani (eds), *Postcolonial Transitions in Europe*, London: Rowan and Littlefield

GLC (1985) *The London Industrial Strategy*, London: Greater London Council

GLC (1986) *The London Labour Plan*, London: Greater London Council

Gobineau, A. (1999 edn) *An Essay on the Inequality of Human Races*, New York: Howard Fertig

Gott, R. (2008) Obituary for Orlando Fals-Borda, *The Guardian*, 26 August

Gramsci, A. (1968 edn) *The Modern Prince and Other Writings*, New York: International Publishers

Grant, W. (2020) 'Decolonising the curriculum', *Political Quarterly*, 91(1): 103

Grayson, J. (2010) 'Borders, glass floors and anti-racist popular adult education', in M. Mayo and J. Annette (eds), *Taking Part? Active Learning for Active Citizenship and Beyond*, Leicester: NIACE, pp 156–68

Habermas, J. (1986) *Theory of Communicative Action*, Cambridge: Polity Press

Haley, A. (2011) *Roots*, New York: Vanguard Press

Hall, B. (2022) *Madiba and Engaged Scholarship: Remarks in Celebration of Nelson Mandela Day at Rhodes University*, Makhanda, South Africa, 18 July

Hall, B., Clover, D., Crowther, J. and Scandrett, E. (eds) (2012) *Learning and Education for a Better World: The Role of Social Movements*, Rotterdam: Sense

Hall, S., Critcher, C., Jefferson, T., Clarke, J. and Roberts, B. (2013 edn) *Policing the Crisis: Mugging, the State, and Law and Order*, Basingstoke: Palgrave Macmillan

Harvey, D. (1990) *The Condition of Postmodernity*, Oxford: Blackwell

Hatherley, O. (2020) *Red Metropolis*, London: Repeater

Henley, J. (2023) 'Young people more likely to doubt merits of democracy – global poll', *The Guardian*, Monday 11 September

Hicks, D. (2021) *The Brutish Museums*, London: Pluto

Hinden, R. (1945) *The Colonial Problem*, ABCA

Hinds, D. (2014) *Mother Country: In the Wake of a Dream*, Hertford: Hansib Publications

Hochschild, A. (2016) *Strangers in Their Own Land: Anger and Mourning on the American Right*, New York: New Press

Holland, J. and Blackburn, J. (eds) (1998) *Whose Voice? Participatory Research and Policy Change*, London: Intermediate Technology Publications

Hope, A. and Timmel, S. (2001) *Training for Transformation, Revised Edition*, Zimbabwe: Mambo Press

Hunter, J.D. (1991) *Culture Wars: The Struggle to Define America*, New York: Basic Books

Hunter, J.D. and Wolfe, A. (eds) (2006) *Is There a Culture War?*, Washington DC: Pew Research Center Brookings Institute

Huntington, S. (1996) *The Clash of Civilisations? The Debate*, New York: Foreign Affairs

Hurston, Z.N. (2007 edn) *Their Eyes Were Watching God*, London: Virago

Ibbott, R. (2014) *Ujamaa: The Hidden History of Tanzania's Socialist Villages*, London: Crossroads

IDAF (1974 edn) *Apartheid and the British Worker: A Handbook for Trade Unionists*, London: IDAF

Innes, L. (2022) 'Lalage Bown: adult educationist whose work helped transform approaches to literature in Africa', *The Guardian*, Saturday 22 January

Jackson, H. (2021) *People's Republic of South Yorkshire*, Nottingham: Spokesman

Johnson, R. (1979) ' "Really useful knowledge": radical education and working class culture' in C. Clarke, C. Critcher and R. Johnson (eds), *Working Class Culture*, London: Routledge, pp 75–102

Joseph-Salisbury, R., Ashe, S., Alexander, C. and Campion, K. (2020) *Race and Ethnicity in British Sociology*, Durham: British Sociological Association, https://www.britsoc.co.uk/publications/race-and-ethnicity-in-british-sociology/

Kane, L. (2012) 'Forty years of popular education in Latin America' in B. Hall, D. Clover. J. Crowther and E. Scandrett (eds), *Learning and Education for a Better World*, Rotterdam: Sense, pp 69–83

Kapoor, A., Youssef, N. and Hood, S. (2022) *Confronting Injustice: Racism and the Environmental Emergency*, Greenpeace and Runneymede Trust

Kasrils, R. (ed) (2021) *International Brigade Against Apartheid*, Johannesburg: Jacana Media

References

Keith, K. (2011) *From Civilization to Participation*, unpublished PhD thesis, Goldsmiths University of London

Kenny, S., Taylor, M., Onyx, J. and Mayo, M. (2015) *Challenging the Third Sector*, Bristol: Policy Press

Kim, C. (2020) 'Commentary', in C. Kim and F. Moran (eds), *Steve McQueen*, London: Tate Gallery, pp 1–9

King, D. (1978) Apartheid in Practice, posters displayed in David King exhibition, *The World Must Change*, curated by Rick Poynor in 2022 at the Standpoint Gallery, Coronet Street, London

Kitson, F. (2010 edn) *Low Intensity Operations*, London: Faber and Faber

Komba, D. (1995) 'Contributions to rural development', in C. Legum and G. Munari (eds), *Mwalimu: The Influence of Nyerere*, London: James Currey, pp 32–45

Koram, K. (2022) *Uncommon Wealth*, London: John Murray

Laginder, A-M, Nordvall, H. and Crowther, J. (eds), *Popular Education, Power and Democracy*, Leicester: NIACE

Lenin, V. (2010 edn) *Imperialism: The Highest Stage of Capitalism*, London: Penguin

Lepore, W., Sharma, Y., Hall, B. and Tandon, R. (2022) 'Co-constructing knowledge and communities', in R. Evans, E. Kurantowicz and E. Lucio-Villegas (eds), *Remaking Communities and Adult Learning*, Leiden: Brill, pp 79–93

Levy, A. (2004) *Small Island*, London: Review

Loney, M. (1983) *Community against Government*, London: Hutchinson

Lugard, F. (1965 edn) *The Dual Mandate in British Tropical Africa*, London: Cass

Luscombe, R. (2022) 'They're after Mickey Mouse: Biden decries Republicans' Disney reprisal' *The Guardian*, Saturday 23 April

Mackintosh, M. and Wainwright, H. (eds) (1987) *A Taste of Power*, London: Verso

Malcolm, D. (1982) 'Interview with Satyajit Ray' in B. Cardullo (ed) (2007) *Satyajit Ray Interviews*, Jackson, MS: University of Mississippi Press, pp 133–141

Marable, M. (1991 edn) *Race, Reform and Rebellion*, Jackson, MS: University of Mississippi Press

Marcuse, H. (1966 edn) *Eros and Civilization*, Boston: Beacon Press

Marris, P. and Rein, M. (1972 edn) *Dilemmas of Social Reform*, London: Routledge and Kegan Paul

Massey, D. (1987) 'Equal opportunities in the GLEB experience', in A. Cochrane (ed), *Developing Local Economic Strategies*, Milton Keynes: Open University Press, pp 23–34

Matiwana, M. and Walters, S. (1986) *The Struggle for Democracy*, University of the Western Cape, South Africa: CACE

Mayer, A. (1958) *Pilot Project India*, Berkeley, CA: University of California Press

Mayo, M. (1975a) 'Community development: a radical alternative?', in R. Bailey and M. Brake (eds), *Radical Social Work*, London: Edward Arnold, pp 129–43

Mayo, M. (2020) *Community-Based Education and Social Movements: Popular Education in a Populist Age*, Bristol: Policy Press

Mayo, M. (2022) *UNITE History Volume 3 (1945–1960)*, Liverpool: Liverpool University Press

Mayo, M. and Annette, J. (eds) (2010) *Taking Part?*, Leicester: NIACE

Mayo, M., Mendiwelso-Bendek, Z. and Packham, C. (eds) (2013) *Community Research for Community Development*, Basingstoke: Palgrave Macmillan

McGrath, M. (2017) 'Back story: a Unite approach to political education', in M. Seal (ed), *Trade Union Education*, Oxford: Workable Books, pp 100–14

McIlroy, J. (1980) 'Education for the labor movement: United Kingdom experience past and present', *Labor Studies Journal* 4: 198

McLennan, G. (ed) (2021) *Stuart Hall: Selected Writings on Marxism*, Durham, NC: Duke University Press

McQueen, S. (2013) *Twelve Years a Slave* (Feature film)

Meghji, A., Tan, S. and Wain, L. (2022) 'Demystifying the 'decolonizing' and 'diversity' slippage: reflections from sociology', in A. Day, L. Lee, D. Thomas and J. Spickard (eds), *Diversity, Inclusion and Decolonization*, Bristol: Policy Press, pp 31–47

Melzer, S. (2009) *Gun Crusaders*, New York: New York University Press

Miller, A. (1987) *Harold Washington*, Chicago: Bonus Books

Mitchell, M. (1936: 2020 edn) *Gone with the Wind*, Wordsworth Classics

Modern Records Centre, University of Warwick (1953) MSS 126/TG/1887/15 Record of the 15th Biennial Delegate Conference, 1953

Mohun, S. (2022) 'A portrait of contemporary neoliberalism', in G. Albo, L. Panitch and C. Leys (eds), *New Polarizations, Old Contradictions: The Crisis of Centrism, Socialist Register*, London: Merlin, pp 1–20

Morreira, S., Luckett, K., Kumalo, S. and Ramgotra, M. (eds) (2021) *Decolonising Curricula and Pedagogy in Higher Education*, London: Routledge

Moynihan, D. (1969) *Maximum Feasible Misunderstanding*, New York: Free Press

Mudimbe, V. (1988) *The Invention of Africa: Gnosis, Philosophy, and the Order of Knowledge*, Bloomington, IN: Indiana University Press

Newman, I. (2014) *Reclaiming Local Democracy*, Bristol: Policy Press

Newman, M. (2016) *Six Authors in Search of Justice*, London: Hurst

Ngugi wa Thiong'o (1964) *Weep Not, Child*, London: Heinemann (published under his English name of James Ngugi)

Ngugi wa Thiong'o (1965) *The River Between*, London: Heinemann

Ngugi wa Thiong'o (1977) *Petals of Blood*, London: Heinemann

Ngugi wa Thiong'o (1986) *Decolonising the Mind: The Politics of Language in African Literature*, London: Heinemann

Ngugi wa Thiong'o (2005 reprint) *Decolonising the Mind*, Oxford: James Currey

Ngugi wa Thiong'o and Ngugi wa Murii (1982 English Translation) *I Will Marry When I Want*, London: Heinemann

Nkrumah, K. (1965) *Neo-Colonialism, the Last Stage of Imperialism*, London: Thomas Nelson

Nkrumah, K. (1997 edn) 'Tenth anniversary of the CPP 1960', in *Selected Speeches of Kwame Nkrumah*, compiled by S. Obeng, Accra: Afram Publications, pp 1–12

Nyerere, J. (1969) *Nyerere on Socialism*, Dar-es-Salaam: Oxford University Press

Nyerere, J. (1986) *President Nyerere in Conversation with Darcus Howe and Tariq Ali*, London: Race Today

Olusoga, D. (2017 edn) *Black and British: A Forgotten History*, London: Pan

Olusoga, D. (2020) 'David Olusoga talks to Steve McQueen about Small Axe', *Sight and Sound*, 30(10): 24–35

Paine, T. (2004 edn) *Common Sense*, London: Penguin Books

Patnaik, P. (2017) 'The October Revolution and the worker–peasant alliance' *Theory and Struggle*, 118: 20–30

Pollins, H. (1984) *The History of Ruskin College*, Oxford: Ruskin College Library

Ramdin, R. (1987 edn) *The Making of the Black Working Class in Britain*, Aldershot: Gower

Reay, D. (2017) *Miseducation*, London: Pluto

Rhodes, C. (2022) *Woke Capitalism*, Bristol: Policy Press

Robins, S. (2005) 'AIDS, science and citizenship after apartheid', in M. Leach, I Scoones and B. Wynne (eds), *Science and Citizens*, London: Zed Books, pp 113–29

Robinson, A. (1982) 'Conversation with Satyajit Ray' in B. Cardullo (ed) (2007) *Satyajit Ray Interviews*, Jackson, MS: University of Mississippi Press, pp 142–64

Robinson, C. (2019) *Cedric J. Robinson*, edited by H.L.T. Quan, London: Pluto

Robinson, C. (2021) *Black Marxism*, London: Penguin

Rodney, W. (1976) *How Europe Underdeveloped Africa*, London: Bogle

Rowbottom, S. (2022) *Daring to Hope: My Life in the 1970s*, London: Verso

Rowbottom, S., Segal, L. and Wainwright, H. (2013 edn) *Beyond the Fragments: Feminism and the Making of Socialism*, London: Merlin Press

Sanghera. S. (2021) *Empireland*, London: Penguin Random House

Savage, M. (2022) 'Four in five people in the UK are "woke", poll reveals', *The Guardian*, 1 May

Scottish Education and Action for Development (1990)

Seifert, R. (2022) *UNITE History Volume 2 (1932–1945)*, Liverpool: Liverpool University Press

Sikakane, J. (1977) *A Window on Soweto*, London: IDAF

Simon, B. (1992) 'The struggle for hegemony, 1920–1926', in B. Simon (ed), *The Search for Enlightenment*, Leicester: NIACE, pp 109–26

Smith, D. (2022) 'Buffalo killings "will fuel Republican embrace of great replacement theory"', *The Guardian*, 22 May

Smith, M. (2020) 'How unique are British attitudes to empire?', YouGov, 11 March

Smith, Z. (2007 edn) 'Introduction', in Z.N. Hurston, *Their Eyes Were Watching God*, London: Virago, pp vii–xxiv

Spickard, J. (2022) 'How would a world sociology think? Towards intellectual inclusion', in A. Day, L. Lee, D. Thomas and J. Spickard (eds), *Diversity, Inclusion and Decolonization*, Bristol: Policy Press, pp 157–69

Steele, T. (2010) 'Enlightenment public: popular education movements in Europe, their legacy and promise', *Studies in the Education of Adults*, 42(2): 107–23

Tandon, R. (ed) (2005) *Participatory Research: Revisiting the Roots*, New Delhi: Mosaic Books

Taylor, H. (2019) *Gone with the Wind*, Palgrave with the British Film Institute

Taylor, R. (2013) 'Thompson and the peace movement: from CND in the 1950s and 1960s to END in the 1980s', in R. Fieldhouse and R. Taylor (eds), *E.P. Thompson and English Radicalism*, Manchester: Manchester University Press, pp 181–201

Taylor, V. (2018) 'Social justice perspectives in South Africa's struggle for social transformation' in G. Craig (ed), *Handbook of Social Justice*, Cheltenham: Edward Elgar, pp 157–70

Taylor, V. and Conradie, I. (1997) *'We Have Been Taught by Life Itself': Empowering Women as Leaders: The Role of Development Education*, SADEP in collaboration with DELTA

Thompson, E.P. (1978 edn) *Poverty of Theory*, London: Merlin

Thompson, E.P. (1980a edn), *The Making of the English Working Class*, London: Penguin Modern Classics

Thompson, E.P. (1980b) *Writing by Candlelight*, London: Merlin Press

Tinker, M. (2020 edn) *That Hideous Strength: How the West Was Lost*, Evangelical Press

Trades Union Congress (1981) *Black Workers: A TUC Charter for Equality of Opportunity* London: Trades Union Congress

Turner, J. (2022) 'Stuart Hall's legacies', *London Review of Books*, 44(21): 9–16

Unite (2009) *Unite Education Theory and Practice: Beyond Functionalism*, London: Unite

United Nations (1955) Report of the Ashbridge Conference on Social Development, United Nations

Victoria and Albert Museum (2022) *Africa Fashion*, London: Victoria and Albert Museum von Kotze, A. (1988) *Organise and Act: The Natal Workers' Theatre Movement*, Durban: Culture and Working Life

von Kotze, A. (1996) 'The creating of the word: a feminist model?', in S. Walters and L. Manicom (eds), *Gender and Popular Education*, London: Zed Books, pp 149–68

von Kotze, A. (2018) 'Celebrating Freire – a message of solidarity from South Africa', *Concept*, 9(3): 96

von Kotze, A. and Holloway, A. (1996) *Participatory Learning Activities for Disaster Mitigation in Southern Africa*, University of Natal: Department of Adult and Community Education

Walker, A. (1975) 'In search of Zora Neale Hurston', *MS Magazine*, March

Walters S. '"The drought is my teacher": adult learning and education in times of climate crisis', in *Journal of Vocational, Adult Continuing Education and Training* (JOVACET), 1(1): 146

Walters, S. and von Kotze, A. (2021) 'Making a case for ecofeminist popular education in times of Covid-19', in *Andragoška spoznanja/Studies in Adult Education and Learning*, 27(1): 47–62

Walters, S. (1989) *Education for Democratic Participation*, University of the Western Cape: CACE

Walters, S. and Butterwick, S. (2017) 'Moves to decolonise solidarity through feminist popular education', in A. von Kotze and S. Walters (eds), *Forging Solidarity in Popular Education at Work*, Rotterdam: Sense Publishers, pp 27–38

Walters, S. and Manicom, L. (1996) *Gender in Popular Education: Methods for Empowerment*. London, Zed Books

Ward, M. (1981) *Job Creation and the Council: Local Government and the Struggle for Full Employment*, Nottingham: Spokesman

Ward, P., Banks, S. and Hart, A. (2019) 'Conclusion', in S. Banks, A. Hart and P. Ward (eds), *Co-Producing Research: A Community Development Approach*, Bristol: Policy Press, pp 203–9

Washington, B. (2021 edn) *Up from Slavery*, Orviedo, Spain: King Solomon

Weir, A. (2023) UNITE *History Volume 6 (1992–2010)*, Liverpool: Liverpool University Press

West, L. (2016) *Distress City*, London: IOE Press

Whitehouse, M. (1993) *Quite Contrary: An Autobiography*, London: Sidgwick & Jackson

Williams, E. (2022 edn) *Capitalism and Slavery*, London: Penguin Random House

Williams, R. (1963 edn) *Culture and Society*, New York: Columbia University Press

Williams, R. (1988 edn) *Keywords*, London: Fontana

Williams, R. (ed) (2018 edn) *May Day Manifesto*, London: Verso

Williams, S. (2021) *White Malice: The CIA and the Neocolonisation of Africa*, London: Hurst

Wintour, P. (2023) 'UN admits that it is not on track to end hunger or poverty', *The Guardian*, 19 September

Wolfe, A. (2006) 'The culture war that never came', in J.D. Hunter, and A. Wolfe, (eds), *Is There a Culture War?*, Washington DC: Pew Research Center Brookings Institute, pp 41–73

Wolfers, M. (2007) *Thomas Hodgkin: Wandering Scholar*, Monmouth: Merlin

Wolpe, H. (1985) *Race, Class and the Apartheid State*, London: James Currey

Yahya-Othman, S., Shivji, I. and Kamata, N. (2020) *Development as Rebellion*, Dar-es-Salaam: Mkuki Na Nyota

Yeates, M. (1950) *Discrimination against Coloured People*, WFTU

Index

A

academics 34–5
Academy Awards 126
accreditation for prior experiential learning (APEL) 81
Achebe, Chinua 128–30, 140
Acropolis Museum, Athens 124
Action and Knowledge (Fals-Borda and Rahman) 36
active citizenship 56
active participatory approaches to learning 89
Adah (*In the Ditch*) 135
Adichie, Chimamanda Ngozi 128
adult community education and development 51, 54–9, 61
adult education 22–3, 54, 58–9, 74
adult literacy 55
Africa 51–61
Africa Fashion exhibition (V&A) 125
African American stereotypes 137–8
African National Congress (ANC) 45, 67–8, 71, 77
African Socialism 53, 59, 61, 146
Africa photography exhibition (Tate Modern) 125
Afro Caribbean Enterprise (Sheffield City Council) 113
After Empire (Gilroy) 24–5
After Imperialism (Barratt Brown) 117
Aiello, T. 50–1
Alabama 48
Algeria 27
Ali, Monica 135
Ali, N 34
Alinsky, Saul 79, 107, 108
Ali, Tariq 60
'All lives matter' slogan 2
Amalgamated Engineering Union 71
America *see* US
Amicus (trade union) 86, 92
Amritsar massacre 131
Ananga (*Distant Thunder*) 131, 132
Angola 69, 73
Anthills of the Savannah (Achebe) 129–30
Anthropological Society of London 33
anthropology 33
Anti-Apartheid Movement (AAM) 66–71
anti-colonial thinkers 130
anti-fascist mobilisations 98
anti-imperialist educators 56–9
anti-racism 93–101, 122
anti-racist education 111, 112–13, 122

anti-retroviral (ARV) drugs 44–5
anti-Semitism 40, 94–5, 97–8
Anti-Slavery International 6
apartheid 66–85
  categories of people 67–8
  developing leadership 77–80
  education 67–8, 77–8
  resistance to 73–5
  shared objectives to end 77
  trade union movement 71
  White supremacy rule 77
  see also Black Consciousness Movement (BCM); South Africa
apartheid free zones 70–1
Arday, J. 35
Army Bureau of Current Affairs (ABCA) 56
Arnold, M. 72
Arusha Declaration 59
asylum seekers and refugees
  community education and development 148
  demonstrations 141–2
  hostile environments 34, 120, 146
  schemes to support 105, 111
  sending to Rwanda 26
  social media 149–50
Attlee government 98
austerity 144

B

'Back to Africa' initiatives 53
Baldwin, James 1, 126, 148
Banerjee, Bibhutibhusen 131
Barratt Brown, Michael 112, 116–19, 143, 146
battle of ideas 52
BBC 14
Belgian colonialism 128
Bengal 133
Bengal Famine 131–2
Benin Bronzes 124
Bennett, T. 124
Benn, Tony 99
Berkeley, California 120
Bevin, Ernest 94, 95, 96, 97
Beyond the Fragments (Rowbottom) 23
Bezos, George 15
Bhattacharyya, G. 12
Biden, Joe 16
Bieze, M. 48, 50
Biko, Steve 68, 72–3, 79, 94, 129
Bimala (*The Home and the World*) 133–4
Black, Asian and Minority Ethnic (BAME) 33–4, 100

Black British history 35
Black consciousness 72, 73
Black Consciousness Movement (BCM) 68, 71–3, 79, 145–6
  see also apartheid
Black Liberation 100
Black Lives Matter (BLM) 2, 17, 28, 31
Black Marxism 28
Black people
  apartheid system 67
  in Britain 62–3
  discrimination 63, 115
  fighting union racism 91
  and the GLC 116
  marginalisation 35
  self-organisation 100
  stereotyping 137–8
  US migrations 105
  see also racism; Windrush generation
Black Power Movement 72, 91, 106, 108, 130
Black Radical traditions 28
Black Workers (TUC Charter) 100
blaming victims 12–13
Blunkett, D. 110–11, 148–9
Boas, Franz 137
Bodleian Library, Oxford 70
Bolsonaro, Jair 41
book-learning 50
boomerang effect 61–2, 64
Bottomore, T. 19, 20
Bown, Lalage 58–9, 60
Boycott Movement 68
Braverman, Suella 141
Brazil 67
Bread on the Waters (Fisher) 90
Brewis, G. 121
Brick Lane (Monica Ali) 135
Bristol Bus Boycott 99
Bristol City Council 121
Britain
  black people as a problem 111
  'butler to the world' 4
  Cold War 97
  Colonial Office 54, 58, 90
  Community Development Projects (CDP) 38–9, 63–4
  education programmes 56
  end of empire 110–11
  fantasies of omnipotence 25
  immigration from Commonwealth 62
  imperial legacies 110
  imperial mission 124
  junior partner to US 96
  local authorities 110, 111, 121–2
  migrants from colonies 135–6
  municipal socialism 110–11
  overseas territories 4
  position in the world 96
  post-Second World War 47, 95–6
  post-war community education 54
  poverty 63, 149
  racism and discrimination 63
  trade unions 102–3
  Urban Programme 63
  working classes 117
British empire 6, 25–6, 35
British Guiana 97
British Nationality Act 1948 62, 98
British Sociological Association (BSA) 34
Broad Left 90
Brokensha, David 54, 55
Burlington, Vermont 106
Butterwick, S. 84

C

Cape Town 82
capitalism 12, 118, 143, 147
Caribbean workers 62–3
case studies 44–5, 99
Center for Neighbourhood Development (Cleveland State University) 107
Centre for Adult and Continuing Education (CACE) 76–7, 79
Centre for Local Economic Strategies (CLES) 119–20
Cesaire, Aime 61
Charlotteville, Virginia 17
Chicago 105–6, 107–10
Chicago Workshop for Economic Development (CWED) 108–9
Chile 101, 113–14
Christians and Muslim conflicts 12
Christian Socialist approaches 88
Churchill, Winston 95
Church of England 14
Cities of Sanctuary 105, 120–1
citizen participation 106–7
City of London 110
city planning 105
civil rights 50, 51–3
Civil Rights Movement 106, 142–3
civil society organisations 67
class and class consciousness 22
Clavel, P. 106, 107
Cleveland 107
Cleveland State University 107
climate crisis 83–4
Climate Justice Charter 83
Clinton, Bill 15
Cochrane, A. 116
Cold War 55, 58
Cole, B. 34
colonial freedom 4–5, 97, 142
colonial grievances 57
colonialism 1–2, 24–8
  Britain's cultural heritage 124
  and capitalism 118, 147

Index

as a 'civilising mission' 124
community education and
  development 6–7
contradictory 94
detrimental to working classes 117
former powers' influence 4, 5
learning about 128–31
legacies 110, 121
museums and galleries 125
and slavery 6, 118
and TGWU 94–5
undermining cultures 132–3
see also decolonisation;
  imperialism; slavery
colonial violence 130–1
Colston, Edward 31–2, 121, 123
Commission on Catholic Community
  Action 107
Common Sense (Paine) 18
communicative action 43–4
communism 14
community action networks 82
community development 1, 2
Community Development Block
  Grants 106
Community Development Journal (CDJ) 64
community development programmes 49,
  56, 64, 104, 142
Community Development Projects
  (CDP) 38–9, 63–4
community education 1–3
community education and development 3,
  6–7, 54, 84, 145–8
community organisations 73, 121
Community University Partnership
  Programme (University of
  Brighton) 38
community–university research
  partnerships 38–9
Community Wealth Building
  Movement 120
Conrad, J. 128
contested histories 47–65, 91
  anti-imperialist educators 56–9
  civil rights 51–3
  decolonisation 6–7, 54–6, 59–61
  post-war Britain 61–4
  public museums 124
  US post-slavery 48–51
Convention People's Party (CPP,
  Ghana) 55
cost-of-living crisis 144
counter-insurgencies 62
Cousins, Frank 97
COVID-19 pandemic 81–3, 144
Craig, Gary 34, 64–5
creative approaches 75
Creech Jones, Arthur 57, 58
critical consciousness 26–7, 144

critical theorists 18
critical thinking 46, 78, 148
cultural activists 74
cultural Marxism 11, 17–20, 141
cultural politics 15
cultural racism ('civilisationism') 24–5
cultural strategies 123–5
cultural struggles 74–5, 140
cultural warriors 1, 11, 13–14, 15–16,
  141, 147
culture and working life course 74
cultures 12, 123, 140
culture warriors 3
culture wars 11–29, 123
  battles of ideas 144–5
  and guns 16
  liberation and social justice 28–9
  and politics 16
  and racism 24–8
  religious differences 14–15
  and wokeism 28
Curaçao 4

D

D'Arcangelis, C.L. 84
Davis, M. 91, 93–4, 100
Day, A. 32
Deakin, Arthur 90, 96, 97
decolonisation 4–6, 30–1, 32–3, 96, 142
  colonial grievances 57
  and conscientisation 148
  contested histories 6–7
  continuing process 80, 84–5, 143–4
  cultural domination 139–40
  education in Africa 59–61
  initiatives 32
  and political independence 143
  slavery and colonialism 35
  South Africa 66–7, 84–5
  see also colonialism; slavery
decolonising the curricula 30–3, 39–40,
  45–6, 147
deindustrialisation 64
de Keyser, Ethel 70
deliberative democracy 44
democracy 73, 75–7, 110, 149
Democracy in Crisis (Blunkett and
  Jackson) 111, 148–9
democratically controlled initiatives 120
DeSantis, Ron 16–17
de-schooling 75
Developing Local Economic Strategies
  (Cochrane) 116
development and environmental issues 80
dialects 137–8, 140
Dilemmas of Social Reform (Marris and
  Rein) 64
Discrimination against Coloured People
  (WFTU) 96

165

Distant Thunder (film) 131–2
domestic violence 81
Douglass, Frederick 125
drama 69–70
droughts 83
Du Bois, W.E.B. 48, 49, 51–3, 61, 142, 145
Durban 74, 75
Durban Workers' Cultural Local 75
Du Sautoy, Peter 55
Dworkin, D. 20

E

Eatonville, Florida 49, 136–7
ecofeminism 83–4
economic and political power 51–2
economic development strategies 108–9
education
  apartheid 67–8, 77–8
  decolonisation in Africa 59–61
  post-Civil War 51–2
  and poverty 87
effective accountability 75–6
electoral defeats 41
Elgin Marbles 124
Elkins, Caroline 25
Emecheta, Buchi 134–5
Empire Windrush, HMT 62
empowerment 107
engaging learners 57
environmental issues 80, 83–4
epistemological legacies 42–4
Eros and Civilization (Marcuse) 19–20
Esteli, Nicaragua 114
ethnicity 34
Ethnological Society of London 33
ethnology 33
Eurocentrism 33
European colonialism 33, 42
  see also colonialism
experimental extension courses 57

F

fair trade 119, 143
Fairtrade Foundation 119
Fals-Borda, Orlando 36–7
Fanon, Franz 4–5, 26–8, 72, 130, 142, 143
Far Right governments 144
Far Right populism 17, 40, 41, 98, 148–9
fascism 94–5
feminism 23, 83
Fieldhouse, Roger 21, 69
films 126–8, 139
First World War 94
Fisher, John 90
Florida 16–17
43 Group 98
Foster, J. 93–4, 99–100
Foucault, M. 87

Frankfurt School 17–20
Fraser, Nancy 43
Freeman, Danny 98
Freire, Paulo 1, 4, 5–6, 18, 28, 31, 36, 60, 72, 79, 142, 144, 150
  Pedagogy of the Oppressed 82
Furthering Socialism in a Cold Climate (Jackson) 114

G

Gangacharan (*Distant Thunder*) 131–2
Gasman, M. 48, 50
Gaventa, John 37
Gender and Popular Education (Walters and Manicom) 77
Germany 94
Gerwel, Jakes 75, 78
Ghana 5, 53, 55
Giddens, A. 42
Gikuyu language 130
Gills, D. 109
Gilroy, Paul 20, 24–5, 26
Global South 36
Gobineau, A. 33
Gone with the Wind (Mitchell) 126, 135–6
Gordimer, Nadine 129
Gott, R. 36
Gramsci, Antonio 17–18, 20, 75, 76, 79, 123, 142, 144
Grant, W. 33
Grayson, J. 113
Greater London Council (GLC) 111–12, 114–16, 118–19
Greater London Enterprise Board (GLEB) 114–16
'the great replacement conspiracy' 13
The Guardian 16
gun ownership 15–16

H

Habermas, J. 43–4
Haley, Alex 126
Half of a Yellow Sun (Adichie) 128
Hall, Budd 36–7
Hall, Stuart 20
Hampton Normal and Agricultural Institute (Hampton University) 48
Harlem Renaissance 136
Harvey, David 41
Hayes, Mike 90
Hayes, Pat 90
Heart of Darkness (Conrad) 128
Heinemann African Writers series 128–9, 134
Highlander Research and Education Center 37
Hinden, R. 57
Hinds, Donald 136
Hindu nationalists 134

history curricula 35
HIV/AIDS 44–5, 82
Hochschild, A. 13
Hodge, Peter 54, 55
Hodgkin, Thomas 57–8, 59, 89, 146
The Home and the World (film) 133–4
homosexuality 14
Hope, Anne 79
Horton, Miles 37
Howe, Darcus 138–9
Hughes, Langston 125
Hunter, James Davis 14–16, 17, 24–5
Huntington, Samuel 12
Huntley, A. 84
Hurston, Zora Neale 49, 136–8, 140

I

Ibbott, R. 60, 61
ideas and social change 3–4
Illich, I. 75, 79
immigration controls 62
imperialism 25, 94, 117
  see also colonialism
India 49, 96, 131–4
Indian Independence Movement 133
Indigenous knowledge systems 32
inequalities 13, 52
Innes, L. 58
'In search of Zora Neale Hurston' (Walker) 138
instrumental learning 56
International Confederation of Free Trade Unions (ICFTU) 97
International Defence and Aid Fund (IDAF) 70
internationalism 52
international solidarity 147
  and anti-racism 93–101
  Chilean refugees 113–14
  and fair trade 116–19
  racial disadvantage 111–14
In the Ditch (Emecheta) 134–5
Islamophobia 12
I Will Marry When I Want (Ngugi wa Thiong'o and Ngugi wa Mirii) 130

J

Jackson, Helen 113, 114
Jackson, K. 110–11, 148–9
Jagan, Cheddi 97
Jallianwala Bagh, India 131
James, C.L.R. 126
Janie (*Their Eyes Were Watching God*) 136–7
Jews 97–8
  see also anti-Semitism
Job Creation and the Council (GLC) 116
Joe (*Their Eyes Were Watching God*) 137
Jones, Arthur Creech 57, 58

Jones-Lecointe, Althea 138–9
Jordanhill Project in International Understanding 70
Julien, Isaac 125
Julius Nyerere lecture 81

K

Kenmure Street, Glasgow 121
Kenya 25, 97, 130–1
Kenya Land and Freedom Army (Mau Mau) 62, 130–1
Kenyatta, Jomo 53
Keyser, Ethel de 70
King, David 69
King, Martin Luther 142
Kitson, Frank 61
Kivukoni College (Mwalimu Nyerere Memorial Academy) 60, 61, 89
knowledge democracy 36–40, 101
Knowledge for Change Training Consortium (K4C) 37–8, 87, 101
'knowledge is power' slogan 87
Koditschek, T. 21
Koram, Kojo 61–2
Kunta Kinte (*Roots*) 126
KwaZulu Natal 74–5

L

Labour History Weekend School (T&G London Region) 90
Labour Relations Bill 1953 (British Guiana) 97
Landless People's Movement (Brazil) 67
'Law and Order in South Africa' poster 69
learning and collective betterment 21
Lenin, V. 94
Lepore, W. 39–40
Levy, Andrea 135–6
lifelong learning 80–1
lifeworld 43–4
Llanelli, Wales 141
local authorities 110, 111, 121–2
London Industrial Strategy (LIS) 115
London Labour Plan 115
London Region T&G 90
Lugard, F. 33
Lyceum Theatre 70

M

machine politics 108, 109
Macmillan, Harold 96
The Making of the English Working Class (Thompson) 22, 23
Malaya 97
Mandela, Nelson 68, 71
Mangrove Nine 138–9
Manicom, L. 77
Marable, M. 91, 102, 147
Marcuse, H. 18, 19–20, 21

Marris, P. 64
Marxism 18, 22, 27–8, 60
Marx, Karl 43, 60
Marx Memorial Library and Workers School (MML) 93, 102
Massacre of Amritsar 131
Mass Education in African Society (Colonial Office) 54
Mau Mau (Kenya Land and Freedom Army) 62, 130–1
May Day Manifesto (Williams) 24
Mayo, M. 95
McCluskey, Len 93
McDaniel, Hattie 126
McGrath, M. 90
McQueen, Steve 126, 127–8, 138–9
Merrifield, Juliet 37
migration 98, 136
Miller, Alton 107
The Missing Dimension (SPA) 34, 35
Mitchell, Margaret 126
mobilisations 14, 121, 141
modern slavery 6
Morreira, S. 30–1
Movement for Colonial Freedom (MCF) 97
Mozambique 69, 73
MS magazine 138
multiculturalism 25
multiple epistemologies 40, 41
municipal socialism 110–11
municipal strategies 105, 146
Murray, Robin 118
museums and galleries 123–5
Musk, Elon 149
Muslims 12, 134
Mwalimu Nyerere Memorial Academy (Kivukoni College) 60, 61, 89

N

National Association for the Advancement of Coloured People 50
National Council of Labour Colleges (NCLC) 88–9
National Education Office 101
National Race Equality Committee 100
National Rifle Association (NRA) 15–16
National Viewers' and Listeners' Association (NVLA) 14
National Women's Committee 100
neighbourhood organisations 107
neo-colonialism 5
neoliberal globalisation 110, 144
New Left 20, 118
Newton, Thandie 128
Ngugi wa Mirii 130
Ngugi wa Thiong'o 31, 130–1, 140
Nicaragua 114
Nikhil (*The Home and the World*) 133–4

'9/11' attacks 16
Nkrumah, Kwame 5, 53, 55, 64, 130, 142, 143
No Longer at Ease (Adichie) 129
Northern College, South Yorkshire 71, 112–13, 122, 143
Northern philanthropists 49–50
Northrup, Solomon 126–7
Notting Hill, London 63, 138
novels and films 126–8, 139
Nyerere, Julius 59–61, 68, 89, 132, 142, 146

O

Obi (*No Longer at Ease*) 129
Okonkwo (*Things Fall Apart*) 129
Olusoga, David 62, 63, 139
Open Society Foundation 149–50
oral histories 101
Organise and Act (Von Kotze) 75
Orwell, George 1
'othering' at work 13

P

Paine, Thomas 18
Pan-African Congress (PAC) 53, 68
Pan-Africanism 53
participatory action research (PAR) 30, 36–40, 86, 101–2
participatory democracy 75–6
participatory research 8, 37, 39, 75, 102
Patnaik, Prabhat 27
Pedagogy of the Oppressed (Freire) 82
People's Plan for the Royal Docks 116
People's Republic of South Yorkshire 114
Plato 42
plays 74
police racism 138–9
political education 89–90, 103
Political Education Project (Harold Washington) 109
Political Quarterly 33
Political Weekend School (T&G London Region) 90
popular cultures 20–1
populist politicians 13, 25, 40
posters 69
'post imperial melancholia' (Gilroy) 25
postmodernist critiques 40–1
poverty 39, 87, 109
Powell, Enoch 63, 98, 138
precarious employment 13
Preston, England 120
private collections 124
privileged elites 13
progressive approaches 81, 148–50
progressive cities 105–7, 121
progressive collaborations 104–5
public transport 111

Index

Q
Qureshi, I. 34

R
race 17, 34
Race and Ethnicity in British Sociology (BSA) 34
Race Equality Unit (Sheffield) 113
Race, Ethnicity and Equality in UK History (Royal History Society) 33
Race, Reform and Rebellion (Marable) 91
race traitors 50
racial disadvantages 111–14
racial discrimination 67–8, 105, 115
racial inequalities 42, 111
racial injustice 51–2, 105–6
racial segregation 48
racism 109
  battle of ideas 52
  Black workers 63
  culture wars 24–8
  decolonisation 147
  immigration controls 62
  and the police 138–9
  sociology degrees 34
  and unions 97
  wars on woke 17
  see also Black people
Rahman, M. 36
rainbow coalitions 108
Ramdin, R. 90, 102, 147
rationality 44
Ray, Satyajit 131–4
'really useful knowledge' 87
reasoned arguments 44
Rein, M. 64
Republic (Plato) 42
researching *with/about* communities 39
resentments and fears 12
resettlement schemes 61
resilience and resistance 134–9
Rhodes, Carl 15
Rhodes, Cecil 31
'Rhodes must fall' movement 31
Rhodes University 37
The River Between (Ngugi wa Thiong'o) 130
Robinson, Cedric 28, 42
Robins, S. 44
Rodney, Walter 110
role education 89
role play 82
Roots (Haley) 126
Rowbottom, Sheila 23
Royal History Society 33
Ruskin College, Oxford 56, 60, 88–9, 90, 101
Russian Revolution 52
Ruvuma Development Association (RDA) 60–1
Rwanda 26

S
safe spaces 81
Sanders, Bernie 106, 107
Sandinista government, Nicaragua 114
Sandip (*The Home and the World*) 133–4
Sanghera. S. 25
Santiniketan, India 133
Savile, Jimmy 14
Scottish Education and Action for Development 66
Second World War 47, 54, 95–6
Seifert, R. 94–5
self-organisation 145
self-reliance 61, 72, 145–6
Senghor, Leopold 53
shared objectives 77
Sharpeville massacre 68, 69–70
Sheffield Campaign Against Racism 113
Sheffield, England 70–1, 113–14, 119–22
Shutt, John 119
slavery 1–2
  Britain's cultural heritage 124
  and capitalism 118, 147
  community education and development 6–7
  ending in US 48
  legacies 110, 121
  loss of identity 126
  museums and galleries 125
  novels and films 126–8
  progressive cities 121
  see also colonialism; decolonisation
Small Axe (television series) 138–9
Small Island (Levy) 135–6
Smith, Zadie 138
social and political inequalities 42
social change 3–4
Social Development in the British Colonial Territories (Colonial Office) 54
social hierarchies 42
socialism 52–3
social liberals 14
social movements 66–7, 80, 106, 121–2
Social Policy Association (SPA) 34, 35
social scientists 52
Society for Participatory Research in Asia (PRIA) 37
sociology degree programmes 34
solidarity 82, 84
Sorrow Songs 52
The Souls of Black Folk (Du Bois) 49
South Africa 66–85
  Anti-Apartheid Movement (AAM) 66–71
  Black Consciousness Movement (BCM) 68, 71–3, 79, 145–6

Boycott Movement 68
community action networks 82
decolonisation 66–7, 84–5
HIV/AIDS 44–5, 82
marketisation of higher education 144
National Party 67
opposition to apartheid 68, 73–5
racial discrimination 67–8
reforms 32
'Rhodes must fall' movement 31
State of Emergency 74
Treatment Action Campaign (TAC) 44–5, 82
see also apartheid
South African Development Programme (SADEP) 77–80
South African Students Organisation (SASO) 72, 94
Southern Africa Resources Project 70
South Yorkshire County Council 111–12
Soweto 68
Spanish Civil War 95
Spickard, J. 42
state funding 90
Stowe, Harriet Beecher 126
strategic action 43
street plays 81
student participation 23
sugar industry 124
Swadeshi movement 133

T

Tagore, Rabindranath 133
Tambo, Oliver 78, 84
Tandon, Rajesh 37
Tanzania 36, 61
Tate Galleries 124, 125
Tate, Henry 124
tax havens 4
taxi drivers 98
Taylor, R. 21
Taylor, Viviene 77–80
Tea Cake (*Their Eyes Were Watching God*) 137
'Teach-Ins' 113
TGWU (T&G) 90, 92, 93, 94–101
  National and Regional Advisory Committees 100
Thatcher, Margaret 111–12
That Hideous Strength (Tinker) 13–14
theatres 81
Their Eyes Were Watching God (Hurston) 49, 136–7, 138
Things Fall Apart (Adichie) 128, 129
Third World Information Network (TWIN) 118–19
Thompson, Dorothy 23
Thompson, E.P. 20–4
Till, Emmet 50
Timmel, Sally 79

Tinker, Melvin 13–14, 17–18
Tomori, S. 60
top-down approaches 21
trade relationships 118
Trades Union Congress (TUC) 71, 89, 91, 100
trade union education 89, 91, 102, 145
trade unions 86–103
  anti-fascist mobilisations 98
  anti-racism 93–101
  and apartheid 71
  international solidarity 93–101
  machine politics 108
  participatory action research (PAR) 86
  slavery, colonialism and imperialism 86
  South Africa 71, 73–5
Training for Transformation manuals (Hope and Timmel) 79
transformative education 78
Treatment Action Campaign (TAC) 44–5, 82
Trump, Donald 13, 16, 41, 120
trust in politicians 149
truth claims 40–2
Tuskegee Industrial and Normal Institute (Tuskegee University) 48–50, 145
Twelve Years a Slave (film) 126–8

U

Ujamaa villages 59–61, 146
UK *see* Britain
Uncle Tom's Cabin (Stowe) 126
under-developed economies 117–18
unequal and exploitative relationships 143
UNESCO 38
unions 89–91
United Democratic Front (UDF) 71, 73–4
United Nations 49, 54
Unite History Project (UHP) 86–7, 92–3, 98, 101–2, 145
UNITE History Volume 1 (Davis and Foster) 93–4
UNITE History Volume 2 (Seifert) 94–5
UNITE History Volume 3 (Mayo) 95
UNITE History Volume 4 (Foster) 99–100
UNITE History Volume 5 (Davis) 100
UNITE History Volume 6 (Weir) 100–1
Unite the Right rally 17
Unite the Union (Unite) 92–3, 99
University Extension 22
University of Brighton 38
University of the Western Cape (UWC) 75, 76, 78, 81
Up from Slavery (Washington) 49
US
  and British politics 142–3
  civil rights 51–3
  Cold War 55
  cultural conflicts 14–16

'the great replacement conspiracy' 13
internal migration 136
post-Civil War 47, 52
post-Reconstruction 48
post-slavery 48–51
progressive cities 105–7
storming the Capitol building 41
unions 91
violent oppression 48
'useful knowledge' 87
USSR 15, 52

V

Victoria and Albert Museum (V&A) 125
Vietnam war 106
villagisation policies 61
von Kotze, Astrid 74, 81–4

W

Walker, Alice 138
Walt Disney World 16–17
Walters, Shirley 75–7, 80, 83–4, 145
Ward, Michael 115, 116, 119
War on Poverty 64, 106, 142–3
War on Terror 25
Washington, Booker T. 48–51, 137, 145
Washington, Harold 107–9
Weber, Max 43
Weep Not Child (Ngugi wa Thiong'o) 130
Weir, Adrian 09, 100
West Africa 57–8
Western Enlightenment 41, 42
Western Marxism 18
West Indian Development Committee 99
White Commonwealth countries 62
White Eurocentric curricula 35
Whitehouse, Mary 14
White people
  social equality 50
  South Africa 67
  wounded by colonialism 26

White supremacist conspiracy
  theories 28
White supremacist violence 13, 17
White supremacy 31, 77
Wigg, George 57
Williams, Raymond 12, 20–4, 89, 123, 140
Windrush generation 62–3, 120, 136
  see also Black people
woke and wokeism 6, 17, 28
'woke capitalism' (Rhodes) 15
Wolfe, A. 16
Wolfers, Michael 58
women
  academics 35
  cross-campus breakfasts 81
  union representation 100
Women Against Pit Closures 114
Women's Liberation 100
worker–peasant alliances 27
workers' education 87–91
Workers Educational Association
  (WEA) 21, 22, 56, 57, 88–9, 90
Workers Education Trade Union
  Committee (WETUC) 89
Working against Racism (TUC) 91
working-class education 88–9
World Bank 61
World Federation of Trade Unions
  (WFTU) 96–7
'The World Must Change' exhibition 69
Wortley Hall, Yorkshire 71
The Wretched of the Earth (Fanon) 26
Wright Mills, C. 92
written languages 130

X

X, Malcolm 72

Z

Zimbabwe 73

www.ingramcontent.com/pod-product-compliance
Lightning Source LLC
Chambersburg PA
CBHW070043040426
42333CB00041B/2180